·turess —
·1 her

The Achievement of Margaret Fuller

The Achievement
of
MARGARET FULLER

Margaret Vanderhaar Allen

The Pennsylvania State University Press
University Park and London

The lines from "At Melville's Tomb" are reprinted from *The Complete Poems and Selected Letters and Prose of Hart Crane*, Edited by Brom Weber, with the permission of Liveright Publishing Corporation. Copyright © 1933, 1958, 1966 by Liveright Publishing Corporation.

Library of Congress Cataloging in Publication Data

Allen, Margaret Vanderhaar.
The achievement of Margaret Fuller.

Bibliography: p. 194.
Includes index.
   1. Ossoli, Sarah Margaret Fuller, marchesa d', 1810–
1850—Criticism and interpretation. I. Title.
P52507.A4   818'.3'09   79-1732
ISBN 0-271-00215-8

To Frank Allen

In lazy Apathy let Stoics boast
Their Virtue fixed; 'tis fixed as in a frost;
Contracted all, retiring to the breast;
But strength of mind is Exercise, not Rest:
The rising tempest puts in act the soul,
Parts it may ravage, but preserves the whole.
On life's vast ocean diversely we sail,
Reason the card, but Passion is the gale;
Nor God alone in the still calm we find,
He mounts the storm, and walks upon the wind.

Pope, *Essay on Man*

Contents

Contents

Preface

Margaret Fuller's personal charisma and the high drama of her life and death have, ironically, camouflaged many of her finest achievements. Since her death in 1850 several biographies have told her story partially. Most of these dwell on the romance of her life and the tragedy of her death but neglect her ideas. There are few editions of her writings and letters, none of them complete, and few explorations of her thought. A contemporary of Emerson, Thoreau, and Hawthorne—and intellectually their equal—Margaret Fuller has been relatively unnoticed as a thinker and literary woman since her death. In this book I have explored some reasons for this disproportionate neglect. Fortunately she is at last beginning to receive well-deserved recognition. A brilliant start toward critical assessment has already been made, with Bell Gale Chevigny's *The Woman and the Myth: Margaret Fuller's Life and Writings*, and with Barbara Welter, Ann Douglas, and Susan Phinney Conrad, each of whom has devoted a lengthy chapter to Fuller in their recent books. Paula Blanchard's excellent biography is the necessary starting point for those who wish to know about Fuller's life. My own study was virtually complete by the time these books were published, but I have benefited from them all.

There could be no better time than now for a discovery of Margaret Fuller. The industrial era, which has dominated the nineteenth and twentieth centuries in Western society and shaped our lives in ways we know and ways we do not know, begins to seem obsolete. It no longer promises the good life but seems to be the chief obstacle to the good life. The assumptions of industrialism were once useful: that human beings must conquer and exploit nature, for instance, or that progress is measured by economic expansion and the ever-spiraling consumption of material goods, or that specialization, efficient management, and scientific overlordship bring about that "progress." These concepts, and the actions they govern, only dehumanize us more completely and threaten our physical and psychic survival, threaten even the planet earth itself. Now an exciting and momentous vision of life is taking shape, one based on very different assumptions. This vision has yet to be crystallized and fully articulated, and it is a long way from becoming an established social norm. It is founded on a reverence for nature and a realistic acceptance of the need to cooperate with our natural environment; on the importance and beauty of individual development and self-realization for all people, not merely the privileged few; on the desirability of living for less materialistic goals than consumption and a higher place in the pecking order. It knows the destructiveness of ideology and the need for open-minded, free-spirited, adventurous exploration. Margaret Fuller knew, lived, and wrote about these things. She was born not only far ahead of *her* time, but even ahead of *our* time.

This book is not primarily a biography. For those relatively unacquainted with Fuller, I have given some essential facts of her life and death in the first chapter. Those who know Fuller will find this overly familiar ground, no doubt. I have not written about all of her achievements. No single book can do them justice. Her extraordinary success in friendship, the educating of countless unnamed children and young persons, the help and consolation she generously gave to the ill, the wretched, and the dying, the selfhood she created and was true to, devotion to her family, the unique texture of her daily existence—all these achievements deserve to be honored. My main concern is with Fuller's ideas and where they led her. In exploring these, I discovered the labyrinthine and sometimes deliberate obfuscation of her reputation, the subject of Chapter 2. Two intellectual giants of her age, Emerson and Goethe, so profoundly influenced Fuller that no clear understanding of her achievements is possible without recognizing the parts they played; their influence is examined in Chapters 3 and 4. Succeeding chapters each explore one aspect of her manifold accomplishments.

Many women active in intellectual milieus, the arts, and politics, in Fuller's time and now, have known the degradation that comes from being trivialized, relegated to the periphery of action and accomplishment, praised for the wrong reasons, or ignored. This is changing, but it has not changed enough. Fuller has been the victim of these and other prejudices against her sex, and as long as they exist, they obstruct her great intellectual and moral leadership. It is, to say the least, a shocking waste of genius.

Portions of Chapters 5, 8, and 10 previously appeared in the *South Atlantic Quarterly* and the *Southwest Review*. My special thanks to Ann Douglas and Wilma Ebbitt for their perceptive criticisms of the manuscript and their many helpful suggestions for its improvement; Henry L. Golemba for his kindness in reading and commenting on the chapters about Fuller's literary criticism; the Lehigh University Library for allowing me access to their collections; the Houghton Library; the New York

Public Library; and the Bethlehem Public Library. The book has bene-fited greatly from the invaluable criticisms of my beloved husband, Frank. More than that: without his faith and encouragement I would never have dreamed of or begun this book; without his generous help and patience I would never have finished it.

Margaret Vanderhaar Allen

Bethlehem, Pennsylvania

CHAPTER 1

Who Was Margaret Fuller?

During her turbulent life and for years after her death in a shipwreck at the age of forty, nearly everyone knew the name of Margaret Fuller. She was famous on both sides of the Atlantic, and with fame she became a subject for gossip. Few could remain indifferent to her. She inspired love or loathing, friendship or enmity, or a curiously ambivalent attraction-repulsion. So colorful was the living woman that she has partly obscured her own hard-won accomplishments.

Though a product of her century, her country, her region, and her family, she transcended all these. Her origins did not wholly define her. She always claimed the right to define herself, to discover where and with whom she belonged. An aura of active, conscious, willed development surrounds her life, which is alien to the docility and passiveness usually associated with nineteenth-century femininity. This principle of active intelligence—in Margaret Fuller also a loving intelligence—made her richly human. "Extraordinary generous seeking" was a motto (from Goethe) that as a girl she adopted for her life and urged her friends to adopt. The expansive, bold quality of her ambitions seemed to spring from the expansive, youthful America she was born into, a country that could perceive no limitations on its divinely ordained progress. The interplay between her own strivings, her own indomitable sense of herself, and the obstacles the world implacably placed before her is surely one of the chief sources of her enduring fascination.

She was born Sarah Margaret Fuller in Cambridgeport, Massachusetts, on May 23, 1810, the first child of Timothy and Margaret Crane Fuller. The Fullers were of Puritan stock and counted distinguished clergymen and landowners among their members. One of them, Margaret's grandfather, voted in the Massachusetts convention against accepting the United States Constitution, because it recognized human slavery. The Fuller men possessed great energy and self-esteem. They were well-educated, principled, outspoken, and frequently tactless; Sarah Margaret shared these qualities.

1

Timothy Fuller was an ambitious young lawyer, a Unitarian and Harvard-educated, when he married Margaret Crane, the beautiful daughter of Major Peter Crane of Canton, Massachusetts. The Cranes were another devout Puritan family, and Margaret Crane, recalled by her famous daughter as a "fair and flower-like nature," was a sweet-tempered, self-effacing woman. She was a shadowy, remote figure in Sarah Margaret's childhood because of her frequent illnesses, pregnancies, and preoccupation with the younger children. Another daughter, born soon after Sarah Margaret, died in 1812, and after her came Eugene, Lloyd, Ellen, Richard, William Henry, and Arthur.

Timothy Fuller, hoping for a son as his first-born, decided to give Margaret the education he had intended for an oldest son. He was a strong-minded, independent man, something of a rebel himself: he lost first place in his Harvard graduating class because he had taken part in a student rebellion on the campus. Though busy with his profession, he kept up his classical reading and closely supervised Margaret's early education. Timothy had read Mary Wollstonecraft's *A Vindication of the Rights of Women*, with its eloquent plea for the education of women. He set out to make his daughter a paragon of intellectual and moral perfection; he taught her Latin and several other languages, history, literature, and mathematics. A demanding teacher who insisted on discipline and accuracy, he tutored her after completing his own day's work. She would study Virgil in the late evening hours, then go to bed haunted with nightmares about wild horses trampling her. Or she would sleepwalk, or experience fits of near-hysteria brought on by excitements too intense for her childish constitution. As an adult, Margaret Fuller believed that these long late hours of rigorous study and a lack of outdoor play and exercise had ruined her health and deprived her of a normal childhood.

The pattern of Margaret's early life, atypical of most girls at that or any other time, was a recognizable one for many of the early woman suffragists: a first-born girl whose education was guided by the father, while the mother remained in the background, either as an invalid or as the nurse of the younger children. Later in life these highly motivated women regarded their fathers with ambivalence, as instigators of the desire for "unwomanly" achievements. These women were often preoccupied with efforts to define women's nature and role.[1]

Her father, her books, and churchgoing dominated Margaret's childhood. Paula Blanchard in her biography describes in detail the feminine milieu of Margaret's youth—her mother's influence, her girl and women friends, her schoolmates. Margaret had little formal schooling except for a term or two at Dr. Park's genteel academy for young ladies in Boston, and a stay at the Misses Prescott's school in Groton, forty miles from Boston, in 1823–24. There Margaret found the other girls frivolous and rude, and they thought her precociously developed intellectual powers strange. The rigorous education she had received from her father—reminiscent of the education of John Stuart Mill by his father—was rare enough for a boy, unthinkable for a girl. The normal education for a girl stressed religion. Her world was to be the family, and it was a commonplace of pedagogical thought that overexertion of the brain could severely damage a girl's female functions and domestic propensities. "The subduing of the will, acceptance of self-abnegation, development of excessive altruism were the desired educational goals."[2] A girl learned the social graces—music, sewing, languages, a little history, a little poetry—that enabled her to compete more advantageously in the marriage market. Her education guided her toward a useful life as wife and mother. Any serious mental exertion or intellectual challenge conflicted fundamentally with her destined role, and girls did not study "masculine" subjects like mathematics, theology, Greek, and the natural sciences. Education was conducted largely through memorization, for both sexes, but far less independent reasoning was required of girls than boys.[3]

Though she later became the center of a brilliant circle of friends and admirers, Fuller's accounts of her early childhood stress its loneliness, its bookishness, its premature development and too-severe discipline, its disturbed nights. She experienced little emotional warmth or closeness from either parent. Piety and churchgoing were keystones of her upbringing. Her loving, affectionate nature was stifled, her mind emphasized disproportionately. But though she accounted her childhood unhappy, her family was stable and close, her parents loving—in their way.

Her father's educational regime may have been emotionally harmful, but it unquestionably developed and strengthened her mental powers. It also gave her a view of the world that few American girls or women then had access to. Margaret's unusual education was a pillar of her later achievement, and like all extraordinary achievement, it exacted its price.

During the years Margaret was growing up, Timothy Fuller was active in politics. He had fervent Jeffersonian convictions and served in the Massachusetts legislature and the United States Congress. A strong supporter of John Quincy Adams and a foe of the entrenched Federalists, Timothy remained loyal to Adams and to the struggling young republic during its critical early decades. When Adams was President in 1826, Timothy Fuller gave a gala ball for him at his house on Dana Hill in Cambridge. Margaret, then an awkward adolescent, presided as hostess. She often filled this role for her father, partly because he wished it, and partly because of her mother's burdens with childbearing and childrearing. That festive evening was the peak of Timothy's political career.

Soon afterward his party, the Democratic Republican party of Thomas Jefferson, fell into a schism. Timothy's side eventually lost out to the faction called Democrats, led by Andrew Jackson.

After the Groton school term, Margaret lived for the next nine years with her family in Cambridge, where she formed many lasting friendships. In 1833 Timothy moved his family to a farm in Groton. He had worked so hard and so vocally for Adams in the 1832 presidential election that when Jackson and his Democrats won, the tide of politics turned against him. Later in life, perhaps because of this political defeat for her father, Margaret Fuller seldom spoke well of Jackson and Jacksonians. Timothy, who once told his wife that he found pride as certain a fortress as philosophy, now decided to abandon politics for farming. He also planned to write his political memoirs and a history of the United States.

Margaret detested the change. To her the Groton farm was a dreary provincial outpost, far removed from her Boston and Cambridge friends. Gregarious, talkative, intensely curious, she needed a congenial circle and mental stimulation. On the farm she felt unutterably deprived. She devoted herself to domestic tasks and tutoring the younger children. This experience on the Groton farm, and a realistic turn of mind, kept her from later romanticizing "the soil" and farm work, as did some other Transcendentalists, such as the Brook Farm commune members, whom she steadfastly refused to join. She generally preferred life in cities among men and women to life among animals and crops. She was not devoid of feeling for nature—on the contrary, she loved it, revered it, was renewed by it—but she was a highly social and urbane woman, and isolated farm life did not suit her.

When Timothy Fuller died suddenly of cholera in 1835, he left a large family with meager financial resources. Margaret was twenty-five, and on her shoulders rested most of the family responsibility. She felt ill-equipped for it. Her bookish childhood had not prepared her to manage a large family. Society neither trained girls to be heads of families nor accorded them its privileges, such as owning property. University education was traditional for the Fuller men, and Margaret assumed the responsibility of providing it for her brothers. Not until the last of the Fuller sons graduated from Harvard many years later did Margaret feel relieved of this financial obligation. The need to earn her own living and to help provide for her family remained a constant pressure through most of her life. Financial security was never one of her advantages.

Though her father, her brothers, and most of her male friends in New England were Harvard-educated, Margaret Fuller was mostly self-educated. She took up where her father had left off. Her prodigious intellectual gifts and a marked literary talent had become evident early and were nurtured by her wide reading in history and literature. Before the age of twenty, she knew French, Italian, and German, as well as Latin and some Greek. She came to maturity during the New England renascence; thus her native capabilities fortunately met with a mentally hospitable atmosphere that nourished them. "Very early I knew that the only object in life was to grow," she once remarked.[4] Feeling the limits of her education, she was eager to complete it in Europe. The rudimentary state of art and culture in America at that period made this imperative. But her father's death and ensuing family responsibilities forced her to cancel the much-desired tour. Bitterly disappointed, she had to content herself with New England for the time being. Later in life she outgrew New England, feeling it was too limited for her.

The determined course of mental and cultural self-improvement she followed set her life apart from most young women. The early nineteenth century brought a marked change in the status and role of women. In colonial America, women had played an essential economic role, both in the home and outside of it. In addition to childbearing and childrearing, women produced, prepared, and preserved food. They made candles, soap, shoes, and rugs. Spinning, weaving, clothesmaking, poultry breeding, and butchering were among their essential productive activities. In the Revolutionary era "they ran mills, plantations, tanyards, shipyards and every kind of shop, tavern and boarding house. They were gate keepers, jail keepers, sextons, journalists, printers, 'doctoresses,' apothecaries, midwives, nurses and teachers."[5] Even though men controlled the basic commodity of preindustrial society, the land, colonial women did have some property and legal rights. Widows in particular enjoyed many of the social and economic freedoms of men. However, the system remained firmly patriarchal, and women derived their identity from men— father, husband, or son.[6]

The economic shift between 1800 and 1830, brought about by the Industrial Revolution, changed women's relation to society. Although it relieved them of much hard physical labor, it otherwise constricted them, and by 1840 women's position had deteriorated significantly. Work outside the home was condemned rather than approved, most occupations and the training for them became professionalized and closed to women, and they lost their legal and property rights.[7]

With the rise of manufacturing and the movement away from the self-sufficient agrarian homestead to the production and marketing of a single cash crop, men's sphere also changed.[8] At the same time that the Industrial Revolution provided vastly expanded possibilities for men's activities, it also cut them loose from their close ties to the homestead. Men greeted these altered social realities ambivalently. New opportunities meant new temptations; greater risks could mean greater disasters.

So their exhilaration was probably mixed with fear. As men's need of women's economic labors outside the home lessened, their need of women's steadying (they hoped) moral influence increased.

These years thus saw the beginning of what has been called the "cult of the lady" or the "cult of true womanhood," a concept of woman based on piety, purity, submissiveness, passivity, and the domestic virtues. With her sphere defined as the family and the church, woman was exalted as a morally superior being whose mission was to ennoble man, while remaining dependent on him. She was trained above all to obedience. While men made money and built a nation, women's role became a redemptive one.[9]

Margaret Fuller's vigorous quest to expand her intellectual and cultural horizons was in itself an act of at least partial rejection of the destiny her society had prepared for a woman. Ann Douglas remarks: "Since there was no overt institutional encouragement or acknowledgement of Fuller's intellectual progress, it had to appear both self-motivated and subversive."[10] She so often had to be sustained and propelled by her own ego that it is not surprising that others saw ego prominent in her. In the cult of true womanhood, ego had no place.

It would be misleading to overstress Fuller's erudition. She had many other gifts besides a first-rate mind, for example, a talent for leadership. Her father, Margaret herself, her admirers, and even her detractors acknowledged that her natural role was that of a queen. She liked being the center of attention. But she was an accessible queen, not an aloof one. She attracted men, women, and children by her gaiety, her sense of humor, her generosity, her warmth and womanliness, and most of all by her intuitive sympathy with everyone who came into her personal orbit. Her conversation has become legendary. She could amuse, delight, inspire, and convey perfect understanding, all at the same time. Many people who knew her, women and men, said that no one had ever understood their inmost selves as Margaret had.

Many people disliked her, however. An obviously brilliant woman never has an easy time. Some thought her arrogant or affected, some found her quick-witted sallies merciless, and some were intimidated by her. Men frequently were put off, at least initially, by her plainness or by some personal mannerism, such as her habit of half-closing her eyes while she talked. After her death, Emerson and Poe left written recollections that emphasized physical traits they found unattractive. As a result, posterity pictures Margaret Fuller as a homely woman with an overdeveloped brain. We may safely conclude that we have received a distorted, highly subjective picture from these writers. A woman of distinction has

6

always been subjected to extensive comments on her beauty or lack of it. If she possesses it, it obscures her other, earned merits; if she lacks it, it vitiates those merits. She may or may not feel it unfair, but a woman expects her looks to count heavily for or against her. They will never be ignored. As a girl Margaret Fuller knew she was neither beautiful nor especially graceful; she longed for those charms and agonized over their absence. She did have an abundance of fair hair, a full figure, expressive gray eyes, and a mobile, sensitive face. Never oblivious to appearance, she always dressed as well as she could afford. Many girls and women admired her personal style.

Those who became acquainted with her usually lost any first dislike. Dr. Johnson said of Richard Savage that "it was his peculiar happiness that he scarcely ever found a stranger whom he did not leave a friend." A gift for friendship was one of Margaret's outstanding talents. All her life she evoked, and returned, love. Yet, surrounded by friends and admirers, she often was lonely.

For eight years after her father's death she taught and studied, wrote and translated. She taught French, German, Italian, and Latin in the Temple School in Boston, directed by Bronson Alcott. Alcott, a Transcendentalist educator and theoretician (and idle dreamer to many), believed that a child's innate intuitive powers should be evoked in the educating process. He discarded the conventional rote learning, repetitive drills, and corporal punishment in favor of education-by-conversation, in the Socratic tradition. Margaret tutored private pupils, in addition to those at the school, and kept up so demanding a program of studies for herself that her health gave way, and she had to leave the Temple School. Shortly afterward the wrath of Boston descended on Alcott: his teaching methods were avant-garde, his school was interracial, and his discussions about how children are born were frank and uninhibited. Margaret Fuller valiantly defended Alcott, though she thought some of his pedagogical premises were naive and overly optimistic. Alcott's school did not survive the controversy. He always thought highly of Margaret and spoke eloquently of her after her death.

In 1837 Fuller accepted an offer to teach at the Greene Street School in Providence, Rhode Island. Providence was to her another outpost, and she felt culturally exiled there. She busied herself with literary labors and produced her first published work, a translation of *Eckermann's Conversations with Goethe*. She also attended occasional political rallies and found them stimulating. After two years in Providence she resigned her teaching position, feeling the need to earn her living some other way. Her health was poor, and she wanted to return to the Boston-Cambridge area. In 1839 she moved with her family to Jamaica Plain, near Boston.

Seeking a way to use her talents and still earn money—the ways to do so being exceedingly limited for a woman at that time—she began her famous Boston Conversations, a series of weekly discussions for women on a wide range of subjects. Twenty-five women signed up for the first series, which cost twenty dollars. Two assumptions gave rise to the Conversations: that women had little opportunity for an education that would exercise their minds, and that women longed for such education. Margaret Fuller undertook to supply it. The Conversations succeeded brilliantly, and more were scheduled. With Margaret as their guide, the women discussed mythology, ethics, demonology, creeds, the fine arts, poetry, the ideal, education, and questions such as "what is life?" One series was opened to men. The Boston Conversations, which will be discussed again in Chapter 9, continued until 1844. They were the nearest thing in New England to a European *salon*. Sometimes they were targets of ridicule. The English writer Harriet Martineau found it pretentious and inappropriate that these well-dressed women, the elite of Boston, should idly discuss the nature of life in a drawing room while slavery poisoned the moral life of the American nation. But those who attended the Conversations never forgot them. Their impact was felt on women's education for the rest of the century.

Fuller's influence on women was great, and her friendships with them warm and enduring. But she often felt that women's milieu (as then defined) was too narrow for her, and inevitably she entered male-dominated realms. In the nineteenth century male and female roles were so strictly defined that to move between them, or attempt to fulfill both as Fuller did, was exceedingly difficult and fraught with conflict, as we shall see in later chapters. In her friendships with men like Emerson, Theodore Parker, George Ripley, James Freeman Clarke, Frederick Hedge, and William Henry Channing, the leading lights of the Transcendental movement and some of the most vigorous and creative minds of that era, Fuller approached them as an equal. She was the first woman member of the Transcendentalist Club and the editor of, and frequent contributor to, the *Dial*. The Transcendentalists believed in equality for women, and in her longest piece for the *Dial*, "The Great Lawsuit: Men vs Men, Women vs Women," Fuller examined the knotty problems of women's rights and sexual roles. Most Transcendentalists were rebellious Unitarians and indefatigable theorists, interested in Romanticism, dedicated to liberal, even radical reform. Transcendentalism also meant a commitment to experience over erudition, a principle that Fuller liked.[11]

Her books began to appear: two translations, *Eckermann's Conversations with Goethe* (1839) and *The Correspondence of Fräulein Günderode and Bettina von Arnim* (1842). After a trip to the Great Lakes and western prairies in 1843, Fuller wanted to write a travel book. For the research she was allowed to use the Harvard library, the first woman so privileged. *Summer on the Lakes* was published in 1844. These books, especially *Summer*, were moderately successful, though Fuller was never wholly single-minded about authorship. Often dissatisfied with her intellectual attainments, she wished for a life of more action and emotional fulfillment.

Her reputation grew, and her books made her known outside New England. In 1844 she accepted an offer from Horace Greeley, the crusading newspaperman and publisher, to write reviews and criticism for his *New York Daily Tribune*. Greeley wanted his paper to uplift the public, morally and culturally, and the *Tribune* was a practical center for much of the radical reformism of the day. This major step in Fuller's life became a milestone in American journalism. Up to this time women had entered journalism only sporadically.[12] Margaret Fuller was one of the first women to earn a living at full-time journalism; after the Civil War many others entered the profession. At the time she accepted Greeley's offer, she was the most distinguished literary figure to write for an American newspaper. Her New England friends were dismayed that a woman of her literary talents would take up newspaper writing, but she correctly believed that the transition from New England to New York would be beneficial for her life and her work. It also paid much better than any work she had done before.

At Greeley's invitation, she lived with him and his wife Mary in their Turtle Bay home amid the green pastures and wooded lanes of Manhattan. From an exclusive concern with literary and artistic culture, her interests now broadened to embrace social and political problems as well. In addition to reviewing books and concerts for the *Tribune* and mingling with New York literary figures, she visited prisons and asylums and hospitals. Her lengthy articles made her a pioneer in investigative and sociological journalism.

Greeley and Fuller, despite differences, generally got along well together. They had a strong personal bond in their mutual devotion to Greeley's son Pickie. Greeley's marriage was difficult, and Margaret soon became his confidante. Some of Greeley's biographers hint that his feeling for Margaret was deeper and more emotion-laden than a business friendship usually is.[13] But she directed her own romantic feelings elsewhere; she was falling in love with James Nathan, a young German Jewish businessman interested in art and music. Though Mrs. Greeley was fond of Nathan, who called on Margaret at the Turtle Bay residence, it soon became too awkward for them to meet there, and Greeley disapproved of the whole affair. Clandestine meetings with Nathan followed, some at her doctor's office, until she moved from the Greeleys' home to

9

rooms of her own. It was not the first time she had fallen in love; there had been romances in New England, some of them one-sided and most of them ending painfully for her. But this affair was decidedly more ardent, more adult. It was growing in intensity when Nathan suddenly left New York for his native country, a departure that decidedly improved Horace Greeley's spirits.[14] Nathan seldom wrote unless he wanted some favor, and Margaret never saw him again. Ungallantly, Nathan refused her pleas for the return of her letters. He eventually married and remained in Europe. Her letters passed to Nathan's son, who released them for publication in 1904, as *Love-Letters of Margaret Fuller*.

During her years in New York Margaret Fuller's writings increased steadily in number and quality. She revised "The Great Lawsuit," and Greeley published it in 1845 as *Woman in the Nineteenth Century*, an enormously successful book both in America and abroad. In 1846 a collection of her critical pieces was published as *Papers on Literature and Art*. Fuller's outspoken literary criticism made her some bitter enemies: James Russell Lowell, for one, disliked her comments on his work and left a spiteful satiric portrait of her in "A Fable for Critics." These years of independence and pronounced personal growth were productive and on the whole happy, insofar as her restless, aspiring nature ever permitted happiness.

In 1846 a wealthy young Quaker couple, Marcus and Rebecca Spring, friends of Margaret and of the Greeleys, offered Margaret the opportunity to accompany them on a tour of Europe in exchange for some help with the care of their young son Eddie. Hoping to see James Nathan there, Margaret accepted eagerly. Her brothers were now educated and on their own, her sister Ellen was married, although not happily, and no obstacle remained to the fulfillment of her long-postponed wish for a European trip. In August 1846 she sailed for Europe with the Springs, arranging with Greeley to send back reports for his *Tribune*.

Europe surged with currents of revolution, which soon caught her up. For a time, though, she enjoyed the Europe of culture and art that she had come to discover. In England and France she met Wordsworth, Carlyle and his wife Jane, George Sand, Chopin, Mickiewicz, Mazzini, and other writers, artists, and political figures. Margaret and the Springs arrived in Italy early in 1847, and she joyfully discovered her true spiritual home at last, in Rome. She wrote that had she found it years earlier, the entire course of her life would have been different. In Rome, during a visit to St. Peter's Cathedral, she met the handsome young Marquis Giovanni Angelo d'Ossoli. Soon she was seeing him constantly. Greeley and Emerson several times wrote letters urging Margaret to come home to America, but she decided to stay in Rome, even though the Spring family planned to return.

"I cannot rest from travel; I will drink life to the lees," she might have said with Tennyson's Ulysses. Though Ossoli urged her to marry him, Margaret refused. She left Rome and flung herself into a whirlwind tour of Italy. Ossoli told her that she would return to him, and she did, in the autumn of 1847. Gradually politics and passion absorbed her more and more. Rome and most of Italy moved toward revolution, and Margaret awaited the birth of a child. In September of 1848 a son, Angelo, was born in Rieti, a small town in the hills outside Rome where she had lived incognito that summer.

The date of Margaret Fuller's marriage to Ossoli is not known with certainty; there is even some doubt that it ever took place.[15] Margaret's pregnancy dictated a secret marriage. And for young Ossoli to openly plan a marriage to an older American Protestant woman of decidedly liberal views would have estranged him from his Catholic aristocratic family; he would inherit nothing. In addition the times were hectic and confused. Rome struggled in the throes of revolution. (The complexities of Roman revolutionary politics are discussed in Chapter 10.) All over Italy popular uprisings erupted against the ruling Austrians. In Rome Pope Pius IX first encouraged the people's nationalist aspirations, then withdrew his leadership and, fearful for his life, surreptitiously left the city. In 1849 Mazzini assumed leadership of the newly proclaimed Roman Republic. The Catholic powers of Europe joined in the attempt to reestablish Papal authority in Rome. The French sent an army to crush the rebels and restore reactionary rule. Though Ossoli's family was aristocratic, he supported the Republic and fought with the rebels as a captain in the Guarda Civica.

During the French bombardment, siege, and invasion of Rome, Ossoli's life was in constant danger. The baby remained in Rieti, which his parents thought safer for him, but after communications were cut off during the siege and travel became impossible, Margaret's anxiety was intense. Asked to direct a hospital for war casualties, she carried out her duties with grace and courage. In all the tumult, experiencing war's brutalities firsthand, in perpetual fear for Ossoli's life, separated from her child, she nevertheless continued to write her dispatches for the *Tribune*. She was the first American woman war correspondent under combat conditions.

She sent her last dispatch on the day the Roman Republic fell. After a month of siege, the French army entered Rome in July 1849. The defeat of the revolution and the end of the Republic meant that Margaret and her husband were forced to flee. They went immediately to Rieti to

11

claim their child. Ossoli was cut off from his inheritance, and the couple had almost no money. The Ossolis traveled to Florence, where Margaret made friends with Robert and Elizabeth Browning, enjoyed a beautiful, tranquil domestic life, and wrote tactful letters to friends and family in America who learned with amazement of her marriage and motherhood. She also completed a history of the Roman revolution, begun during her solitary pregnancy in Italian villages. She thought this book was the best thing she had ever written.

At last the family booked passage for America, traveling on a slow cargo ship because they had so little money. Margaret had premonitions of disaster. The ship's captain died of smallpox, which little Angelino contracted. He soon recovered, but this respite from disaster was brief. In July 1850, within sight of New York, their ship, the *Elizabeth*, was wrecked in a storm off Fire Island. For twelve hours the ship foundered, while beach pirates stood and watched passively, making no attempt to go for help or put out a boat to bring in survivors. The captain's widow and some of the crew survived, but Margaret, her husband, and her child drowned. Of the three, only Angelino's body was recovered.

Margaret Fuller's death was like the final act of some momentous tragic drama. She seemed almost an American Byron, another lacerated, impatient spirit who defied convention, attracted excitement, danger, and passion, fought in a revolution in a distant land, died prematurely, and became a romantic legend. Like the Ulysses of Tennyson's poem, she hungered for life and yearned "to follow knowledge like a sinking star, beyond the utmost bounds of thought." So much sense of mystery and of waste is evoked by such a life that perhaps it can never be contemplated with detachment. But if we cannot be unimpassioned, we can try to be fair. Thirteen decades have elapsed since that shipwreck off Fire Island. It is time to penetrate misty legend and look hard at who Margaret Fuller was, and what she did.

CHAPTER 2

The Factitious Margaret Fuller

The wreckage had scarcely been recovered from the sands of Fire Island when the creation of a Margaret Fuller myth began. There was of course genuine shock and grief at her death, and friends in Europe and America felt the wrench of her passing. Yet there was also, in America at least, a perceptible sigh of relief. Mid-nineteenth-century Americans, on the whole, preferred not to cope with the challenges to their most cherished beliefs and biases that Margaret Fuller embodied. She was returning to America no longer Miss Fuller the intellectual spinster, the literary blue-stocking, but an exiled revolutionary with a handsome husband much younger than herself, and a child certainly conceived, if not born, out of wedlock. She was returning too as an avowed socialist, and socialist views had undoubtedly colored her history of the Italian revolution, the manuscript of which went down in the shipwreck. Elizabeth Browning and others whom Margaret Fuller knew in Florence had been shocked at her left-leaning views.

Yet the active, growing body of socialist thought in America would have supported Fuller in proclaiming socialist ideas. Horace Greeley and his *Tribune* encouraged Fourierist socialism, for example, and socialist experimentation was in the air. So her political opinions did not alarm them the most. Not a woman of half-measures nor of compromises, and having fused in her own experience the New World and the old, she would quite likely have prodded her compatriots toward cosmopolitan-ism, an internationalist view, and a maturity of outlook like her own. But Americans were not yet ready for such a viewpoint, and they were unwilling to be made even more painfully conscious of their cultural and intellectual deficiencies. The American stance toward Europe still veered between slavish imitation and truculent defiance of its culture and thought; few could accept and assimilate Europe as Fuller had done.

Furthermore, this woman, who had courageously defended Goethe and George Sand against charges of immorality, now needed a moral tolerance for herself that her compatriots were not prepared to give. She suspected this before she sailed for America, commenting shrewdly,

"Goethe says that there is nothing men are slower to forgive than singular behavior for which no explanation is forthcoming."[1] When the news of the shipwreck reached Boston, some believed it was just as well, and Emerson wrote to Carlyle, a little too complacently perhaps, "She died in happy hour for herself."[2]

But Margaret Fuller had far too strong an impact on those who knew her to be conveniently forgotten. A myth began to grow up around her memory, and many truths about her life became distorted in the process. The real Margaret Fuller had been strong willed, independent, spontaneous, stubbornly alive, allowing no one to manipulate her. Dead, she was more easily "arranged." Her friends, with the tacit cooperation of her family, immediately created an image of her as they wanted the world to remember her. Margaret had enough facets to her soul to furnish material for a hundred biographers, said one friend.[3] So they chose what fit the image they wished to project and ignored or destroyed the rest.

They agreed that they owed her some memento, even a biography. If her body had not been washed out to sea, perhaps a fine cemetery vault or a crypt in a chapel would have sufficed. Those who first worked on the memoir were Emerson, one of her oldest and closest friends; W.H. Channing, a Unitarian clergyman of socialist views who had known her in New York; and Samuel Gray Ward, who with his wife Anna had been her close friends in New England. Ward wrote to Emerson, "How can you describe a Force? How can you write the life of Margaret?"[4] Later he stepped aside, and James Freeman Clarke, another Unitarian clergyman and friend, replaced him. Clarke had once studied the German writers with Margaret and had edited a journal called the *Western Messenger*, to which she frequently contributed. From New York Horace Greeley introduced a commercial element; he insisted that the memoir appear as soon as possible, within months, he hoped, in order to capitalize on the current peak of interest generated by Margaret's tragic death. No one person was responsible for the project. Emerson knew that one editor should take charge, though he rejected the task. The plan was to gather written reminiscences from those who had known her, particularly the famous, and to combine them with her letters, poems, and journals. These, with the editors' comments, would constitute a biography.

Between business enterprise and the clergy, Margaret Fuller's interests were not well served. Her own papers—all that remained of her now—were scattered about and abominably mishandled from the start. Some were lost in the shipwreck. She had lived in many places and had entrusted her papers to various persons for safekeeping. Some papers that she had left with friends in London were guarded with bulldog tenacity;

the friends believed that the only honorable thing was to burn them, now that Margaret was dead. Carlyle, at Emerson's request, pried the papers away from their scrupulous guardians, but, inexplicably, they never arrived in America. Accounts of Margaret written by Robert Browning and Mazzini likewise failed to reach America and could never be traced.

Transatlantic mails were the least of the bungling. Those who worked with her papers in America displayed a carelessness that bordered on contempt. Sections from her letters and journals were ruthlessly blue-penciled, chopped, and altered by Emerson, Channing, and Clarke. They judged it too dangerous to let her speak for herself any longer—a privilege allowed only to the living. "We must meet in the Autumn, & learn what may be told, or may not," wrote Emerson in 1851 to Charles Newcomb, another friend who had some of Margaret's letters.[5] If Fuller's letters, mostly to and about persons then living, were judged in any way injurious to those persons' reputation or privacy, they were censored. Her editors also scanned her private journals with inquisitorial thoroughness for any unorthodox opinions.

The result was the *Memoirs of Margaret Fuller Ossoli*, which appeared in the United States and England in 1852. Greeley had been right: there was immense interest, and the book was widely read and reviewed. The *Memoirs* solidified the Margaret Fuller myth that, with a few later alterations or additions, prevailed for well over a hundred years.

Like many myths, its basis lay partly in truth and partly in the personal needs of those who perpetuated the myth. The Margaret Fuller of the *Memoirs* was presented to the world as a saintly and pious paragon of nearly every virtue, a joyless semimartyr who led an adventurous life, but who, apart from the interest of her inspiring personality, left behind her no written or other works of any value. The *Memoirs* give us a plaster saint, someone too excessively good to be real: devoted to truth, courageous, heroic, unsparingly generous, deeply religious, a suffering spirit tirelessly leading all her friends to Higher Things, an elevating moral teacher and lover of Christian virtue. In all these respects, the editors tailored an image of Fuller to conform exactly with the stereotype of "the true woman," an ideal of womanhood that prevailed for much of the nineteenth century in America.[6] Apart from her brilliant conversation, which safely departed with her last breath, Fuller's intellectual achievement was disparaged or underrated or ignored. Also ignored were her pleasures and worldly successes—and the pagan in her. Fuller's imagination was called deficient and her writing pronounced inferior and so dismissed from serious consideration. Her vocation in life, said her editors, was to be a friend, The Friend, and effusive testimonies from her friends flow like sugar syrup. A truthful account was not the purpose of the *Memoirs*.

The *Memoirs* strongly emphasize Fuller's sufferings as well as her virtue. (The cult of true womanhood decreed that women must expect suffering and submissively endure it as their lot.) She did suffer; she usually worked in spite of great difficulties—poverty, poor health, loneliness—and she talked of her woes often, seeming to want pity or consolation from others. Yet she herself might say proudly with Ulysses, "All times I have enjoyed greatly, have suffered greatly, both with those that loved me, and alone." The *Memoirs* omit entirely the great enjoyment and the triumphs. They dwell excessively on her sufferings and include many morbidly introspective passages from her adolescent journals and letters. The impression emerges that Margaret Fuller led a pathetic, sad life, with few rewards except shining virtue to counterbalance all that misery. For the modern reader, to whom plaster saints are not as attractive as they once were, the *Memoirs of Margaret Fuller* is nearly unreadable. Chaotic, disorganized, and formless, it has too much piety and mournfulness, too little fact. Carlyle complained of this, saying that the book lacked a clear, concise narrative, and that if you asked factual questions, "You are answered (so to speak) not in words, but by a symbolic tune on the bagpipe, symbolic burst of wind-music from the brass band."[7] Yet since her death, Margaret Fuller's reputation in America and abroad has been formed more by this book than by any other single source, and biographies still draw heavily on it.

Emerson, Channing, Clarke, and the others blew the bagpipes for virtue, friendship, and suffering because the age demanded it. If a woman was not a True Woman, she was worthless, even a monstrosity. Knowing and respecting Fuller, these men wished to safeguard her reputation. Incapable of challenging society's conception of womanhood, they manufactured a Margaret Fuller of whom society could approve. Thus their motives were partly admirable, even generous. They had revered her and wanted others to do so. They wanted to protect her, to build her a monument, said Emerson, against the crowds of the vulgar who were taunting her.[8]

Yet they themselves did not, perhaps could not, come to terms with her as she was. What she did, what she thought, what she stood for—all these opposed Victorian prudishness, hypocrisy, and sickly overprotection of a "weaker sex." She had challenged the patriarchy of which her editors were bulwarks. She had been strong, independent, and honest, and she had not hidden or fled from her (and others') sexuality. The tenacious ethic of purity in the Victorian age, the prevailing image of women's role, and Fuller's thoroughgoing feminism all help to explain the emergence of a Margaret Fuller myth. Free thought? an irregular marriage? Let us forget all that and bury it, let us canonize her instead, they said. It is so much easier and makes us feel so much better. Thus they avoided dealing with the eroticism that so terrified them; they avoided the need to cope with her challenge to society's prejudices and injustices.

The whitewash of the *Memoirs* may have been motivated by guilt as well as timidity and generosity. The facts of Fuller's life lead to an inescapable sense of tragic waste, an Aristotelian fear and pity at a life and an extraordinary talent prematurely cut off. Fuller's American friends had good reason to feel they had contributed to the blighting of her life. Horace Greeley, for example, praised her extravagantly in the *Memoirs*, and in his own autobiography called her the most extraordinary woman America had yet produced. Yet Greeley, who paid Fuller ten dollars for each of her dispatches from Europe, had refused to answer her letters when he learned of her unconventional marriage, and he dropped her from the *Tribune*. This financial and emotional hardship dampened Fuller's hopes that Greeley would publish her book on the Roman revolution. Another friend, even closer than Greeley, who had reason to feel guilt was Emerson, who had often been selfish, narrowminded, and less than honest toward Fuller. The *Memoirs* have an exaggerated, almost unreal quality. Overcompensation for their own guilt, their failures of friendship, may have helped produce all that wind-music from the brass band.

It is easy to criticize Margaret's friends for their failures and not to recognize how much they were prisoners of their age and its concepts— as we all are. Still, there was evasion, lack of courage, and an almost abject bowing to public opinion. If Margaret's reputation was served, the truth was not. What price virtue—or its counterfeit?

The makers of the *Memoirs* were not the only ones who perpetuated the Margaret Fuller myth. The public loved its combination of high drama and titillation and its moral lesson: as Barbara Welter remarks, Margaret Fuller's life showed nineteenth-century women the hazards and pitfalls of intellectual and personal emancipation.[9] Fuller's own family eagerly cooperated in the myth. Her brother Arthur, also a clergyman, undertook to collect and publish some of her writings after Emerson refused the task. Arthur Fuller too was singlemindedly bent on presenting to the world only the pious Christian face of his famous sister (as was another brother, Richard, who years later wrote to T.W. Higginson insisting that Higginson's biography stress her religiousness, wisdom, and high moral character). Arthur selected and prepared essays and poems for publication with this end in view. For example, he emphasized verses, not intended for publication, that were little more than jottings from her church-going hyperreligious youth. Arthur changed her critique of the French novelists by omitting her praise of George Sand, whom the American reading public thought to be a scandalous and immoral proponent of free love.[10] However, Arthur and Richard Fuller were the only persons close to Margaret who cared enough about her writing to want it published after her death. So, although Arthur Fuller does perpetuate a partial and distorted image of her, he at least preserved much of her work in print.

In succeeding years Margaret Fuller continued to be both overpraised and underestimated, either exalted to sainthood or ignored. When the New York publisher Evert Duyckinck produced his influential *Cyclopaedia of American Literature* in 1855, he based his sketch of Fuller on Emerson's section of the *Memoirs* and concluded with her death, remarking: "So perished this intellectual, sympathetic, kind, generous, noblehearted woman."[11] The post-Civil War generation of New England Transcendentalists and reformers canonized her for her humanitarian principles and for her feminism, the suffragist movement being well under way by then. In their periodicals the names of Emerson, Theodore Parker, and Margaret Fuller appeared again and again "like the names of the apostles in a history of the Christian Church."[12] As an old man James Clarke said that it would be worth dying for the chance of meeting Margaret again in heaven.[13] He had done his best to ensure that she would not be truthfully known on earth.

A new controversy erupted in the 1880s when Nathaniel Hawthorne's son Julian published a biography of his father that contained excerpts from his notebooks. (Hawthorne's notebooks, after his death, had been thoroughly censored by his wife, as Fuller's had been by Emerson. But Hawthorne's have since been largely recovered by scholars; Fuller's have not.) The controversial passage consisted of slanderous gossip Hawthorne heard in Italy about Margaret and her husband, followed by a malicious diatribe against her.[14] The most charitable statement in this long, vitriolic passage is that a kindly Providence had mercifully wrecked the ship that brought all three Ossolis back to America. If Margaret had to face slander like this, we are tempted to agree with him.

Hawthorne's comments stirred up a furor, for though the principals were dead, their families were not, and Margaret Fuller's partisans took up the cudgels in her behalf. The controversy eventually died down, though it was resurrected briefly in academic circles in the 1930s.[15] But Hawthorne's *Italian Notebooks*, in which the offensive passage appeared, circulated more widely than anything written by Margaret Fuller or her literarily inept brothers, and so the abusive attack long passed among many for a genuine portrait of her.

Hawthorne and Margaret Fuller knew each other well in Concord. She had nothing but high praise, even affection, for him as a writer and as a man, but Hawthorne's reaction to her was more intense and more confused. Some critics say Hawthorne, despite his attacks, liked Margaret Fuller; others insist he never liked her. He used Fuller's passionate, imperious personality as the prototype, or one of them, for Zenobia in *The Blithedale Romance* (1852), which grew out of Hawthorne's experiences at Brook Farm, where Fuller was a frequent visitor. Henry James thought that Zenobia was the finest thing in the book. He said that she was Hawthorne's only definite attempt to represent character in his novels. In spite of James's warnings not to compare the image too strictly with the model, readers did so.

Zenobia, whose name comes from a queen in antiquity, possesses a regal bearing and great influence over others. Proud, self-willed, mocking, and generous, she speaks eloquently about the deprivations and humiliations women were forced to endure. Zenobia is surely one of America's most attractive fictional feminists. Her frank sensuality is not lost on the reticent, perceptive Miles Coverdale.

> "I am afraid," said Zenobia, with mirth gleaming out of her eyes, "we shall find some difficulty in adopting the Paradisiacal system for at least a month to come. Look at that snow-drift sweeping past the window! Are there any figs ripe, do you think? . . . As for the garb of Eden," added she, shivering playfully, "I shall not assume it till after May-day!"

Miles reflects: "These last words, together with something in her manner, irresistibly brought up a picture of that fine, perfectly developed figure, in Eve's earliest garment." We may well admire Hawthorne's boldness in writing such a passage in America in 1852, and the boldness of mind that enabled him to portray the woman in the feminist without demeaning either.

There are parallels between Margaret Fuller and Zenobia other than feminism and temperament. Zenobia too is a superb conversationalist. Zenobia habitually wears an exotic flower of rare beauty in her hair, as Margaret Fuller did, at least when she conducted her famous Conversations. It is difficult to see why Hawthorne used the flower for Zenobia unless he wished to make the identification explicit. Zenobia, like her prototype, met a tragic, untimely death by drowning: she died for love. Zenobia's self-inflicted death suggests that a feminist, the world being what it is (or was), is better off dead. Modern critics now think that Zenobia is a composite of several women—transformed by Hawthorne's artistry and imagination—but the names of Zenobia and Margaret Fuller still remain linked.

Hawthorne seems to have been deeply ambivalent about Margaret Fuller.[16] Just as something of Fuller is infused into Zenobia, so something of Hawthorne himself is infused into Miles Coverdale, and one central theme of *Blithedale* is Zenobia's impact on Miles and his struggle to hide it from the world and from himself. Passing from fiction to life, we recall that, although Hawthorne sometimes engaged in extended conversations with Fuller on long walks through the woods and long moonlit boat rides on the river, he married a woman who was in nearly every respect the opposite of Margaret. Sophia Peabody Hawthorne conformed to the cult of the "true woman" with scarcely any deviation, and though she could unreservedly admire her husband's books, she could not provide the criticism he needed. As Henry James tactfully put it, Hawthorne's taste in women was "conservative." Like many other artists and men of intellect, Hawthorne preferred submissive, dependent women rather than strong, independent women for long-term relationships. But he could not quite get Margaret out of his system, and Zenobia is one of the most vivid characters he ever created.

Behind the vitality and warmth of Zenobia, however, stands that startling passage in the *Italian Notebooks*. The contradiction is only apparent. Hawthorne recognized Margaret's sexuality and passionate nature, responded to it, and was terrified of it and of his own passionate sexuality, actual or potential. The hostility and contempt expressed in the *Italian Notebooks* reveal Hawthorne's inability to be objective about Fuller. It has been suggested that Hawthorne, who was fond of beautiful, pure women, would have judged Margaret more leniently if she had been beautiful.[17] The passage, with its allusions to her "defective, evil nature," implies that Hawthorne took the Puritan view, including Puritan intolerance, and regarded Fuller as sinning through intellectual pride. Inevitably, therefore, she was betrayed by the flesh, that is, through her passion for a young, handsome man who could not appreciate her or offer her anything intellectually. She had sinned—Hawthorne called it "a total collapse in poor Margaret, morally and intellectually"—and she was justly punished. What to conventional opinion was Fuller's finest achievement, love and marriage, was ignominy in Hawthorne's view. In his condescending "she proved herself a very woman after all, and fell as the weakest of her sisters might," I see the harsh, unspoken condemnation: they can never amount to anything, these women, poor weak creatures, for all their pretensions. The abusiveness of Hawthorne's attack reveals how powerfully and fundamentally Fuller had challenged both patriarchy and Puritanism. Paula Blanchard's comment is incisive: "There is no possible way that anyone can accuse Margaret of being evil—if he is thinking of Margaret herself. But Hawthorne was not; he was thinking of what she represented to him."[18]

We may conjecture that the artist, the man, and the intellect in Hawthorne were attracted to and interested by Margaret; but to the Puritan and the male supremacist in him, she was the enemy, to be attacked unmercifully. Ultimately it is impossible to decide whether or not Hawthorne "liked" Margaret Fuller, and it is probably not terribly important, except for the damage he did to her reputation after her death.

Fuller had, we see, an intense impact on her generation and her century. Almost every imaginative mind of her age bore some trace of her influence, said Van Wyck Brooks. Oliver Wendell Holmes, who knew Margaret when they were schoolmates, made her the protagonist of his novel *Elsie Venner*. Henry James, who as a small boy was stunned when Washington Irving brought his father the news of her drowning, used the Margaret Fuller legend in *The Bostonians* and other novels. George Eliot wrote a sanctimonious and conventional review of the *Memoirs* for the *Westminster Review*, but she admitted privately that she had been very much moved by them, and by Margaret Fuller. (Eliot, precariously balancing an irregular liaison of her own with a desperate need for respectability and public approval, would hardly have been likely to stress the defiant and unconventional in Fuller's life, particularly her life in Italy.) Mazzini and the Polish poet Adam Mickiewicz had been in love with her: Mazzini offered her marriage, and Mickiewicz wanted to divorce his wife so that he could marry Margaret.[19] "Gray-headed men of today, the happy companions of her youth, grow young again while they speak of her," wrote Julia Ward Howe in 1883.[20]

Fuller's personality and her dramatic life have always received more attention than her work. She has never lacked for biographers, although some have made her story a maudlin soap opera, and others have produced Freudian psychohistories. "Margaret was a great creature," said Carlyle in 1854, "but you have no full biography of her yet. We want to know what time she got up in the morning and what sort of shoes and stockings she wore."[21] A definitive biography was impossible as long as Fuller was not acknowledged as a major literary and cultural figure in her own right. Until recently, she was seen merely as her friends' friend, her father's daughter, a whetstone on which the genius of others was honed, a frustrated feminist in quest of love, or an eccentric curiosity.

Thus it is hardly surprising that, for many, knowledge about Margaret Fuller has been a tangle of guesses, hints, prejudices, and apocryphal stories. The twentieth century developed its own versions of the myth. One of these came from the influential historian-critic Vernon L. Parrington. Though he sympathized with her achievements and admitted that she had been caricatured, Parrington merely developed the new myth of radical rebel. He called her a sensitive emotional barometer whose life epitomized the rebellion against Puritanism and Yankee materialism. Partly true, to be sure, but a barometer is a passive mechanism on which something else is registered. She was neither thinker, scholar, nor artist, asserted Parrington.[22] Margaret Fuller as a mindless, passive rebel has been a popular twentieth-century version of the Fuller personality cult, and it too perpetuated the delusion of her insignificance as a thinker or writer.

In her own time and long afterward, Margaret Fuller stirred strong reactions. She seemed to awaken murky, half-articulated fears in the Puritan consciousness. She represented something genuinely new in American experience, which seemed threatening to many, men and women alike.

The new dimension of American life that Margaret Fuller embodied, like America itself, had its roots in Europe. To understand her, we cannot look only at America. Too much of her thought and experience was nourished by Europe and eventually flowered there. Her friends called her "the Yankee Corinne" and compared her to Madame de Staël. More recently she has been compared to Mary Wollstonecraft.[23] Margaret, as those who knew her acknowledged, was a self-made woman, and Corinne, the heroine of De Staël's immensely popular novel by that name, influenced her self-creation. Consciously or not, Fuller seemed at times to be acting out the role of Corinne, creating her own myth. "Life imitates art," observed Oscar Wilde, and Margaret as a girl imitated literary models—Corinne's author as well as Corinne—partly because of the absence of models among the adult women in her milieu.[24] Corinne was to young women of the Romantic age what Werther was to young men.

The novel's popularity in Europe and the United States has faded, but it does retain a certain charm, despite its contrived plot. Corinne is an independent young woman of great aristic gifts and a sensitive, sympathetic nature, who lives in Rome and feels herself Italian in temperament and natural affinity, though born of English stock. Corinne achieves fame with her poetic gifts and attracts the intelligent, the gifted, the socially aristocratic, and the merely curious. She meets a handsome young Englishman, Lord Oswald, and they fall deeply in love. In the course of their romance they travel throughout Italy—the book served as a useful travel guide as well as a romance, one of those unique De Staël blends of practicality and emotional extravaganza. Through a series of misunderstandings, Oswald and Corinne separate. He returns to England, where he falls in love with and marries a pretty and submissive young woman, a more conventional domestic type than Corinne. This girl is eventually discovered to be Corinne's half-sister; through other twists of the plot, Corinne follows Oswald to England, but her generosity and self-abnegation prevent her from interfering with what she thinks is his own preference and his happiness. Distraught, she returns to her beloved Italy, where she languishes and finally dies of a broken heart, a martyr to love and a victim of the crushing obstacles that society puts in the path of the superior woman.

Though Margaret Fuller seems to have regarded Corinne as something of a weak-willed ninny, she and her own friends were enchanted with the idea of the sybilline *improvvisatrice*, who by her wit, intellect, talent, and personality was the center of a circle of admirers, who found the conventional woman's role unbearably stifling, but who nevertheless longed deeply for love and paid severe penalties for that love. Margaret Fuller, like Corinne, found her spiritual home in Italy, though Anglo-Saxon by birth and heritage; and many of the men who loved her chose, like Lord Oswald in the novel, to marry women with few talents and virtues beyond domestic ones.

Corinne's creator, Madame de Staël, also significantly influenced Margaret Fuller, who once asked a teacher, "Now tell me, had you rather be the brilliant De Staël or the useful Edgeworth?—though De Staël is useful too, but it is on the grand scale, on liberalizing, regenerating principles, and has not the immediate practical success that Edgeworth has."[25] Aside from differences in wealth and social class, the similarities are striking. Both women had fathers prominent in public life. Both had an overly intellectual, precocious childhood, deficient in bodily exercise and emotional nurturing. Though Fuller's father and De Staël's mother carefully supervised their education, parental discipline was felt much more than parental love. Both Fuller and De Staël were dazzling conversationalists, fascinating others through sympathy and personal charm where they could not attract through physical beauty. Both women had a penchant for acting, a love of commanding the center of the stage, and a flair for self-dramatization. Both women had passionate, enthusiastic natures and yearned for the heroic in life and in literature. Both studied German literature and thought; in fact, De Staël's *De L'Allemagne* helped to inspire Fuller to begin their study. But neither woman contented herself only with learning and writing. Both wanted more active careers. As mature women they became more deeply involved in politics than anything else. Madame de Staël's political maneuverings took place on the perilous stage of revolutionary and Napoleonic France, Margaret Fuller's in revolutionary Italy. Both women had an impassioned love of freedom and contempt for tyranny; De Staël defied Napoleon when no one else in Europe dared to. Both women were prominent literary critics, who through personal influence and through their writing had a great impact on their age. Both, after other experiences with love and toward the end of turbulent lives, married men much younger than themselves, handsome, completely unintellectual, but totally devoted. Neither woman lived beyond middle age.

Public reception of these women was similar too. Both were lionized, the European far more than the American. Both were controversial, in part because they often took unpopular stands as a matter of principle. And both suffered from the confusions of being female in a world that normally rewarded only men for political, intellectual, and artistic accomplishment. " 'Tis an evil lot, to have a man's ambition and a woman's heart," lamented Margaret Fuller. A remark by one of De Staël's biographers applies equally to Fuller: "Her unforgivable sins were her independence, her defiance of public opinion, her ruthless pursuit of happiness, and her conscious superiority. In a woman these were sins only exceptional minds could forgive."[26]

Margaret Fuller, in her time, found almost no exceptional minds to forgive her. Those who could neither understand nor forgive manufactured a myth instead.

CHAPTER 3

Emerson

In the drama of Margaret Fuller's life, death, and continuing legend, Emerson was one of the most important actors. As mentor, friend, co-worker, and chief guardian of her reputation after she died, Emerson was closely associated with Fuller for many years. She has often been regarded as his satellite, one of several minor figures in a group dominated by him. Some have seen her achievements as a mere adjunct to Emerson's.[1] Both these fallacies quickly dissipate on learning more about Fuller, and about how Emerson both shaped and stifled her achievements.

When they met in 1836, Emerson's public reputation was established and growing. Though he was only a few years older than Fuller, she looked up to him as a mentor and guide. She had heard him preach— some of his sermons, she said, were milestones in her intellectual history—and she wanted to know him personally. Through her effort and the help of mutual friends, Emerson invited her to Concord for a visit in the summer of 1836. Fuller often made an unfavorable first impression, and she made one on him. In a letter to his brother, written during her first visit, Emerson complimented her as an intelligent and accomplished lady, "quite an extraordinary person for her apprehensiveness, her acquisitions & her powers of conversation."[2] But in his private journal he remarked that the worst guest was one who "comes into the quiet house sometimes in breeches sometimes in petticoats and demands of his entertainer not shelter and food, but to find him in work."[3] Fuller did not come to Concord for chitchat; already she was making intellectual demands on Emerson. The breeches, if not the petticoats, were metaphorical, but the phrase reveals Emerson's bewilderment about whether she was masculine or feminine in character. To have intellect and use it as she did was considered masculine (Emerson and others habitually complimented her work by calling it manly or masculine), but her personal attractiveness was unambiguously feminine.

Emerson and his wife Lidian soon succumbed to Margaret's magnetism, and friendship quickly developed. Letter followed letter between Margaret and Waldo, as he was called by those close to him—except for his wife, who called him "Mr. E." Early letters expressed joy at the new friendship, hope for its ripening, and eagerness to arrange future meetings. Both delighted in sharing ideas, books, and literary enterprises. Their intercourse stimulated two fertile minds, and Emerson soon found he could scarcely live without that intercourse. The unmistakable impression from Emerson's letters and journals is that Margaret Fuller aroused in him an emotion, even an ardor, uncharacteristic of this sober, calmly sane, and dignified former clergyman. Like so many young persons of her generation, Fuller found in Emerson a man of lofty ideals and cultivated intellect who could articulate the high, if vague, aspirations toward which she struggled. Her mental life enlarged in scope and became more stable and inward through her association with him. But she assumed, without foundation, that because Emerson understood the life of the mind and the spirit, he understood also the life of the heart. That he did not led to bitter misunderstanding between them.

Temperamentally they were very different. Fuller was sociable and gregarious; Emerson was a lover of solitude. Time and again in his letters to her, he expressed his preference for a quiet life, set apart from the crush of human activity. For his chosen life of thought, he felt he needed isolation. Fuller detested a life apart from a vigorous, active society; she never forgot those miserable years on her father's farm at Groton. Despite his preference for the secluded pastoral life, Emerson often tired of his isolation and begged Margaret to relieve him of it. He would sometimes complain of receiving no letters from her to brighten his solitude. Once, at the end of a cold Massachusetts winter, he wrote that he wished for letters from her every day. He would beg her for visits: "Are you not ready to come up hither & make the bright days brighter or the grey ones tolerable? . . . Do I not need music & enchantments? Will you not bring me your charitable aid?"[4] She nearly always responded to his pleas for relief from solitude. She broadened his social life by making all her own friends accessible to him, friends like Caroline Sturgis, Sam Ward, Anna Barker, and Charles Newcomb. Margaret Fuller took him out of himself as no one else could, and Emerson soon found her indispensable.

With no other woman in his entire long life did Emerson experience such a fruitful intellectual communion. Fuller gave him the novels of George Sand; he took credit for introducing her to most of English literature, though she had read extensively under her father's tutelage and together with James Freeman Clarke. She, more receptive to art forms than Emerson, introduced him to the ballet, which he found immoral and therefore abhorrent. One reason Fuller became a better literary critic than her mentor—at least a better practical critic, though her critical theory was less philosophical than his—was that she responded to art *qua* art, while Emerson's moralism and philosophical inclinations distorted his taste and judgment of art. Fuller did not see this, however, and, assuming his interest in art coincided with her own, tried to educate him. She brought him portfolios of prints and sketches of Guercino, Piranesi, Raphael, Leyden, and others; she accompanied him to the new Boston art museum, the Atheneum. And knowing German better than he, she instructed him in pronunciation. More important, she refused to let him dismiss Goethe as lightly as he was first inclined to do, bringing him around to a reluctant admiration for Goethe's genius.[5]

The work of Fuller and Emerson on the *Dial*—she was its first editor, he was its second and last—has been studied more than any other aspect of their collaboration. This journal helped establish a uniquely American criticism and literature; it would not have been possible without their joint efforts. Many persons contributed to the *Dial*, but Fuller and Emerson guided and supported it, as well as provided large amounts of copy for it. The *Dial* lasted only four years, had a small circulation, and failed financially, but it had an enormous influence in America and abroad.

There was more to their association than delight in each other's company or the stimulus of ideas or the sharing of cultural experiences. Episodes of grating and painful misunderstandings shadowed their friendship. In the summer of 1840 Margaret and her friend Caroline Sturgis accused Waldo of coldness and incapacity to love. He protested, but before the disagreement died down, their mutual friend, Anna Barker, announced her engagement to another member of their circle, Sam Ward. The announcement evoked violent feelings in Margaret Fuller, who had once been in love with Sam Ward and also probably with Anna Barker. Emerson had been infatuated by the beauty and charm of southern-bred Anna, whom he saw as the beautiful Récamier to Fuller's De Staël, and he too felt an uncharacteristic state of emotion, which he detested and feared. Like the German Romantic writers their circle was reading, they all made a cult of friendship and glorified the ideal of Friendship, which the Barker-Ward engagement threatened. A series of intense, almost incoherent letters passed back and forth in the autumn of 1840 among Fuller, Emerson, Sturgis, Barker, and Ward, but by November the storm had passed. A calmer period succeeded it. A year later, though, Emerson still wrote bitterly to Caroline Sturgis about the capriciousness, instability, egotism, and ridiculous fanaticism of lovers, presumably with Anna and Sam in mind. This murky episode raised some terrifying demons of jealousy, desire, and fear of loss of love, and it left scars.

In mid-1841 Margaret renewed the confused argument about her relationship with Waldo. From the available evidence of their letters and journals, usually circuitously expressed in grandiloquent language, she seems to have expected more warmth and love from their friendship than she had so far received, more totality of commitment. She insisted she had no wish "to violate the sanctity of relations,"[6] presumably a reference to Emerson's being married, though it is hard to understand how Fuller can have expected an intense and exclusive love from a married man to have no relevance to his marriage. (Bell Gale Chevigny's analysis of this complex friendship sheds light on Fuller's state of mind here.[7]) At this stage in her life Fuller, like many people who are difficult to understand, craved to be understood. "I felt that you did not for me the highest office of friendship, by offering me the clue of the labyrinth of my own being," she accused him.[8] Insisting that she understood him perfectly, she asked petulantly why he could not understand her. "Why do I write thus to one who must ever regard the deepest tones of my nature as those of childish fancy or worldly discontent?"[9] Emerson, answering, admitted his icicle nature and acknowledged that he could not give her what she desired. "There is a difference in our constitution," he told her. "We use a different rhetoric. It seems as if we had been born & bred in different nations. You say you understand me wholly. You cannot communicate yourself to me. I hear the words sometimes but remain a stranger to your state of mind."[10] It was true. Margaret understood and eventually accepted Waldo for what he was; he could not understand her, and there is little evidence he ever seriously tried to. A number of Emerson's other friends—Thoreau for one, the poet Ellery Channing for another—had the disillusioning experience of asking for bread and receiving a stone. Emerson knew that he often failed his friends. He knew he had failed Margaret. Waldo told her, in effect, that by temperament or choice or both, he could not and would not be the kind of friend or lover she wanted and needed. For a long time she could not accept this. Only years later did she realize that Emerson would always subordinate persons to ideas and the rewards of personal relationships to the reward of contemplating the Ideal. "Persons are fine things, but they cost so much!," he noted in his journal. "For *thee* I must pay *me!*"[11] Evidently that was too high a price.

The conflict was painful and unsettling for them both, Margaret with urgent emotional needs that demanded fulfillment, Waldo admitting he could not fill them, but begging for her friendship anyway. There was probably a strong sexual undercurrent in this friendship that neither alluded to, an element that could be neither resolved nor surmounted. "She and Mr. Emerson met like Pyramus and Thisbe, a blank wall between," said one who knew them both.[12] Although her demands on him were urgent, he made demands on her too and could never understand why she was dissatisfied with their relationship. He said to her irritably, "I was content & happy to meet on a human footing a woman of sense & sentiment with whom one could exchange reasonable words & go away assured that wherever she went there was light & force & honour."[13] The unspoken question is clear: "Why must you be so unreasonable?" He expected her to delight, dazzle, inspire, and entertain him, never considering the price of such perpetual sweetness and light to her. "It costs Corinne no exertion to radiate the image of her on my retina," he wrote in his journal. "Yet how splendid the benefits!"[14] Once he greeted her as "ever to me a friendly angel with a cornucopia of gifts."[15] Waldo felt he very much needed Margaret and her gifts:

> And now what will you? Why should you interfere? See you not that I cannot spare you? that you cannot be spared? that a vast & beautiful Power to whose counsels our will was never party, has thrown us into strict neighborhood for best & happiest ends? . . . Allow me to serve you & you will do me a kindness; come & see me & you will recommend my house to me; let me visit you and I shall be cheered as ever by the spectacle of so much genius & character as you have always the gift to draw around you.[16]

Like many artists and men of intellect who are single-minded in the pursuit of their vision, Emerson apparently used whatever other persons might offer him with little intent of reciprocating. The givers, unfortunately, could not always accept being subordinated to such high and impersonal goals. One reason fewer women than men have achieved the highest reaches of art and thought may be that most women have been unwilling to use and thus subordinate other persons as means to those abstract ends. Women have historically tended to subordinate art and intellect to the concrete needs of human beings.

Emerson's need for Margaret Fuller is underlined by the frequency with which he urged her to move to Concord permanently. One of his fondest plans was for a society of kindred spirits, a kind of university composed of choice souls like herself, Alcott, Parker, Sturgis, Ripley, and others. "What society shall we not have!," he exclaimed to her. "What Sundays shall we not have! We shall sleep no more & we shall concert better houses, economies, & social modes than any we have seen."[17] Margaret once or twice agreed, thinking their friendship might prosper thus, but she knew she could not earn a living for herself in Concord and regretfully told him so.

The death of Emerson's son Waldo in early 1842 drove every other consideration from his mind, and by summer of that year the crises with Fuller were largely over. A calmer, mellower friendship ensued. During an August visit to Concord, she took a walk with him to Walden Pond and later wrote in her journal, "I feel more at home with him constantly, but we do not act powerfully on one another. He is a much better companion than formerly, for once he would talk obstinately through the walk, but now we can be silent and see things together."[18] Another day during the same visit she wrote, "Waldo and I have good meetings . . . my expectations are moderate now; it is his beautiful presence that I prize, far more than our intercourse."[19] About this time, Fuller relinquished her post as editor of the *Dial*, and they saw and wrote each other less often. Emerson, relieved that no more demands were being made on him, returned to his dream of a small society of cordial spirits united on a free and nonmaterial basis in Concord. As long as Fuller lived, he never gave up that dream. Even after he learned of her marriage, he wrote, in a letter neither of them knew would be the last between them:

> I . . . had vainly imagined that one of these days, when tired of cities, our little Concord would draw you to itself, by the united claims of four families of your friends,—but surprise is the woof you love to weave into all your web. Well, we shall only postpone our claim a little more patiently. . . . You may stay in Italy, for now, but all the more we shall want you & must have you at last.[20]

Waldo Emerson and Margaret Fuller seem to have been in love with each other. Those who think of Emerson as an idealized, sexless, above-it-all saint or sage, instead of a man, will doubtless reject this suggestion. The possessiveness and intensity on both sides characterizes love more than friendship, though admittedly Fuller had many intense friendships. Their quarrels had the marks of lovers' quarrels, their reconciliations were like lovers' reconciliations. A repentant Margaret Fuller wrote in June 1841:

> Dearest Waldo, By the light of this new moon I see very clearly that you were quite in the right and I in the wrong. . . . Now will you not as soon as you sincerely can write to say that you will bear no thought of this unless I behave again in this ungracious way and then you must tell me what I said this time and check my impetuous ways. I wanted this afternoon as soon as you were really out of the house to run after you and call as little children do kiss and be friends: that would not be decorous *really* for two Editors, but it shall be so in thought, shall it not?[21]

This make-believe was even more noticeable with Waldo, who frequently called Margaret a child or adopted an attitude of paternal benevolence. It was perhaps an unconscious disguise for their love or an effort to render it harmless, or a way to find relief from the transcendental loftiness of their *Dial* labors.

They expressed their love in many ways—in the tenderness and generous concern they so often showed for each other's well-being and happiness, for example. Emerson turned to Margaret Fuller to share his moments of supremest happiness or deepest sorrow, as at the birth of his daughter Edith or the death of his son Waldo. His continuing solicitude about Margaret's periodic ill-health, his efforts to arrange for publishers for her writings, and a host of large and small favors he did for her, all belie the accusations she made and he acknowledged, that he was cold and uncaring. Waldo was often generous. Yet each demanded from the other more than it was possible to give in return.

This intense interest of Fuller and Emerson in each other, however sublimated, was not so rarefied that it escaped Mrs. Emerson's notice. Though she was Margaret's loyal friend and attended her Conversations, Lidian Emerson was sometimes extremely upset at the amount of time her friend spent with "Mr. E." Chevigny points out the dishonesty of both Fuller and Emerson in not recognizing this.[22] Waldo apparently saw no conflict in his relationships with Margaret and his wife. His love for Margaret was associated in his mind with that pure platonic love glorified by Dante in the *Vita Nuova*. Fuller influenced Emerson to read and translate that work, and many rhapsodic passages in his journals show that the *Vita Nuova* best expressed his own love for Margaret.[23] Apparently she was to Waldo a holy person or savior who would lead him on divine upward paths toward a truly "New Life."

While Emerson envisioned his friend as leading him upward on heavenly paths, she was interested in more earthly ones. Gradually she expected less and less from him. She saw that their friendship must exist on his terms or not at all. She began to feel the need to broaden her life, to grow beyond the limits marked out for her by Emerson's serene world of lofty thought and platonic love. When Horace Greeley offered her a job and a home in New York, she accepted. She poured much of her hurt and bitterness at Emerson's rebuffs into a last article for the *Dial*. "Thought always convinced me that I could not have been so shallow as to barter heart for anything but heart," she wrote. "I only, by the bold play natural to me, led you to stake too high for your present income. I do not demand the forfeit on the friendly game."[24] Looking to the poets, she found parallels in the uneven friendship between Wordsworth, "who so early knew, and sought, and found the life and the work he wanted, whose wide and equable thought flows on like a river through the plain," and Coleridge, whose "nature was ardent, intense, variable in its workings, one of tides, crises, fermentations."[25] She wrote in her journal, on the eve of her departure for New York: "Leave him in his cell affirming absolute truth. . . . He keeps true to his thought, which is the great matter. . . . My inmost heart blesses the fate that gave me birth in the same clime and time."[26]

In New York, Fuller grew even further apart from Emerson. They continued to correspond, and occasionally they met, but he disapproved of her newspaper work, thinking it too lowly an enterprise for her talents. She became more and more involved in social and public issues. New York exhilarated her: it had exasperated Emerson. He had disliked its superficiality and materialism; she delighted in its opportunities. "The air of Wall Street, the expression of the faces of the male & female crowd in Broadway, the endless rustle of newspapers all make me feel not the value of their classes but of my own class—the supreme need of the few worshippers of the Muse—wild & sacred—as counteraction to this world of material & ephemeral interest," wrote Emerson, always true to his vocation.[27] But in New York Margaret Fuller began at last to find herself, as a woman and as a writer. She loved New York, loved "the vast tides of life that flow through her," and thought that only some great poem could express that life.[28] She found in New York that "twenty months have presented me with a richer and more varied exercise for thought and life, than twenty years could in any other part of these United States."[29] Emerson's secluded life of contemplation was not for her.

Fuller's high regard for Emerson never changed, and when she went to Europe she did much to spread his reputation there. She gave his essays to influential writers like Sand and Mickiewicz, who circulated them in French intellectual circles. When her *Papers on Literature and Art* was translated into French, its critique of Emerson aroused further interest in him. Emerson always showed a kindly solicitude for her, rejoicing when she wrote she was happy, expressing concern when she wrote of distress. But he did not know all the sources of her happiness, nor could he help her when she was in trouble. He wrote to her in Rome that he wanted to help her financially but found it impossible because of his own debts. "To serve you in the smallest part, you whom I have never offered to serve, would be a happiness."[30] Emerson was not to have that happiness. When he went to Europe in the autumn of 1847, they did not meet at all.

Still, Waldo continued to think of her as the Margaret he knew in Boston and Concord: "How much your letter made me wish to say, come live with me in Concord! . . . I mean yet to coax you into Mrs. Brown's little house opposite to my gate," he wrote her from Manchester in March 1848.[31] He never dreamed that she was then anxiously awaiting the birth of her child; he knew only that she was ill and poor. Gravely concerned, he did his best to rescue her. Several times he wrote commanding her to take the first available steamer to Marseilles, join him in Paris, and sail home to America. Because of her pregnancy and her liaison with Ossoli, about which he knew nothing, such an arrangement was clearly impossible. Emerson learned of the new husband and child only when it became public knowledge in 1849. He was dumbfounded, like everyone else who had stereotyped her as Miss Fuller, bluestocking and spinster. Emerson's remark to Elizabeth Peabody, that he couldn't understand why anyone would want to marry Margaret,[32] showed his characteristic obtuseness where she was concerned.

For Fuller Emerson always remained the symbol of a noble calm and stability of life such as she never enjoyed. During the bombardment of Rome, separated from her baby, anxious about her life and Ossoli's, she received a letter from Emerson and replied to it: "If ever you know of my life here, I think you will only wonder at the constancy with which I have sustained myself, ... Meanwhile, love me all you can. Let me feel that, amid the fearful agitations of the world, there are pure hands, with healthful, even pulse, stretched out toward me, if I claim their grasp."[33] Contradictorily, perhaps, her apprehension about Emerson's judgment of Ossoli made her reluctant to return to America. "I expect that to many of my friends, Mr. Emerson for one, he will be nothing, and they will not understand that I should have life in common with him," she wrote to her sister.[34]

Though Emerson was a background figure during Fuller's years in New York and Europe, he reentered the picture prominently at her death. As soon as the news of the Fire Island shipwreck reached Concord, he dispatched Thoreau to the site to obtain information and to recover whatever he could from the wreckage. In his journal Emerson recorded his shock:

> On Friday, 19 July, Margaret dies on rocks of Fire Island Beach within sight of & within 60 rods of the shore. To the last her country proves inhospitable to her, brave, eloquent, subtle, accomplished, devoted, constant soul! If nature availed in America to give birth to many such as she, freedom & honour & letters & art too were safe in this new world. ... I have lost in her my audience.[35]

On further reflection, he apparently adapted easily enough to her death, even felt it had been propitious. "She died in happy hour for herself," he wrote to Carlyle a month later. "Her health was much exhausted. Her marriage would have taken her away from us all, & there was a subsistence yet to be secured, & diminished powers, & old age."[36]

Almost immediately after her death, W.H. Channing asked Emerson to write Margaret's biography. Emerson, wondering in a letter to Sam Ward whether he could obtain the materials, and whether it would be publishable, said "I think it could really be done, if one would heroically devote himself, and a most vivacious book written."[37] But though Emerson made assiduous efforts to locate her papers, and though he helped prepare the *Memoirs*, such heroic devotion was not forthcoming from him.

After the *Memoirs* appeared, Margaret Fuller's brother Richard wrote to Emerson in December 1852, suggesting that he prepare an edition of her writings for a share of the profits. Emerson must have felt he had done enough by this time, for he begged off, saying that his eyes were weak and his working time too short. "I hardly know who is a proper party to take charge of Margaret's papers—I think they require to be put into the hands of an original writer, to make them really publishable," he wrote Richard Fuller, and he concluded somewhat lamely by offering a few letters and papers for such an edition.[38] Nine months later, Richard Fuller asked Emerson to write an introductory preface to a volume of Margaret's essays for $100. But he refused even this offer, claiming he had lectures to give and *English Traits* to prepare.

Margaret Fuller, not foreseeing that she would die at forty, had made no arrangements for the collection and proper editing of her writings. Yet she was concerned about the preservation and safety of her papers. In addition to the parcel she entrusted to her London acquaintances, she left another trunk of papers with an agent in Paris. On several occasions in Italy when she believed her life in danger, she took documents and letters about her marriage to her friends Emelyn Story and Lewis Cass, the American consul. Years before, she had sent Emerson poems with the admonition to keep them carefully with others she had given him. "You will then have a complete inventory of my emblems & trappings '*in case of death.*' Have you safe those I gave you of the All Saints Day &c.? I cannot find my copy & though I presume it is only mislaid, feel uneasy lest they should pass out of existence, for to me they are the keys of dear homes in the past. So I commend them to your care."[39] Because of their friendship she trusted Emerson, but her trust was to prove misplaced. He was clearly the most suitable person to take charge of her papers, collect them and edit them, or else arrange for some competent person to do it. He had worked with her, writing and co-editing, for a longer time and more closely than with anyone else. He was more qualified to undertake such an edition than any of her other friends and relatives.

Why then did Emerson refuse the editorship when Fuller's family and friends turned to him?

There are several possible reasons. Emerson had no scruples about subordinating all else to his own work, which must go forward no matter what claim of friendship had to be sacrificed. He also may have felt somehow betrayed by her marriage, which "would have taken her away from us all," and acted out of vindictiveness. Perhaps Emerson did not think Fuller's writings were worth his efforts. He never respected the integrity of her papers, as is clear by his mutilation of them in preparing the *Memoirs*. If he could suggest burning them, he probably would not want to edit them. When Emerson told Richard Fuller that some "original writer" should work them over to render them publishable, he showed his doubt of their intrinsic merit. On the other hand, Emerson did make long and detailed efforts to recover as many of her letters and papers as he could. An interesting passage from his journal while he was working on her *Memoirs* indicates his opinion of her work:

> Miss Peabody ransacks her memory for anecdotes of Margaret's youth, her self-devotion, her disappointments, which she tells with fervency, but I find myself always putting the previous question. These things have no value unless they lead somewhere. If a Burns, if a De Staël, if an artist is the result, our attention is pre-engaged; but quantities of rectitude, mountains of merit, chaos of ruins are of no account without result;—'tis all mere nightmare; false instincts; wasted lives.
>
> Now, unhappily, Margaret's writing does not justify any such research. All that can be said is that she represents an interesting hour and group in American cultivation; then that she was herself a fine, generous, inspiring, vinous, eloquent talker, who did not outlive her influence; and a kind of justice requires of us a monument, because crowds of vulgar people taunt her with want of position.[40]

In the Fuller *Memoirs* as well as in his own journals, Emerson disparaged her writing. She was a sentimentalist, deceived by her fancy; she wrote opaquely; and she had no talent for writing of nature, he said.[41] Most of Fuller's friends thought her conversation better than her writing, an opinion with which she agreed. Emerson merely concurred with the received opinion. He placed no value on her written works after her death.

Yet when she was alive, Emerson praised her work highly and urged its publication. Of her planned life of Goethe he told her, "I know that not possibly can you write a bad book [or] a dull page."[42] She responded gratefully, seeking his encouragement. When her translation of *Eckermann's Conversations* with her preface appeared, Emerson called it a brilliant statement. Several months later, after reading some of her journals, he wrote her that he hoped they soon would be published. He prefaced his negative criticisms of her "Essay on Critics" in the *Dial* with these remarks: "It has, like all these pieces that I read of yours, a certain merit as a whole, beyond the merit of the details. All these pieces have the rare merit of being very readable." Of her autobiographical sketch, "The Magnolia of Lake Ponchartrain," he said, "The Magnolia is a new Corinna with a fervid Southern eloquence that makes me wonder as often before how you fell into Massachusetts. It is rich and sad—sad it should not be—if one could only show why not!—but the piece will have a permanent value." In July of 1841 he wrote her, "I admire with all the world the article on Goethe." In November: "I read with pleasure & pride the paper on the composers." Receiving her essay for the *Dial* entitled "Entertainments of the Past Winter," he answered, "It calms me with the sense of so much possession, for it is a fine *manly* . . . criticism on the men & things before us, so flowing too & so readable that I am glad & proud of my friend."

No such lavish praise appeared in Emerson's comments after her death.[43] Why was there such a discrepancy?

Every possible answer to this question puts Emerson in an unfavorable light. He may have been flattering Margaret Fuller. He may have wished to spare her feelings by hiding his true opinions. He may have feared her displeasure if he said she wrote badly. Perhaps he feared losing her friendship or her love. Or Emerson, who accused the female mind in general and Margaret Fuller's mind in particular of an inability to be impersonal, may have allowed his judgment to be swayed by her personal magnetism. In all the drama of his relationship with her, Emerson may have been swept into glowing praise for her writings that later evaporated and vanished with her existence. The inescapable conclusion is that Emerson was either insincere or confused about Fuller's writings. At best, he lacked a clear, consistent standard by which to judge authorship.

Emerson's relationship with Margaret Fuller and his treatment of her work, both before and after her death, become more understandable seen in the context of his thinking about women, or Woman, that abstraction so much discussed in the nineteenth century. However magnetic or superior the individual woman might be, she was always circumscribed by the limitations of Emerson's thinking about the female sex. To his contemporaries Emerson seemed to be a progressive, enlightened thinker about women's rights, though in reality he was highly conventional and antifeminist. Some of his antifeminism derived from the social mores of the patriarchal society, some from the heritage of Puritanism, and some from his individual temperament.

The Transcendentalists applied their unshakable conviction of human dignity and equality to all individuals without restriction. The Transcendentalist period in New England broadened the theory and practice of human rights inestimably; for example, it fueled the Abolitionist movement. Women also responded to its liberating influence. Encouraged by the Transcendentalist reexamination of male and female roles, they began setting aside the traditional restrictions on their activities. Women of all classes emerged from the home to educate themselves and to organize for human rights, to lecture, write, edit, and publish.

Emerson supported women's rights in theory and said he believed women should have all the political rights and the right to own property.

Yet when women took action and planned a Woman's Rights Convention in 1850, Emerson wrote to Paulina Davis, an organizer, that he opposed public conventions as a method of obtaining redress. Like Fuller, he was skeptical of organized reformers and their schemes. He told Paulina Davis:

> Perhaps I am superstitious & traditional, but whilst I should vote for every franchise for women,—vote that they should hold property, and vote, yes & be eligible to all offices as men . . . I should not wish women to wish political functions, nor, if granted assume them. . . . A woman whom all men would feel to be the best, would decline such privileges if offered, & feel them to be obstacles to her legitimate influence.[44]

Emerson clearly perceived the suffering of women, to which many passages in his journals attest. "If women feel wronged, then they are wronged," he told Paulina Davis in the same letter. Though Emerson sometimes grew bored with Fuller's lengthy discussions of women's rights and wrongs, at least he knew her position: "Margaret Fuller testifies that women are slaves," he once noted in his journal.[45] He realized too that women would have to find their way for themselves:

> Man can never tell woman what her duties are: he will certainly end in describing a man in female attire . . . No. Woman only can tell the heights of feminine nature, & the only way in which man can help her, is by observing woman reverentially & whenever she speaks from herself & catches him in inspired moments up to a heaven of honor & religion, to hold her to that point by reverential recognition of the divinity that speaks through her.[46]

Nevertheless, Emerson did not or could not follow out the implications of these insights, and his views about women often failed to rise above stereotyped roles. "Woman should not be expected to write or fight or build or compose scores, she does all by inspiring man to do all. The poet finds her eyes anticipating all his ode, the sculptor his god, the architect his house. She looks it. She is the requiring genius."[47] Emerson praised one woman he knew, Sara Ripley, by writing of her passivity and submissiveness. "She is feminine in her character, though she talks with men. She has no disposition to preach, or to vote, or to lead society. She is superior to any appetites or arts."[48] In one especially striking passage, he wrote sensitively of women's humiliating situation in society, yet immediately he blunted the insight with the patronizing conclusion that they, like children, did not perceive the degradation:

> *Woman.* It is the worst of her condition that its advantages are permissive. Society lives on the system of money and woman comes at money & money's worth through compliment. I should not dare to be woman. Plainly they are created for that better system which supersedes money. But today,—In our civilization her position is often pathetic. What is she not expected to do &

suffer for some invitation to strawberries & cream. Mercifully their eyes are holden that they cannot see.[49]

Emerson's most forceful and unequivocal antifeminist statements appear, in a wondrous irony, in an address he made to the Woman's Rights Convention in Boston in 1855. The lecture is a dismal compendium of almost every cliché ever designed to prevent women from thinking and acting for themselves by asserting their utter inability to do so. With all the weight of the moral authority his age had ceded to him, Emerson announced decisively that women's place was in the shadow of their husbands and children.

> The life of the affections is primary to them, so that there is usually no employment or career which they will not with their own applause and that of society quit for a suitable marriage. And they give entirely to their affections, set their whole fortune on the die, lose themselves eagerly in the glory of their husbands and children. . . .
>
> No mastery in either of the fine arts . . . has yet been obtained by them, equal to the mastery of men in the same. The part they play in education, in the care of the young and the tuition of older children, is their organic office in the world. . . . Up to recent times, in no art or science, not in painting, poetry, or music, have they produced a master-piece. . . .
>
> There are plenty of people who believe women to be incapable of anything but to cook, incapable of interest in affairs.[50]

This charge, Emerson went on to say, was well-founded. However, he admitted that women exerted a decorative, civilizing influence, like that of dancing-masters and the etiquette of old-world courtiers.

> Society, conversation, decorum, flowers, dances, colors, forms, are their homes and attendants. . . . More vulnerable, more infirm, more mortal than men, they could not be such excellent artists in this element of fancy if they did not lend and give themselves to it. They are poets who believe their own poetry. They emit from their pores a colored atmosphere, one would say, wave upon wave of rosy light, in which they walk evermore, and see all objects through this warm-tinted mist that envelops them.

Not that women were devoid of moral qualities. They excelled in one: "The omnipotence of Eve is in humility. . . . This is the victory of Griselda, her supreme humility."

Emerson discoursed on women's lack of self-control, their excessive moodiness, their subjectivity, their narrowness, their variable constitutions, and the necessity for them to accept men as their guardians. Most insulting of all, he implied that women wanted no change in their situation and would be pained and embarrassed if they had the rights "a few" were asking.

From today's perspective, this is a disgraceful performance. It is impossible to know how women received it then. But the address makes clear that Emerson's Transcendentalist stance on the broadening of human possibility, human rights, and equality stopped short of women. When these principles threatened the societal base of patriarchy, when women like Margaret Fuller actually tried to live by them, the patriarchy had to be uncompromisingly reasserted. Women's subordinate position was immutable.

Fuller never wholly realized the virulence of Emerson's antifeminism. Not surprisingly, her own eloquence about the condition of women fell on stone ears where he was concerned, although he had seemed to encourage it, for example, by publishing her feminist tract in the *Dial*. Many besides Fuller looked to Emerson for leadership, guidance, wisdom. The semblance of enlightened views and conduct is often crueler than open bigotry, when appearance drops away to reveal hollowness at the core. Fuller once felt that cruelty with special keenness, when her *Dial* tract was being considered by Horace Greeley for publication as a book. Greeley agreed to publish it if Emerson would write the introduction. Fuller asked him, and he promised to do so. After much procrastinating he finally begged off the task, pleading that he had too much work of his own. Apparently Emerson did not want his name closely linked with Fuller's impassioned feminism and outspoken criticism of society. Though Greeley eventually published the book, she was sorely disappointed when Emerson reneged on his pledge.

Emerson had surely been closer to Fuller than any man she ever knew except Ossoli, her husband. Yet after her death, Emerson left in her *Memoirs* this evaluation, which judges her by standards she spent her life struggling to escape:

> Of the few events of her bright and blameless years, how many are private, and must remain so. In reciting the story of an affectionate and passionate woman, the voice lowers itself to a whisper, and becomes inaudible. A woman in our society finds her safety and happiness in exclusions and privacies. She congratulates herself when she is not called to the market, to the courts, to the polls, to the stage, or to the orchestra. Only the most extraordinary genius can make the career of an artist secure and agreeable to her. Prescriptions almost invincible the female lecturer or professor of any science must encounter; and, except on points where the charities which are left to women as their legitimate province interpose against the ferocity of laws, with us a female politician is unknown. Perhaps this fact, which so dangerously narrows the career of a woman, accuses the tardiness of our civility, and many signs show that a revolution is already on foot.
>
> Margaret had no love of notoriety, or taste for eccentricity, to goad her, and no weak fear of either. Willingly she was confined to the usual circles and methods of female talent.[51]

There lay her tragedy, of course, or at least part of it, a tragedy that Emerson refused to understand and did nothing to avert.

Some of Emerson's antifeminism, and his problems with Fuller, came from his fear that women were a snare or trap, literally or metaphorically. Several passages in his journals reveal that fear explicitly. He also feared and distrusted passion, as have so many American writers and thinkers before and after him.[52] Though Emerson apparently rejected the straitened thinking of his Puritan forebears, traces of it lingered and led to a suspicion of women, as well as a frank distaste for writers whom he judged to have led or advocated immoral lives—writers like Goethe or Sand or the socialist theoretician Fourier.

Margaret Fuller challenged Emerson, sexually and intellectually. She was "an affectionate and passionate woman"; distrusting passion, he necessarily distrusted her. "You would have me love you," he wrote of her in his journals, where he was often more honest than in his letters. "What shall I love? Your body? The supposition disgusts you. What you have thought & said? Well, whilst you were thinking & saying them, but not now. I see no possibility of loving any thing but what now is, & is becoming; your courage, your enterprize, your budding affection, your opening thought, your prayer, I can love,—but what else?"[53] It is difficult to say whether she sensed that Emerson was thinking such thoughts during their visits and conversations. Maybe she thought them too, about him; some of her rapturous passages about the way Emerson looked in his blue cloak hardly sound platonic.

In the *Memoirs* Emerson dwelt at length on a few of her physical traits he found unattractive. Those passages shed light on Emerson's ambivalent sexual response to Fuller. They also show how prominently the physical element loomed when Emerson (and so many other men) attempted to deal with notable women. Madame de Staël, who knew about the confusions evoked in others by a superior woman, wrote acidly: "Men of intellect, astonished to meet rivals among women, can judge them with neither the generosity of an adversary nor the indulgence of a protector. In this new conflict they follow neither the rules of honor nor of kindness."[54]

Emerson's personal relationships were damaged by his cold and egotistic nature, his inability to sustain any feeling of compassion. For example, before he went to Europe in 1847 he thought that Londoners like Carlyle surely exaggerated the poverty and suffering there. But once in England, Emerson changed his view. He wrote to his wife from Manchester:

Ah perhaps you should see the tragic spectacles which these streets show, these Manchester & those Liverpool streets, by day & by night to know how much of happiest circumstance, how much of safety of dignity & of opportunity belongs to us so easily that is ravished from this population. Woman is cheap & vile in England—it is tragical to see—Childhood, too, I see oftenest in the state of absolute beggary. My dearest little Edie [their daughter], to tell you the truth, costs me many a penny, day by day. I cannot go up the street but I see some woman in rags with a little creature just of Edie's age & size, but in coarsest ragged clothes, & barefooted, stepping beside her, and I look curiously into *her* Edies face, with some terror lest it should resemble *mine*, and the far-off Edie wins from me the halfpence for this near one. Bid Ellen & Edie thank God that they were born in New England, & bid them speak the truth and do the right forever & ever; and I hope they & theirs will not stand barefooted in the mud on a bridge in the rain all day to beg of passengers. But beggary is only the beginning & the sign of sorrow & evil here.[55]

Emerson's wife, who also suffered because of his coldness, attested that he was deeply impressed by the sufferings of others. Yet his compassionate response passed as quickly as the sight that evoked it. When Emerson on that same trip met and mingled with the English aristocrats he so much admired, he talked with them of "the splendid privileges of these English palaces, to which . . . the world never had anything that could compare."[56]

Emerson did not connect privilege and penury. When he saw beggars, he gave them pennies and rejoiced that he and his daughters were prosperous Americans. Margaret Fuller, seeing those same sufferings, threw all her energies into alleviating them at their source—the structure of the society that incubated beggars or allowed them. She failed in those efforts and nearly lost her life in the process. Emerson set himself to understand the world, Fuller to change it.

Emerson's high-toned moralism often interfered when some situation required compassion. An instance of this was his reaction to the suicide of Anna Barker Ward's brother. Emerson wrote to Fuller: "S.G.W. [Sam Ward] writes me that Anna's brother Jacob has killed himself. I have never seen him. Sometimes we see that that act may be great, but it very seldom is so: More often it is as Adam Smith said the greatest piece of impertinence that a man can be guilty of."[57] Moralizing over tragedy seems callous in the face of desperate suffering. Perhaps Emerson sensed that concern for individual pain would have interfered too much with his goals and his vision, but eventually one comes to question the ultimate value of a vision so devoid of human compassion. There have been too many visions like that.

Emerson found in Margaret Fuller "the presence of a rather mountainous ME."[58] He disliked egotism in a woman. Fuller's pride and self-love were great, to be sure—who else would have said with such offhand assurance, "I now know all the people worth knowing in America, and I find no intellect comparable to my own"?[59] Yet her pride in herself made possible her achievements in spite of overwhelming obstacles. Paradoxically, her egotism even led her to respond to the needs of others: self-love allowed love of others, because she assumed their aspirations were as godlike as her own, their needs as urgent, their sufferings as intense. Emerson's egotism differed: it prevented him from feeling what others needed. His first recorded thought at Fuller's death, "I have lost in her my audience," shows that he valued her not for herself but only insofar as she reflected him. That, for Emerson and for most other men in his century, was Woman's value: to inspire and uplift and purify and listen to Man. Inevitably he thought egotism in a woman was entirely inappropriate to her subordinate, passive role. We know now that Emerson's splendid exhortations about self-reliance and independence of spirit were not meant for women. He perceived women primarily as adjuncts to himself. He simply could not conceive that they might have or desire any independent existence, work, or thought. This fact explains much of his failure to do justice to Fuller's writings, for after she died, neither she nor her works had much reality to him. "Absent from you I am very likely to deny you," he once told her.[60] Emerson's denial of Fuller after her death has profoundly influenced her reputation and has been a major barrier to recognition of her achievement.

Admittedly, persons (male or female) were far less important to Emerson than ideas, and human love far less important than the "something higher" he spoke of repeatedly in his essays and journals. He found personal love too undependable, because it was mutable, unpredictable. Margaret Fuller had recognized almost from the start Emerson's mistrust of human beings:

After the first excitement of intimacy with him,—when I was made so happy by his high tendency, absolute purity, the freedom and infinite graces of an intellect cultivated much beyond any I had known,—came with me the questioning season. I was greatly disappointed in my relation to him. I was, indeed, always called on to be worthy,—this benefit was sure in our friendship. But I found no intelligence of my best self; far less was it revealed to me in new modes; for not only did he seem to want the living faith which enables one to discharge this holiest office of a friend, but he absolutely distrusted me in every region of my life with which he was unacquainted. The same trait I detected in his relations with others. He had faith in the Universal, but not in the Individual Man; he met men, not as a brother, but as a critic. Philosophy appeared to chill instead of exalting the poet.[61]

Emerson found only the Ideal worthy of his allegiance and devotion, though Carlyle and others warned him against too much abstractness and otherworldliness. Some passages from his journals describe ecstatic encounters with this Ideal realm, which was to him a source of permanent beauty and tranquility. Of one such mystical experience he wrote,

"Instantly the world in which I had lived so long becomes an apparition & I am brave with the celestial blood that beats in my heart whilst I worship the new beauty, & I am ready to die out of Nature and be born more fully into the new America I have found in the West."[62]

The conflict between Emerson and Fuller arose from a fundamental philosophic difference. One sought permanence and beauty in the Ideal, subordinating individual persons to that entirely spiritual ideal, and one sought the beauty and happiness of existence on the earth among persons and their created works. Shortly before she left for New York, Margaret Fuller had a last long evening walk with Emerson, and they came to an understanding about their differences. "We agreed that my God was love, his truth."[63] That summation was not generous enough to herself, for Fuller was motivated as much by devotion to truth as by the wish to give and receive love. Emerson tried to apprehend existence by thought alone, but Fuller knew that intellect was only a part of the meaning of her humanity. "With the intellect I always have, always shall, overcome," she wrote, "but that is not the half of the work. The life, the life! O, my God! shall the life never be sweet?"[64] She aimed for a wholeness of life that Emerson did not dream of. In pursuit of her goals, she became entangled in what Yeats calls "the fury and the mire of human veins," but always she served her gods well.

Emerson simplifed his life considerably by deciding to reign through the mind. Consistent in his aims, he allowed no one, not even Fuller, to draw him out of the domain for which he knew himself best suited. Through it he wielded great moral and intellectual leadership, and almost alone he succeeded in bringing a raw, immature America to respect the life of the mind whose dignity he embodied. In a country where the free search for truth was and is so strewn with obstacles, he pursued his own path against the tyranny of public opinion. Fuller understood that too. "I already see so well how these limitations have fitted him for his peculiar work, that I can no longer quarrel with them," she said. "I feel how invaluable is a cool mind, like his, amid the warring elements around us. As I look at him by his own law, I understand him better; and as I understand him better, differences melt away."[65]

Though Fuller apparently resolved her difficulties with Emerson, a clear understanding of this intricate relationship is exceedingly difficult to reach. Certainly there were defects on both sides. Yet we end by having to forgive Emerson for so much more. These pages on Emerson will seem too harsh to some persons. It is not my purpose to assault his undeniable greatness. I approached this study with all the reverence, admiration, and goodwill that most Americans share for this wise, humane thinker-teacher. Only after exploring the details of Emerson's relationship to Fuller did I glimpse another side of him. I saw there a distressing paradigm of many male-female relationships—tinged with in-justice, exploitation, emotional defects and emotional demands, the man successful and admired by the world, the woman at war with that world or with herself. Behind Emerson's shining words I discovered another, hidden Emerson, but the public and the private Fuller are the same woman. She did not bifurcate her words.

Fuller knew what she owed Emerson, and she was grateful. When she left New England, she made this epitaph of her friendship with him. "Farewell, O Grecian sage," she wrote. "Your excellence never shames me. You are intellect—but I am life."[66] Always loyal to her friends, she knew that, however flawed their relationship, he had changed her for the better. "From him I first learned what is meant by an inward life. . . . His influence has been more beneficial to me than that of any American," she once said in tribute to him. "I am always aware that I am far larger and deeper for him. His influence has been to me that of lofty assurance and sweet serenity. . . . He stops me from doing anything, and makes me think."[67] She accepted Emerson as he was: "Do not find fault with the hermits and scholars. The true text is: 'Mine own Telemachus, He does his work—I mine.' "[68] The parallel is excellent: the sober Telemachus' domestic and religious pieties contrast to Ulysses' impatient search for more life and new experience. Ulysses-like, Margaret Fuller struck out beyond the boundaries Emerson set for her, but ever afterward, his name was destined to be linked with hers.

CHAPTER 4

Goethe and Humanism

No one influenced Margaret Fuller's thought and life as much as Goethe, the master-spirit of the era. If Emerson was her most beneficial American influence, Goethe was the strongest European one. Students of Goethe have spoken of his remarkable gift for bringing out the best in them, for freeing the ego from stultifying layers of intellectual knowledge and rediscovering the true sources of selfhood. Goethe knew well that he was a liberator of the self, for its realization in both art and living. "Through me," he said, "they [younger poets] realized that, just as men live from within outwards, so the artist must work from within outwards, since he, no matter what disguise he wears, can bring only his individuality to light."[1] The liberation Fuller achieved and tried to help others achieve would have been impossible without Goethe.

She discovered Goethe at a time when the New England intellectuals of the 1820s and 1830s were making their first enthusiastic acquaintance with German thought and literature. The pilgrimages of leading American educators to Germany, Carlyle's articles explaining and popularizing German literature between 1827 and 1832, the appearance in America of De Staël's influential *De L'Allemagne*—all these helped kindle American interest in Germany and helped overcome some, though not all, of the isolation and immaturity of American culture. From its inception the new American Romantic movement drew on Germanic sources. The first stirrings of a native American literary and cultural movement coincided with an especially fertile and creative epoch in German literature and owed much to it.[2]

The Transcendentalists found in German thought the inspiration and support for many of their own unorthodox ideas. Transcendentalist periodicals such as the *Dial* and the *Harbinger* contained many articles about German writers, and at Brook Farm the Germans were diligently studied. The Transcendentalists adopted the German belief that innate truth exists intuitively in each individual mind; the correspondence between mind and nature and the habit of explaining abstract concepts by analogies with nature; preoccupation with the interior life and a rejection

45

of the merely external; disdain for society as it was, and a fondness for utopian visions; dislike of practical life with its financial, business, and worldly affairs; and a neo-Platonic preference for a loftier, truer, more satisfying ideality over a mean, ignoble, and unsatisfying reality.

Margaret Fuller began studying German in 1832, stimulated by the enthusiasm of Carlyle and De Staël. After three months she read the language with ease, and for years afterward German literature was a principal part of her studies. She taught it, talked about it, wrote articles about it, wrote imitations of it, and made numerous translations, some unpublished. She was especially receptive to German Romanticism, though familiar with German classicism as well. The poems, dramas, and essays of Tieck, Lessing, Körner, Novalis, Jean Paul Richter, Schiller, Heine, Klopstock, Uhland, and Schelling were among her readings. Literature and esthetics interested her more than philosophy and metaphysics, and though she tried to read some of the more abstract works—those of De Wette, Jacobi, Fichte, and Herder—she found them nearly incomprehensible.

Fuller advanced the knowledge of German literature in America through her writing, teaching, and conversation. This has been well documented.[3] But how the Germans influenced her has scarcely been explored, because she has always been regarded as a minor figure in a major movement, rather than important for herself. Many characteristics of her thought and writing style derive largely, if not wholly, from the German Romantic writers. She studied them at a formative time, and they fed her starved emotional life. Fuller shared with them the cult of friendship, mystical pietism, interest in the occult, preoccupation with subjective inner states of mind and feeling, and a disdainful impatience with the "real," "practical" world. Her convoluted, disorganized, willfully cryptic literary style, as well as her inability to find any suitable form for her writing, also shows their influence. Some German Romantics exalted fragments over finished production, and they thought form in literature was an unworthy goal for a writer, two ideas that still have wide currency and vociferous support. Without understanding how thoroughly she had been immersed in the German Romantics, one might conclude that Fuller's writings of that period reflected merely callowness, ignorance, or eccentricity. After she left New England, those traits were less evident in her work; some vanished entirely. Gradually the Romantics' hold on her imagination diminished, although she continued to write pioneering critiques of German literature when she lived in New York.

Goethe was not, strictly speaking, a Romantic. As much classical as Romantic, as much modern as either, he transcends any school or movement. Fuller discovered Goethe in the year of his death, 1832. "It seems to me as if the mind of Goethe had embraced the universe," she wrote to James Clarke, who shared her interest in Goethe and studied with her. "I have felt this lately, in reading his lyric poems. I am enchanted while I read. He comprehends every feeling I have ever had so perfectly, expresses it so beautifully; but when I shut the book, it seems as if I had lost my personal identity."[4] Sometimes she turned for relief from "the immense superiority of Goethe" to a writer like Novalis, whose "one-sidedness, imperfection, and glow . . . seem refreshingly human to me." The "glow" she meant was that of emotions. Her ardent nature led her to prefer writers who addressed and nourished the emotions, and to the neophyte, Goethe often seems aloof, dispassionate. Yet she kept on reading Goethe even when repelled by him. "I don't like Goethe so well as Schiller now," she told Clarke. "That perfect wisdom and *merciless* nature seems [sic] cold, after those seducing pictures of forms more beautiful than truth. Nathless, I should like to read the second part of Goethe's Memoirs, if you do not use it now."

Goethe soon became the most important figure in Fuller's mental world, though her interest in other German writers did not diminish. In a dozen years she read most of his major works, translated several, and planned to write his biography, which would be the first in English. She knew she needed to go to Europe for research, but could not go because she lacked the means. Emerson tried to help by asking Carlyle to send books. She collected materials on Goethe and had a promise of publication for the biography, but then she had to take the teaching position in Providence to support herself and help her family. Ill health—she was frequently prostrated by racking headaches and other unspecified ailments—also kept her from completing the book. But though she never wrote the biography, from these efforts came two important essays on Goethe for the *Dial*, and a third which prefaced her translation of *Eckermann's Conversations*. These pieces helped introduce Goethe to an interested American reading public.

That interest seems remote from us now, because it has declined so markedly. Few literate Americans are familiar with Goethe's life or the range of his thought or with works other than *Faust*, though to know Goethe only from *Faust* is like knowing Shakespeare only from *King Lear*. Goethe, safely established as a classic, has diminished to an industry for a few scholars and a rich source of quotable epigrams. He knew that his work would never have mass appeal. "My works cannot be popular," he told Eckermann. "They are written, not for the multitude, but only for individuals who desire something congenial, whose aims are like my own."[5] Not many great writers have mass popularity, and it is interesting to speculate on why so few today know and enjoy Goethe.

The arch-Puritan T.S. Eliot, who helped form Anglo-Saxon taste and literary values in the twentieth century, showed little interest in Goethe and much preferred Dante. The continuing eminence of the Romantic movement and visionary poets like Blake has perhaps blunted us to the power of Goethe's unvisionary, worldly genius. Goethe's emphasis on psychic health and sanity may not interest the contemporary mind; madness is more literarily fashionable. Perhaps Goethe was so lionized in his own century that a reaction inevitably set in. Or, in this democratic century, Goethe's hostility to democracy may alienate us from him. And of course his idiom is not current.

People do not talk of Goethe now, but they talked of him when Margaret Fuller lived and wrote. Even before Fuller discovered him, Goethe had enthusiasts and detractors in America. Fuller and other discerning reader-critics like Edward Everett, John Lothrop Motley, James Freeman Clarke, and F.H. Hedge tried to publicize his work, certain that his leavening influence would have great benefits. Yet these efforts on his behalf could not entirely remove the Puritan hostility to Goethe, a lurking suspicion that he was a morally subversive writer. Some prominent New Englanders of Fuller's day, such as Longfellow, while professing admiration for Goethe, denounced him as sensual and immoral. The influential educator George Bancroft thought Goethe indecent, vulgar, base, and immoral for representing vice so alluringly.

It was not only Americans who objected to Goethe. De Staël remarked on his lack of patriotism, aloofness from daily life, and offenses against good taste. In Europe he was recurrently attacked by miscellaneous bigots, prudes, idealists, philistines, liberals, radicals, and superpatriots. (One of these attacks was by Wolfgang Menzel, whom Fuller challenged in one of her *Dial* essays.) In England, De Quincey rejoiced that Goethe was not widely read there and charged him with immorality and impiety.

Clearly Goethe evoked strong, even fanatic response. "Goethe is the greatest genius that has lived for a century, and the greatest ass that has lived for three," Carlyle once exploded. "I could sometimes fall down and worship him; at other times I could kick him out of the room."[6] Many Transcendentalists and other Americans found Goethe subversive because he was un- or anti-Christian, skeptical, worldly, unsympathetic to democracy, and not devoted to the "highest" aims of life and poetry. They may also have found him suspect because he frequently delighted in life. Philosophically the Transcendentalists were closer to Kant—the term *transcendental* derives from Kant—than to Goethe, who rejected Kantian subjectivism and considered himself a spiritual heir of Spinoza. Interestingly, Americans ignored one aspect of Goethe's thought that would have confirmed their own cherished beliefs: his emphasis on the inherent value of action, work, and practical life as opposed to idle speculation, useless theory, or fruitless contemplation. Carlyle, admiring and publicizing those pragmatic tenets of Goethe, helped set the tone for the Victorian age in England. Carlyle transformed Goethe into a Victorian idol, conveniently ignoring his paganism, and did more than anyone else to make him known in the English-speaking world. Yet Americans have never really understood or accepted Goethe.

Emerson, who so often expressed the American mind and taught it what to think, was equivocal about Goethe. Both Fuller and Carlyle tried to win Emerson over to their own enthusiasm, but they did not succeed. Emerson, predictably, disapproved of Goethe's morals as well as his "velvet life," meaning his place in the court at Weimar.[7] Pushed and pulled by Carlyle and Fuller, Emerson reluctantly came to admire Goethe as a writer and called him "the pivotal mind in modern literature."[8] In his essay on Goethe in *Representative Men*, as well as in his *Dial* essay "Modern Literature," he so diluted and qualified his praise of the poet that he tore down with one hand what he purported to exalt with the other. Emerson called Goethe "the poet of prose, and not of poetry" and said he was too egotistic to have much moral influence.[9]

> That Goethe had not a moral perception proportionate to his other powers is not, then, merely a circumstance . . . but it is the cardinal fact of health or disease; since, lacking this, he failed in the highest sense to be a creator, and, with divine endowments, drops by irreversible decree into the common history of genius. He was content to fall into the track of vulgar poets and spend on common aims his splendid endowments, and has declined the office . . . of a Redeemer of the human mind.[10]

Obviously disappointed at not finding in Goethe the "Physician" of humanity,[11] Emerson seems to have wished him to be more like Jesus. But this American thinker enunciated what he and his age expected a poet to be. "I dare not say that Goethe has ascended to the highest grounds from which genius has spoken," said Emerson. "He has not worshipped the highest unity; he is incapable of self-surrender to the moral sentiment. There are nobler strains in poetry than any he has sounded. There are writers poorer in talent, whose tone is purer and more touches the heart."[12]

Though Emerson commended Goethe as a teacher and applauded the dignity he brought back to literature, his own Puritan-Calvinist bias was everywhere apparent: "[Goethe] was entirely at home and happy in his century and the world. None was so fit to live, or more heartily enjoyed the game. In this aim of culture, which is the genius of his works, is their power. The idea of absolute, eternal truth, without reference to my own enlargement by it, is higher."[13] Goethe's ability to enjoy life and be fit for it, Emerson implies, is less than admirable. One can scarcely imagine two less compatible minds than those of Emerson and Goethe, for Emerson, the rigorous moralist, distrusted and misunderstood human passions; he was skeptical of Goethe's unconcern with political issues and unsympathetic to the esthetic traditions of the Renaissance that Goethe embodied.[14]

Margaret Fuller partly agreed with Emerson, though she was a much fairer and more sympathetic interpreter of Goethe. They probably discussed Goethe many times, because reflections of Emerson's stance appear in her essays on Goethe. Her own intellectual development was largely a process of the struggle between the Emersonian view, with its roots in the Puritan-Transcendentalist-moralistic view of life and art, and Goethe's broader, more worldly, humanist view. She did not gradually reject the one and come to accept the other. She accepted parts of both, and the tension between them animated her thought.

Although Fuller was more receptive to Goethe's thought than most other Transcendentalists, her birth, education, heritage, and social group shaped her life and beliefs in ways thoroughly alien to what Goethe stood for. Though she refused to be entirely defined by them, she was ineluctably a product of her time and place. Clergymen, ex-clergymen, or clerical students dominated her intellectual and cultural milieu.[15] And even Transcendentalists not directly connected with the ministry, like the poet Jones Very, had deeply imbibed religion and religious fervor. Transcendentalism, like Puritanism and Unitarianism before it, was a highly intellectual phenomenon, with its moral rigorism, hidden asceticism, and disdain for the sensual nature of humankind. The monklike Thoreau embodies these qualities even more than Emerson. The religious and clerical nature of this germinal American movement called Transcendentalism has not been fully recognized. Any history of that movement deals with interminable religious controversies, hair-splitting over obscure points of doctrine, accusations of heresy, and counterprotestations of orthodoxy. Tremendous amounts of energy and mental effort fueled those doctrinal battles, fought like matters of life and death. Today the unimportance of those ancient clerical controversies indicates the vastly altered place of religion in American intellectual life. From our irreligious milieu we try to understand that hyperreligious age in which Margaret Fuller lived the first thirty-four years of her life. Not surprisingly, she often found it suffocating, even while it shaped her thinking. In fleeing New England, she escaped that religiosity. Apparently Fuller had no interest in theology, religious theory, or religious debate, though many of her fellow Transcendentalists seemed interested in little else. Even if she had been, theology had always excluded women, though religion was the single nondomestic realm allowed to them.[16]

Yet Fuller derived great strength from her religious origins. Puritanism has engendered force of character, sense of purpose, and firmness of will, individually and nationally. "Huguenot conscientiousness," Fuller called it in one of her *Tribune* articles.[17] American Puritanism has too often meant narrow, rigid moral codes severely enforced by the self-righteous and punished by ostracism or worse. It has often meant bigotry, small-mindedness, anti-intellectualism, philistinism about art, and suspicion of beauty. But it has also meant the pursuit of high moral standards, publicly and privately, and a refusal to settle for corruption in political systems or individuals. Margaret Fuller struggled against the bondage of her Puritan heritage, but she also shared its strengths. She was acutely uncomfortable with moral compromise. Always she aspired to the highest standards and goals, for herself, for others, and for societies and nations. She would never take refuge in cynicism or indifference when her lofty standards were not met.

So she was not much like Goethe. She was highly moralistic, emotional, and idealistic. Fraught with inner conflicts and plagued by ill health, she seldom achieved a harmonious relation with society. Egalitarian and democratic in her sympathies, she loved freedom and helped its cause in a revolution. In some ways she was more like Schiller than Goethe. But in the process of wrestling with Goethe, new powers, ideas, and capabilities developed in her. Formed by Puritanism, her American heritage, she was re-formed by Goethe and European humanism. The outlook that emerged blended the characteristics that we conventionally associate with classicism and Romanticism. Some of this outlook came naturally to her, some was acquired. It shaped her views on art, politics, and most social questions, and to understand those views, we must study that fusion.

In her critical essays on Goethe, Fuller's moral idealism is apparent. Goethe's inveterate realism both attracted and dismayed her. Henry James once quoted a French critic on Goethe: "It will astonish many persons to learn that Goethe was a great scorner of what we call the ideal. Reality, religiously studied, was always his muse and his inspiration."[18] The reality of Goethe's private life made Fuller uneasy, although she insisted that she would not allow her knowledge of his life to interfere with her judgment of his works. Since most of her contemporaries lacked such objectivity, she paradoxically had to defend Goethe's alleged immorality and unspirituality, the very grounds on which she found fault with him. She, a Puritan, defended Goethe to other Puritans. Many were shocked that a woman even dared to discuss such things. But though her essays on Goethe show an objectivity, sympathy, and comprehension of him possessed by few others of her milieu, she nevertheless was disappointed at what she, with Emerson, thought of as Goethe's deficient moral sense. Madame de Staël said of Goethe: "Le poète sait rétablir l'unité du monde physique avec le monde moral; son imagination forme un lien entre l'un et l'autre."[19] If Emerson understood this truth not at all, Fuller understood it only dimly.

This and other differences between Fuller and her mentor Goethe have led some to conclude that her entire life underscores her failure to live Goethe's teaching. Others find her so much a kindred spirit to Goethe that they deny she was a Transcendentalist. Margaret Fuller belongs wholly neither to Goethe nor to Transcendentalism, though she took much from both.

In general, Goethe humanized and liberated Fuller. He helped free her from the narrower confines of the Puritan mentality and revealed to her a life governed by principles other than immutable moralism. Her natural tendency was tolerance, and Goethe's broader tolerance enlarged her own. Fuller once noted that Americans were politically tolerant but spiritually intolerant, an ironic legacy of those who came to America to vindicate the rights of conscience. A disadvantage of immutable moralism is that it forces one to reject so much human behavior, so many individuals. The position of throwing up one's hands in horror is not conducive to embracing. One of Fuller's strengths was her sympathetic attention to all kinds of people. Whatever was human aroused her interest. In softening and modifying her moralism, Goethe increased her access to human beings and human experience.

Goethe educated Margaret Fuller to be a citizen of the world. This world held his interest, not some vague "higher" world. Goethe helped cure Fuller of an unhealthy spirituality, redirecting her vision and her efforts along saner, more fruitful, and more earthly lines. He liberated her from parochialism and showed her how to become cosmopolitan without sacrificing her nationalism or her patriotism. She could thus be interested in other peoples and cultures and ways of thinking, without being diminished as an American and a patriot. At a time when Americans were just beginning to create their national literature and formulate its principles, Goethe was already thinking of a world literature. "National literature is now rather an unmeaning term," he said. "The epoch of World-literature is at hand, and everyone must strive to hasten its approach."[20] Fuller did this in her literary criticism, as we shall see, and became the most cosmopolitan American critic of her time. Few of her compatriots were as much at home in Europe as she was, and in this, Goethe's cosmopolitan influence can also be seen.

Fuller's feminism also owed something to Goethe. Nineteenth-century New England had shown her only narrow and dismal possibilities for

women, stifling their intellectual development, demanding of them do-
mesticity and submissiveness. Through Goethe she began seeing what a
woman might be and become. Though Goethe was not a feminist in the
modern sense of the term, women inspired him, and he genuinely liked
them, though he also used them. The broad range of female characters in
his works delighted Fuller, and she discussed some of them in *Woman in
the Nineteenth Century*. She saw immediately that Goethe's women had
strong, separate identities: they were interesting *as* individuals. "All
these women, though we see them in relations, we can think of as
unrelated. They all are very individual, yet seem nowhere restrained."[21]
It was a revelation to her that Goethe allowed women to freely develop
their own abilities and talents; he did not define their existence by their
relations to others. "In all these expressions of Woman, the aim of Goethe is satisfactory to me," she wrote. "He aims at a pure self-subsistence,
and a free development of any powers with which they may be gifted by
nature as much for them as for men."[22]

These were wonders barely dreamed of in America in 1843, where
women had just begun awakening to their individual potential. Fuller
thought Goethe discerned the future development of women. His work,
she wrote, "bodes an era of freedom like its own of 'extraordinary generous seeking,' and new revelations. New individualities shall be developed
in the actual world."[23] By the actual world she meant the world outside
the home and family, which needed one specific type of woman to function there and forbade all other feminine types and talents their flowering. Fuller tried to bring into actuality in her own life the possibilities
suggested by Goethe. She hoped she could thus show the way for other
women to follow.

Goethe often used images of light to describe human and natural processes, and for Fuller he opened the shutters of a darkened room. With her
entire mental life illuminated, she looked out and saw beyond the confines
of the room. Goethe redirected her gaze, and she was never satisfied
afterwards with a narrow scope. Thus Fuller's liberation meant emphasiz-
ing more than one or two sides of her character. Goethe advocated a
many-sided harmonious development of all human qualities. This was
termed *self-culture* in Fuller's time, a new phrase for an old ideal traceable
back through the Renaissance to classical Greece, and popular with many
of the Transcendentalists. Fuller's personal growth from childhood had
been heavily weighted on the side of intellect and spirituality. Her Roman
and Christian—not Hellenic—education stressed study, religion, and the
sense of duty. As a result, her physical and emotional health had been
impaired, and her esthetic needs starved. To balance these deficiencies,
she gravitated toward German Romanticism. Goethe, however, showed
her most fully the ideal of self-culture that she strove after during much of

her adult life. Developing all her powers and talents became not only desirable but imperative for Fuller. She literally set about creating herself. All who knew her acknowledged her success. Even those who disliked her admitted that she had made of herself a work of art.

The concept of self-culture was suspect to some of Fuller's associates. They did not prefer an impoverished personality, but they feared the consequences of opening that Pandora's box, the old Renaissance ideal of the harmoniously developed human being. James Clarke, in Fuller's *Memoirs*, considered it his duty to teach that self-culture was not the highest aim of life, since the salvation of the soul has at its core a "profound selfishness."[24] To enter the kingdom of heaven, admonished Clarke, we must renounce perfect development here; Margaret's commitment to self-culture, he said, brought her into severe conflict with her surroundings, "which seemed so inadequate to the needs of her nature," and into conflict with her duties to relatives and friends.[25] The entire passage severely judges what Fuller strove to achieve. It sounds especially sour coming from a man who once avidly studied Goethe, the friend who most encouraged Fuller in her Goethean studies.

Margaret Fuller's friends were also alarmed by her interest in occult and mystical phenomena, which found encouragement in her studies of Goethe and the German Romantics. Hypnotism, numerology, the meaning of dreams and omens, clairvoyance, astrology, the significance of apparent coincidences, and psychic manifestations were important to her. Emerson wrote one of the best available accounts of Fuller's occult interests in the *Memoirs*. But he decisively stated that Margaret's occultism showed her paganism, and that occult interests generally were superstitious and puerile. Still, he admitted, "this propensity Margaret held with certain tenets of fate, which always swayed her, and which Goethe, who had found room and fine names for all this in his system, had encouraged; and, I may add, which her own experiences, early and late, seemed strangely to justify."[26]

Emerson's denunciation of her occult interests echoes the bitter wars waged by the Christian clergy for so many centuries against superstition and occultism. We are reminded too that witches were once burned in New England, and although no one called Margaret Fuller a witch, her friends often spoke of something "foreign" about her.

Goethe's idea of the *dämonisch*, which he insisted was not to be confused with conventional ideas of a devil or evil force, especially fascinated Fuller. Goethe describes it in his autobiography:

> He thought he could detect in nature—both animate and inanimate, with soul
> or without soul—something which manifests itself only in contradictions, and

which, therefore, could not be comprehended under any idea, still less under one word. It was not godlike, for it seemed unreasonable; not human, for it had no understanding; nor devilish, for it was beneficient; nor angelic, for it often betrayed a malicious pleasure. It resembled chance, for it evolved no consequences; it was like Providence, for it hinted at connection. All that limits us it seemed to penetrate; it seemed to sport at will with the necessary elements of our existence; it contradicted time and expanded space. In the impossible alone did it appear to find pleasure, while it rejected the possible with contempt.

To this principle, which seemed to come in between all other principles to separate them, and yet to link them together, I gave the name of Demoniac, after the example of the ancients, and of those who, at any rate, had perceptions of the same kind. I tried to screen myself from this fearful principle, by taking refuge, according to my usual habits, in an imaginary creation.[27]

Napoleon exemplified this "demoniac" nature, said Goethe. He was "full of unlimited power of action and unrest; so that his own dominion was too little for him, and the greatest would have been too little."[28] Goethe frequently spoke of the *dämonisch* as a powerful element in every passion, for it found its proper element in love. Herman Melville, who made his Captain Ahab one of the *dämonisch* natures described in Goethe's autobiography, understood the concept well.

Margaret Fuller, in an essay on Goethe, defined *dämonisch* as "gifted with an instinctive, spontaneous force, which at once, without calculation or foresight, chooses the right means to an end," and elsewhere she defined it as "energy for energy's sake."[29] She mentioned it in many letters and journals, and though Goethe insisted that the *dämonisch* was not synonymous with evil, Fuller tended to link them. She wrote to an unnamed friend:

As to the Daemoniacal, I know not that I can say to you anything more precise than you find from Goethe. There are no precise terms for such thoughts. The word *instinctive* indicates their existence. I intimated it in the little piece on the Drachenfels. It may be best understood, perhaps, by a symbol. As the sun shines from the serene heavens, dispelling noxious inhalations, and calling forth exquisite thoughts on the surface of earth in the shape of shrub or flower, so gnome-like works the fire within the hidden caverns and secret veins of earth, fashioning existences which have a longer share in time, perhaps, because they are not immortal in thought. Love, beauty, wisdom, goodness are intelligent, but this power moves only to seize its prey. It is not necessarily either malignant or the reverse, but it has no scope beyond demonstrating its existence. When conscious, self-asserting, it becomes (as power working for its own sake, unwilling to acknowledge love for its superior, must) the devil. That is the legend of Lucifer, the star that would not own its centre. Yet, while it is unconscious, it is not devilish, only daemoniac. In nature, we trace it in all volcanic workings, in a boding position of lights, in whispers of the wind, which has no pedigree; in deceitful invitations of the water, in the sullen rock, which never shall find a voice, and in the shapes of all those beings who go about seeking what they may devour. We speak of a mystery, a dread; we shudder, but we approach still nearer, and a part of our nature listens, sometimes answers to this influence, which, if not indestructible, is at least indissolubly linked with the existence of matter.

In genius, and in character, it works, as you say, instinctively; it refuses to be analyzed by the understanding, and is most of all inaccessible to the person who possesses it. We can only say, I have it, he has it. You have seen it often in the eyes of those Italian faces you like. It is most obvious in the eye. As we look on such eyes, we think on the tiger, the serpent, beings who lurk, glide, fascinate, mysteriously control. For it is occult by nature, and if it could meet you on the highway, and be familiarly known as an acquaintance, could not exist. The angels of light do not love, yet they do not insist on exterminating it.

It has given rise to the fables of wizard, enchantress, and the like; these beings are scarcely good, yet not necessarily bad. Power tempts them. They draw their skills from the dead, because their being is coeval with that of matter, and matter is the mother of death.[30]

This intriguing letter, with its overtones of *Walpurgisnacht*, suggests the reasons for Fuller's great interest in the occult. It illustrates how her Puritanism blended with Goethe's thought. No seventeenth-century Puritan preacher could have expressed better the sense of a mysterious, lurking Luciferian principle in the universe. Through Goethe she defined it and came partly to terms with it.

In acknowledging the existence of supra- or nonrational powers in the universe, Fuller departed from orthodox Christian teachings and from modern rationalism, for both reject occultism as a superstitious, barbaric relic of dark and pagan ages. In this way she allowed Goethe to free her from the limitations of a sterile, too-oppressive rationalism. Transcendentalism itself was a reaction against excessive rationalism, and the spirit of the nineteenth century was preeminently rationalistic and increasingly materialistic. Fuller's occult interests may have been a way of touching more primitive cultures or of loosening the bonds of modern rationalist civilization.

But unlike many primitives, her recognition of nonrational forces did not drive out rationality. In fact, because of the ignorance and charlatanism surrounding occult subjects, she advocated systematic, disinterested study of them. "The facts, the facts, are what we want now, no hasty, ambitious theories, no premature definitions, but carefully examined, distinctly recorded facts!"[31] She urged cooperative scientific efforts to formulate the laws of phenomena like supersensory communication. She never rejected reason nor did she "descend" to superstition. She tried to encompass what undeniably existed—in her own experience and that of others—but was not strictly rational. From Goethe she learned that reason and the suprarational did not necessarily contradict one another. To the rationalist superstition is bondage, and rationalism proceeds by excluding all phenomena it cannot comprehend on its own terms. But Fuller followed Goethe in admitting the existence of mystery, admitting that there were different modes in which existence and power became manifest. She never rejected experience because it had not yet been rationally explained.

At the heart of Margaret Fuller's thought lies the sense of the soul's dynamic evolution through successive stages. In perpetual growth and change she found a fundamental truth of existence. Few poets have articulated this truth better than Goethe or explored more of its possibilities. As "the pivotal mind," he lived at a time when the traditional philosophy of a static, fixed universe was yielding to the view of nature and humanity as mutable, organic, evolutionary. Goethe thought it was the poet's business to understand this. "The Divinity works in the living, not in the dead," he said, "In the becoming and changing, not in the become and fixed. Therefore Reason, with its tendency towards the divine, has only to do with the becoming, the living; but understanding with the become, the already fixed, that it may make use of it."[32]

Transcendentalism was highly receptive to the new ideas, especially from Germany, about the dynamic nature of the soul. The Transcendentalists emphatically rejected the older static schemata, particularly that of Locke, who dominated the thinking of the day in America. The concepts of organic growth and change were fundamental to Transcendentalism:

> This was what has been called the "organic metaphor," the tendency to conceive of reality in terms suitable to living things, to interpret the world by means of analogies with plant and animal life. Among the salient characteristics of such life are growth and change, potentiality and ripeness, creativity, and the interconnection of parts within a complex unit. Thus in Emerson's eyes—he was the most deliberate and subtle of American writers in exploiting this metaphor—nature was not a vast machine but a marvelously integrated diversity, a growing, dynamic, harmonious union of all beings in a single living Body. The Transcendentalists absorbed the organic metaphor from their German and English sources. . . . Its most important meaning for them was in the view it gave of human development. . . . It had not been customary to think of human intelligence as an organic growth. Locke discussed the operations of the mind in essentially mechanical terms; it was with a shock of delight, therefore, that the Transcendentalists realized that the mind *grew*.[33]

Goethe frequently spoke of human life as a progress through successive stages.

People always fancy that we must become old to become wise; but, in truth, as years advance, it is hard to keep ourselves as wise as we were. Man becomes, indeed, in the different stages of his life, a different being; but he cannot say that he is a better one, and, in certain matters, he is as likely to be right in his twentieth as in his sixtieth year."[34]

He sometimes compared human growth to the stages of growth of a plant, an image of metamorphosis as the essential fact of human existence. Referring to moral growth, he said:

Man has various stages which he must go through, and each brings with it its peculiar virtues and faults, which, in the epoch to which they belong, are to be considered natural, and in a manner right. On the next step he is another man; there is no trace left of the earlier virtues or faults; but others have taken their place. And so on to the final transformation, as to which we know not what we shall be.[35]

All this Fuller understood well. "Faust contains the great idea of his life," she wrote, "as indeed there is but one great poetic idea possible to man—the progress of a soul through the various forms of existence."[36] She understood that a person must acquiesce in this process, this progress from form to new form, and not only acquiesce but cooperate and actively seek it. The wager episode in *Faust* expresses this truth. If once Faust says to the passing moment "Stay, thou art so fair," then he has denied life with his consciousness, and Mephistopheles, the great negater, has triumphed.

Goethe expressed the idea also in a less formidable and more realistic work, the two-volume story of Wilhelm Meister. *Wilhelm Meisters Lehrjahre* (apprenticeship) and its sequel *Wilhelm Meisters Wanderjahre* (travels) were widely read by Fuller's contemporaries. Those novels, so popular as *Bildungsromans* in the nineteenth century, reflect the humanism that Fuller was especially drawn to.

To see the humanist basis of the Wilhelm Meister chronicle and therefore understand Fuller's humanism, we need to recall briefly what it has meant historically. Modern mass culture and industrial society have largely eclipsed the heritage of humanism, which has suffered from the strains and conflicts of a fragmented world. Many have lost touch with the humanism that inspired thinkers and artists from Socrates to Milton, from Ben Jonson to Matthew Arnold. That humanism, born in Periclean Greece, revived in the European Renaissance, regarded human beings in this world as the supreme object of interest, study, and love. Reacting against medieval otherworldliness, the humanists of the Renaissance emphasized the dignity and perfectibility of human beings, focusing particularly on education. They believed that education was best accomplished through reason and kindness rather than authority and force. In the Renaissance, and to some extent in Greece, humanists even advocated education for women as well as men. The humanist goal was the well-balanced individual, who developed his or her innate capacities through exercise and use. Stressing intellectual and moral culture, proponents of humanism wished to create a civilization in which cultivated men and women might lead lives of reason, morality, and esthetic satisfaction. Some humanists were Christian, others were not. Goethe's humanism and that of German classicism blended the Christian heritage with the Greek and strongly emphasized individual autonomy and responsibility.[37] In the twentieth century, humanism is threatened by technology. As Jacques Ellul and others have explained, the world of technology is a world of material things, a universe of machines, objects, and processes. In the world of technology human beings are reduced to material objects, so much so that the concept of a distinctively human excellence apart from a technological society scarcely exists any longer. Moreover, in our age the necessity of dealing with and providing for enormous numbers of human beings has made the older humanist emphasis on the individual seem outmoded, impossible of realization, or even irresponsible. So far it has not been imaginatively possible to adapt traditional humanism to the lives of large masses of people, though many thoughtful, humane persons feel the need for such a reconciliation.

Wilhelm Meister's world is a less complicated one. In the *Lehrjahre* young Wilhelm strives for a reasonable and happy life that allows him scope and does not stunt his esthetic faculties. He is reluctant to settle into the constricting merchant's life laid out for him by his family and his social class. Not knowing exactly what he wants to do and be, Wilhelm follows his love for the theater and leaves home to join a traveling company. He serves in turn as actor, writer, producer, promoter, and overall guiding hand. At the height of his success with the troupe, a mysterious voice comes from the wings during a performance of *Hamlet* and urges him to flee. Wilhelm understands that if he stays with the theater, he will not develop further. He may not relax into complacency and enjoy his success, but must reach still further.

The novel's chief concerns are education and living in the world; the two frequently coincide during Wilhelm's years of growth. His education begins in rebellion, when he rejects the paths marked out for him by his family and class. It is furthered as he develops his nature through experiences in many places with many different people. Although he does not understand what he searches for, Wilhelm loves, acts, errs, and grows. Through all this he strives to become what he was meant to be. Margaret Fuller took her motto from the *Lehrjahre:* "extraordinary generous seeking." The *Lehrjahre* presents the educational aim of self-cultivation, yet this is not its only theme. Wilhelm learns from a group of truth-seekers called the Society of the Tower that self-development, although indispensable, is only one step toward a happy, fruitful life. He must henceforth devote himself to actively serving others. Wilhelm's apprenticeship, his learning period, ends when he discovers he is a father and undertakes the education of his son Felix, whose name means happy. Through fatherhood Wilhelm comes to understand the continuity of life.

At the end of the *Lehrjahre*, Wilhelm Meister's education is virtually complete. The *Wanderjahre*, subtitled *The Renunciants*, poses the question "What will be his goal?"[38] Whatever it is, it will necessarily limit him, and so Wilhelm must accept some measure of renunciation, for submission to limitation is the moral foundation of a useful life. Dilettantism, Goethe suggests, is a great evil, because it excludes genuine education and genuine achievement.[39]

The *Wanderjahre* emphasizes social activism. Goethe portrays a group of workers and artisans, a type of society (preindustrial) in which individuals contribute on the basis of their talents and work, but in which they are subordinated to the whole. The concepts of an elite who will leaven society, of hierarchy, subordination, and submission to limitation, suggest a classical stance. A clear sense of community is cultivated among all the members, and Wilhelm brings his son Felix to this group to be educated. At the end of the novel, Wilhelm performs a symbolic act of saving his son from death. After this he decides to become a surgeon.

Many readers in Fuller's time found *Wilhelm Meister* mundane, commonplace, and unheroic—when they were not appalled by its protagonist's "vices" and the "low" company he kept. But the work contains passages of extraordinary beauty, even sublimity. For instance, in Wilhelm's instruction in the three reverences, he learns from the wise elders of the community that reverence does not come easily to human beings, nor do they willingly submit to it. Nature does not impart it, therefore they must learn from teachers. Education should unfold what nature has given each child, yet the child is not an adult until he or she learns reverence for what is above, under, and around, that is, for God, for the material earth that nourishes and endangers, and for people, one's comrades and equals. These reverences, together with the development of a unique self, form the basis for human life in the world. It is essentially a humanist basis, and quite practical as well.

Wilhelm Meister is the opposite of Faust.[40] Both aspire and strive for something beyond their given lot, but unlike Faust, Wilhelm learns that there is or ought to be a limit to one's striving. Wilhelm wants to know how to live: he seeks a unified, happy life. Faust, on the other hand, is the heroic titan who will accept no limits. Wilhelm integrates himself into ordinary human culture and finds a productive and rewarding life in association with others. Faust's genius lies in his transcendence of those things, and by that transcendence he achieves grandeur. In these two extremes, Goethe presented the possibilities open to the modern mind. But Faust has captured the modern imagination, because the heroic man or woman usually has more charisma than the useful one. As Margaret Fuller once said, "Who would be a goody that could be a genius?"[41] Goethe called Faust a subjective, perplexed, impassioned individual whose semidarkness would probably be highly pleasing to humankind, and he was right. Margaret Fuller seemed to follow Faust's path rather than Wilhelm Meister's, yet she grew decisively toward social activism and usefulness, like Wilhelm, rather than toward isolated splendor, like Faust. Unwilling to choose either classicism or Romanticism to the exclusion of the other, she wove both into the fabric of her life.

To the humanist, humankind is a unique species, neither beast nor unbodied being. Because human beings are partly but not wholly physical creatures, the humanist considers analogies between persons and animals to have a limited usefulness and never entirely equates the human with the natural. Thus humanism is incompatible with the ideology of scientific naturalism, or materialistic naturalism, that reigns intellectually in our century. The threadbare literary naturalism that still permeates American writing is also alien to humanism. Traditional humanists assume that people are capable of choice, freedom, and responsibility. People have reason, intellect, will, a moral sense, and feeling, however incipient, darkened, perverted, or crushed these faculties may be in any individual. Some forms of humanism have emphasized the corruptibility of human nature rather than its perfectibility.

Humanism is politically neutral and thus allies itself with either a conservative or a liberal political philosophy. It often surfaces after a period of excesses, seeking to restore a balance when human affairs appear to have gone dangerously awry. When humanism joins conservative politics, it stresses the inherent flaws and imperfections of human nature, the need for moderation and limitation, the predominance of reason and traditional wisdom over emotion or intuition, and skepticism about improving the human lot, individually or en masse. Such was the humanism of Swift, Pope, Burke, and Johnson in the eighteenth century[42] and the neohumanist school of literary critics like Irving Babbitt, Paul Elmer More, and Norman Foerster in the first third of this century in America.

Humanism is equally at home with more leftist political viewpoints. Then it emphasizes the infinite possibilities for human improvement, the need for expansion, change, and aspiration, the importance of the intuitive imaginative faculties over reason, and the extension of personal and political freedom to more and more individuals, groups, and nations. Although they did not apotheosize imagination and intuition, many great figures of the eighteenth-century enlightenment were humanists, or within the humanist tradition. Much socialist thought and some of the forms socialism took in the nineteenth and twentieth centuries had a humanist foundation.

The foregoing helps explain the seeming paradox in Fuller's and Goethe's divergent political sympathies: he was aligned with conservatism and the Weimar aristocracy, she was a revolutionary and socialist at the end of her life, yet neither betrayed their fundamental humanism. Margaret Fuller's steady leftward political movement fulfilled her humanism and did not negate it. But all her activities, personal as well as public, expressed these basic humanist principles and ideas. Her Boston Conversations for women, for example, and much of her journalism in New York were educative in intent: she wished to help prepare civilized, moral human beings to live in a civilized, moral society. The societies she moved in were not yet ready to accept such ideals. She once observed that "the mass has never yet been humanized, though the age may develop a human thought."[43] Humanism has rarely had so devoted an advocate as Margaret Fuller, and to the extent that those societies were un- or antihumanist, she inevitably clashed with them.

Humanism has always valued art. The humanist wishes to find and express the constant elements of human nature and human experience, those that transcend a particular time, place, social class, or wholly personal eccentricity. For the true humanist, art expresses these elements better than any other activity, and, in revealing us to ourselves, forges the links that join all human beings.

The most central and continuous of Goethe's studies focused on art and form. Fuller absorbed from Goethe this love and respect for art as the supreme human expression. After literature, Goethe was most devoted to the plastic arts; he had less temperamental affinity for music, less instinctive response to it. But Fuller found more exaltation and meaning in music than in any other artistic experience, even literature. Goethe thought that the *dämonisch* dwelled in music more than other arts, and music spoke better and more intimately to her restless soul. She did not have the natural eye for painting, drawing, or sculpture that might lead her to fruitful study and sure intellectual grasp of them. Yet from Goethe she knew their importance, and she tried to educate herself and her friends about the visual arts, which were then in their infancy in America.

For most of her life, nothing took precedence over her devotion to art. In this she diverged from her fellow Transcendentalists, for whom art was only one expression of the spirit. Genuine art and poetry reach toward a condition that harmonizes the sensual and spiritual sides of human nature, a truth imperfectly grasped, if at all, by the Transcendentalists. Schiller, feeling that the Kantian disdain for the sensual nature was a defect, recognized the true esthetic ideal in Goethe. "Only when the sensual and the moral natures in man are at enmity with each other must help be sought in pure reason," Schiller said. And again, "Religion opens her arms to him on whom beauty is lost."[44] This suggests why so little significant poetry emerged from the Transcendentalist movement. The Transcendentalists, trying to justify art by showing that it was moral and uplifting, actually confined it in a straitjacket. Theodore Parker, for example, advocated the study of German literature because of its religious qualities, and because it approached the Christian ideal of literary art. Poe fought valiantly to separate art from moral uplift and didacticism, and so did Margaret Fuller, if more subtly and less pugnaciously than Poe. She owed her commitment to the primacy of art largely to Goethe, for she found it nowhere in her own milieu.

The social dimensions of art and the relation of the artist to society especially interested her. Goethe explored this relation in his poetic drama *Torquato Tasso*. Fuller translated the play in 1842, but she could not find a publisher for it, and it remained unpublished until nine years after her death. Exploring the isolation of the artist and his ambivalent feelings toward the nonartists among whom he must live, *Tasso* is a study of a sensitive, passionate, creative person trying to accommodate himself with the world. It is a play full of paradoxes, reflecting, as Fuller noted, the painful relations of genius to his peers who do not understand him. This is a typical theme of the Romantic movement, although the play is as much classical as Romantic in its observation of the unities and in the calm, measured stateliness of its verse. *Tasso*, written in 1790, is also surprisingly modern in dealing so trenchantly with the failure of communication between individuals. Fuller's interest in the play suggests that she had felt the pangs of Tasso's situation. She also liked the play because it showed another Goethe than the self-restrained, serene sage of Weimar that the world paid homage to. The play reveals him as vulnerable, erratic, willful, and even foolish. *Tasso*, she wrote in her essay "Goethe," showed that Goethe's self-control was a quality acquired, not innate, and thus all the more valuable.

The character of Tasso is based on the Renaissance Italian court poet, who is best known for his epic *Jerusalem Delivered*. As the play begins, Tasso has just completed his masterpiece and delivered it to his patron, Alfonso, the Duke of Ferrara, to whose court Tasso belongs. It is springtime in the garden of the Duke's villa, and all is well with Tasso's world. He is a great favorite of the court ladies, especially the Duke's sister, Princess Leonore, who inspired the poem and whom he loves. Tasso's success and favor arouse the momentary envy of Antonio, the Duke's most trusted diplomat, and they quarrel. The men and women of the court love and esteem Tasso, but for each of them he serves some element of self-interest too. The Duke, for example, values Tasso's poem because it redounds to his own glory, and he worries about the poet being wooed away to adorn the competing court of the Medicis. For the Duke, poet and poem serve political purposes, form part of a power structure. Though Tasso is loved, his court friends treat him as a spoiled, helpless child who must be guarded, lectured to, restrained, scolded, and sometimes rebuffed when his enthusiasm does not happen to suit them. Tasso is spontaneous, loving, and generous by nature, but he suffers a deep sense of inadequacy in comparison to the competent, sophisticated Duke and diplomat, and this sense of inadequacy is linked with a touch of paranoia. Thus he does "misbehave," does seem a spoiled, helpless, unruly child.

The ugly misunderstanding destroys the idyll. Efforts to reconcile Tasso with Antonio deepen the rift. No one at court understands why it has happened, though they try. "Alas, that we fail so completely to observe the pure, mute signal of the heart," laments the Princess. Disillusioned and wounded, Tasso impetuously decides to leave the court and go to Rome. "I must be free in thinking and creating," he exclaims. "In action the world hems us in enough." Crushed in spirit, his manhood humiliated, Tasso nevertheless admits that he needs the practicality and rocklike strength of Antonio and thus has to stay at Ferrara's court. A tenuous truce is achieved between poet and court, but at a price.

Goethe said that the theme of *Tasso* was "the disproportion between talent and life."[45] "Poor Tasso in the play offered his love and service too officiously to all," wrote Fuller. "They all rejected it, and declared him mad, because he made statements too emphatic of his feelings."[46] As Tasso says, "If men in their torment must be mute, a god gave me the power to tell my pain." The genius, the passionate soul, the creative person, the loving, spontaneous person—Tasso is all these—bitterly clashes with the demands, the deceits, the restrictions of friends and the world, and yet such a person needs those friends, that world. Goethe usually explored his theme of the individual's developing potentialities in the context of some society. Americans are more fascinated by the solitary hero, the cowboy, the gunman, the outlaw, Natty Bumpo in the wilderness, Amelia Earhart's solo flights, the lonely pioneers making their heroic way—the list is endless. Fuller, though, was fascinated by the range of relationships *within* society portrayed by Goethe. She knew, as he did, the individual's need of society, knew that in society lies the individual's field of action and greatest satisfactions. The importance of society is evident in most of Goethe's mature works, not only *Tasso* and

Wilhelm Meister but in *Iphigenia in Tauris, Hermann and Dorothea, Elective Affinities*, and many others.

The likenesses between Margaret Fuller and Tasso are readily apparent. In some ways the favored darling of her circle, she constantly experienced a sense of incompatibility with that circle. Impetuous, loving, creative, proud, and generous by nature, she needed the society that hemmed her in and crushed her aspirations.

Torquato Tasso is not a tragedy, however. Tragedy is implicit in the play if one regards the incompatibility between society and its Tassos to be fundamental and unalterable.[47] Goethe said, "All that is tragic rests upon an irreconcilable opposition. When compromise occurs or becomes possible, the tragic vanishes."[48] The uneasy reconciliation at the end of the play signifies the reconciliation Goethe sought for himself. To some extent he found it at Weimar, whose Grand Duke Karl August, Goethe's friend and patron, was said to be like Antonio. Goethe tried to reconcile the opposing extremes of experience by balancing or uniting them. This search for reconciliation, this hunger for unity, became a cornerstone of Fuller's thought too, and more will be said about it later. Yet she never quite arrived at that harmonious interior reconciliation that Goethe ultimately achieved, nor did she ever find a happy modus vivendi with society. She had neither a Weimar, a Ferrara, nor any other safe haven.

For the most part she was, unlike Wilhelm Meister, the seeker not the master. Goethe taught the necessity of overcoming rather than falling victim to circumstance, a noble teaching. Such mastery comes to only a few, perhaps; Fuller was not one of them. It is difficult to avoid the conclusion that fate is kinder to some than to others. Kind to Goethe, unkind to Schiller. Kinder to Bach than to Beethoven and Mozart. Kind to Wordsworth, unkind to Coleridge. Kind to Valéry, unkind to Rimbaud. Kind to Emerson, unkind to Poe. Still, fatalism does not help us understand Fuller, who was so seldom passive or fatalistic. Goethe did not write tragedy; Fuller, we feel, lived it. Fuller's life—her aspirations, her struggle to realize them, her successes and her failures—frequently leads us to contemplate such ultimate questions, and to recognize the limits of intellect in answering them, limits that she and Goethe both understood.

Goethe was the great liberator for Margaret Fuller. Through him she formed and remained true to the humanist ideals at the heart of her endeavors: her literary criticism and social thought, her personal relationships, her philanthropy and political activity. Through Goethe, her individuality came to light, and she discovered who she was and what she might become. From Goethe came the sustaining vision toward which her thought and life unfolded.

CHAPTER 5

The Prophecy of a Poet

The legend of Margaret Fuller's life and personality has cast a long shadow over her written works, which have been virtually ignored since her death. Henry James, who never knew her, knew her legend. He wrote that "this impassioned Yankee, who occupied so large a place in the thoughts, the lives, the affections, of an intelligent and appreciative society . . . left behind her nothing but the memory of a memory."[1] This simply is not so, for Fuller left behind a substantial body of work. Several books, many essays, critical articles, sketches, letters, and poems exist, though they are not always easily available at present. Thus she need not be consigned to the dim recesses of insubstantial legend that James pictured and clearly preferred.

Though Fuller regarded herself as a writer by profession, at least after she went to New York, her works have received little attention, for many reasons. Some of her contemporaries judged that they had little merit. Elizabeth Browning, who knew Margaret Fuller in Florence and loved her as a friend, called her "a very interesting person . . . far better than her writings."[2] Considering that so many writers have been far worse as persons, this is an admirable tribute, although misleading. Mrs. Browning rejected Fuller's writings decisively:

> Her written works are just *naught*. She said herself they were sketches, thrown out in haste and for the means of subsistence, and that the sole production of hers which was likely to represent her at all would be the history of the Italian revolution. In fact, her reputation, such as it was in America, seemed to stand mainly on her conversation and oral lectures. If I wished anyone to do her justice, I should say, as I have indeed said, "Never read what she has written." The letters, however, are individual, and full, I should fancy, of that magnetic personal influence which was so strong in her.[3]

Henry James reiterated those words: "She left nothing behind her, her written utterance being naught."[4] James, fond of the terms "haunting," "apparition," and "ghost" in speaking of Fuller, seemed to make a cult of elusiveness. He, like Mrs. Browning, seemed unaware of the vitality, the intelligence, and the ardent social commitment in Fuller's writings, par-

66

ticularly in the last decade of her life. Or perhaps James was aware of these things. Not for nothing did the literary gentlemen of Boston breathe a sigh of relief at her death and the silencing of her "lightning pen."[5]

We have already seen Emerson's part in the unmaking of Fuller's literary reputation. "Her pen was a non-conductor"[6] was only one of the remarks with which Emerson dismissed her writings. He pronounced her unsuccessful as a nature writer, ignoring the fact that she never tried to be one; she had poor powers of observation, he said, and her descriptions of nature were mostly superficial raptures.[7] Faulty as they are, such I-know-best judgments have stood unquestioned for over a century, carrying all the weight of Emerson's authority. Fuller's biographers and anthologizers have echoed and reechoed them. This weighty body of opinion has prevented any serious examination of her work. The fairness, generosity, and level-headedness of her own literary criticism have not always characterized her critics' writings. Even so, a few people have always found her writings valuable: for example, Horace Greeley thought her *Summer on the Lakes* the best American book his firm had published.

Fuller's writings were also neglected because her reputation as a conversationalist far outweighed her reputation as a writer. James Freeman Clarke spoke for Fuller's friends: "Those who know Margaret only by her published writings know her least; her notes and letters contain more of her mind; but it was only in conversation that she was perfectly free and at home."[8] Another friend, the Reverend F.H. Hedge, said that all who knew her concurred that her genius was in talk, not in her writings, which "do her very imperfect justice."[9] Henry James never heard her conversation, yet he accepted these opinions: "Her function, her reputation, were singular, and not altogether reassuring: she was a talker; she was *the* talker; she was the genius of talk. . . . She has left the same sort of reputation as a great actress."[10] James did admit that "some of her writing has extreme beauty, almost all of it has a real interest; but her value, her activity, her sway (I am not sure that one can say her charm), were personal and practical."[11]

The issue of Fuller the conversationalist versus Fuller the writer is complex. The notion prevailed then that women excelled and should excel in conversation rather than writing. Orestes Brownson, for example, thought a woman's intellectual mission, such as it was, was best fulfilled in conversation, "where the gentle, fitful flashes of her mind show to advantage," although of course she could not hope to rival the sustained, penetrating light of a man's discourse, and even the occasional sparks she emitted would never appear if they were not struck against the flint of a man's reason.[12] Brownson's supercilious assumption, typical of his time, was that though women spoke better than they wrote, even their conversation was inferior to men's. Thus they could never escape inferiority, whether they talked *or* wrote. Fuller unconsciously reflected this widespread assumption when she judged herself: "Conversation is my natural element," she said. "I need to be called out, and never think alone, without imagining some companion. Whether this be nature or the force of circumstances, I know not; it is my habit, and bespeaks a second-rate mind."[13] Thinking she had a second-rate mind deprived her of self-confidence, and this inevitably affected her literary career. Those from whom great things are never expected will rarely produce them, and to think oneself second-rate invites this opinion from others.

Apart from the comparative excellence of her performance in either medium, Fuller shrewdly recognized the tactical advantages to be gained in talk, and she suspected that women form their concepts differently from men:

> A woman of tact and brilliancy, like me, has an undue advantage in conversation with men. They are astonished at our instincts. They do not see where we got our knowledge; and, while they tramp on in their clumsy way, we wheel, and fly, and dart hither and thither, and seize with ready eye all the weak points, like Saladin in the desert. It is quite another thing when we come to write, and, without suggestion from another mind, to declare the positive amount of thought that is in us. Because we seemed to know all, they think we can tell all; and, finding we can tell so little, lose faith in their first opinion of us, *which, nathless, was true.*[14]

Another time she said, "These gentlemen are surprised that I write no better, because I talk so well. But I have served a long apprenticeship to the one, none to the other. I shall write better, but never, I think, so well as I talk; for then I feel inspired. . . . My voice excites me, my pen never."[15]

Margaret Fuller's conversation may indeed have been infinitely superior to her writing. But she had no Boswell, and those who wish to know her now must do so through her writings. At least one contemporary opinion rated her writing equal to her talk. Poe, who knew her personally and who reviewed her writings, as she reviewed his, thought her conversation and literary style were much the same. "Her personal character and her printed book are merely one and the same thing," said Poe. "We get access to her soul *as* directly from the one as from the other—no *more* readily from this than from that—easily from either. . . . Her literary and conversational manner are identical."[16] Quoting a passage from her *Summer on the Lakes*, Poe remarked, "Now all this is precisely as Miss Fuller would *speak* it. She is perpetually saying just such things in just such words. To get the *conversational* woman in the mind's eye, all that is needed is to imagine her reciting the paragraph just quoted." Poe scolded her severely for slovenly grammar and hasty disregard of the details of writing, but he praised her style. "In general effect, I know no style which surpasses it. It is singularly piquant, vivid, terse, bold, luminous—leaving details out of sight, it is everything that a style need be." Despite Poe's judgment, received opinion for over a century has persisted in exalting what is irrevocably gone—her life and conversation—and undervaluing what remains—her writing.

To return to the issue of confidence, Fuller's own severe self-criticism is a principal reason her writing has been undervalued. When planning her biography of Goethe she wrote to James Clarke: "Am I, can I make myself, fit to write an account of half a century of the existence of one of the master-spirits of this world? It seems as if I had been very arrogant to dare to think it; yet will I not shrink back from what I have undertaken,—even by failure I shall learn much."[17] Continually plagued by this absence of self-confidence, she needed encouragement from her friends. "When I look at my papers, I feel as if I had never had a thought that was worthy the attention of any but myself; and 'tis only when, on talking with people, I find I tell them what they did not know, that my confidence at all returns."[18]

Modern feminist consciousness allows us the historical perspective to understand Fuller's lack of self-confidence as part of the long history of women's intellectual deprivation. Nearly all writers for many centuries were male. The literary tradition, even when it claimed to transcend gender, was nevertheless embodied mostly in males. (However sexless their art, they acted as males in their personal and social lives, and few today would insist that all these are not intertwined.) Women were denied the education, the mandate, the models, authority, freedom, scope, and encouragement necessary for first-rate writing. When those conditions began to change in Fuller's time, so did women's writing. But the prohibitions against women as artists that existed for many centuries could not be erased in a few decades, and the psychological damage is evident in Fuller's persistent self-doubts about writing and about women as artists.

Frequently she felt her talents lay elsewhere than in writing. Because she had been so moved by Emerson's eloquence, and because she always longed for a life of action and leadership, she wrote, "If I were a man, the gift I would choose should be that of eloquence. That power of forcing the vital currents of thousands of human hearts into ONE current, by the constraining power of that most delicate instrument, the voice, is so intense,—yes, I would prefer it to a more extensive fame, a more permanent influence."[19] But she was not a man. Dr. Johnson once demolished the idea of female eloquence by comparing it to a dog walking on hind legs, making it seem ludicrous for a woman to aspire to public speaking. When

Fuller said she "would" prefer eloquence, she implied that she did not have that choice. To write was deemed, in the Victorian age, more suitable for a woman than to speak in public. (When the first feminists tried to do so, they met jeers and insults.) Lacking any sanction from society for public eloquence, Fuller kept trying to express her creativity in written words. In her journal she reflected, "Who, that has a soul for beauty, does not feel the need of creating, and that the power of creation alone can satisfy the spirit? When I thus reflect, the Artist seems the only fortunate man. Had I but as much creative genius as I have apprehensiveness!"[20] She had creative genius—and a first-rate mind. But she was not fully aware of all the obstructions to their development and expression.

Fuller never solved the problem of form for herself and never found the best vehicle for her expression. "For all the tides of life that flow within me, I am dumb and ineffectual, when it comes to casting my thought into a form. No old one suits me. If I could invent one, it seems to me the pleasure of creation would make it possible for me to write."[21] She sometimes spoke of the deadness of writing for her; it did not sufficiently express the life within her.

She tried several forms, but none pleased her. She wrote many poems, but was never satisfied with them. Though hampered by traditional poetic forms, she could find no others suitable. Her grand ambitions— she once had the plans for three historical tragedies out of a projected six—were not completed. Those who knew her well verified her great potential as a poet. She was, said W.H. Channing,

> fitted by genius and culture to mingle as an equal in the most refined circles of Europe, and yet her youth and early womanhood had passed away amid the very decent, yet drudging, descendants of the prim Puritans. Trained among those who could have discerned her peculiar power, and early fed with the fruits of beauty for which her spirit pined, she would have developed into one of the finest lyrists [sic], romancers and critics, that the modern literary world has seen. This she knew; and this tantalization of her fate she keenly felt.[22]

The discrepancy between Fuller's ideals and achievement is greatest in her poems. Her gift for poetic communication seldom found an effective voice in her poems. Many other Transcendentalists, like Fuller, aspired to poetry but succeeded in prose. Her lyric poems are often moralistic or pious, filled with undigested sadness and dejection. Unable to break out of eighteenth-century diction and conventions, she disparaged her verses as "all rhetorical and impassioned."[23] Poe thought her poetry affected, and Emerson, though moved by her poems, said that they would not stand alone, apart from the persons or circumstances that gave rise to them. Fuller knew that much of her poetry was occasional poetry and said that "for us lesser people [she meant less than geniuses like Goethe or Byron], who write verses merely as vents for the overflowings of a personal experience," it is inexcusable to take the public for a confidant by means of autobiographical poetry not sufficiently universalized and objectified to be of lasting merit.[24] (She would likely have been dismayed by the vast amount of versified autobiography in today's poetry.) As always, Fuller's self-criticism was too harsh. The passion and tension in "The Captured Wild Horse," the delicate harmony of "To Miss R.B.," the good-humored self-mockery in "Imperfect Thoughts," and the frank paganism and rationalism of "Thoughts on Sunday Morning," to mention only a few, make them well worth reading.

Fuller's infatuation with the German Romantics probably contributed to her inability to find a wholly satisfying form for her utterance. Many German Romantics spoke as she did of dissatisfaction with "mere" words, a wish to go beyond existing forms and wield "an enchanter's mirror, on which, with a word, could be made to rise all apparitions of the universe, grouped in new relations; a magic ring, that could transport the wearer, himself invisible, into each region of grandeur or beauty; a divining-rod, to tell where lie the secret fountains of refreshment; a wand, to invoke elemental spirits."[25] Fuller, in describing the kind of poetry she wanted to write, was describing something like the poetry that the French Symbolists developed later in the century. The Symbolists, following Baudelaire, evolved a poetic credo inspired by Poe. Rejecting positivism and logic, sentimentality and didacticism, the Symbolists used words for their sensuous, evocative qualities. Through poetic symbols or *correspondances*, they tried to suggest "les secrètes affinités des choses avec notre âme."[26] Fuller anticipated the Symbolists. Once again her ideas were far ahead of her time. But she could not write the poetry she envisioned. "In earlier years I aspired to wield the sceptre or the lyre; for I loved with wise design and irresistible command to mould many to one purpose, and it seemed all that man could desire to breathe in music and speak in words, the harmonies of the universe. But the golden lyre was not given to my hand, and I am but the prophecy of a poet."[27]

Fuller could not know that people would later question women's use of traditional literary forms. Virginia Woolf once said there is no reason to think the form of the epic or the poetic play suits a woman, any more than the sentence, presently constituted, suits her. Rimbaud, with his compulsion to shatter precedents, announced, "When the endless servitude of woman is broken, when she lives for and by herself, man—heretofore abominable—having given her her release, she too will be a poet! Woman will find some of the unknown! Will her world of ideas differ from ours?"[28] Today we know that the answer is yes. Women now feel freer than ever before to express their sense of life and art. Woolf also said that, despite considerable accomplishments in fiction among women, "it is the poetry that is still denied outlet."[29] Modern feminist questioning of past standards and limitations helps us understand why Margaret Fuller did not write poems of undeniable excellence, and why she found so great a frustration in her inability to do so. She tried to resign herself to using "the slow pen,"[30] but one senses that she substituted prose essays for a literary form she considered superior.

For Fuller ever to have produced a body of finished work of high artistic standards, she would have had to discipline herself in ways for which she was neither inclined nor prepared. When Poe admonished her for slovenly grammar and carelessness with detail, he did so justly. Fuller lacked a formal education, particularly in writing, where mastery comes easily to no one. Whatever its defects, formal education tends to correct such faults. Often she wrote hastily to fill up the columns of the *Dial* when other contributors had not sent their promised material, or to meet her obligations to Horace Greeley, who saw no reason why she could not turn out reams of copy every day, as he did. But writing was only one of her occupations. Household duties and family responsibilities, teaching and tutoring, the demands of friendship, her own continuing studies, and later, active politics absorbed her. Who can say what her writing would be if circumstance had allowed her to give it more time and attention? Life made its claims on her. She acquiesced to some, struggled against others. We sense throughout her life a reluctance to allow art greater claims than the process of living; her writings reflect this choice.

For, after all excuses are made, the fact remains that Fuller's carelessness with detail often makes her writing seem impromptu, or amateurish. She knew how far short she fell of her own standards. "How can I ever write with this impatience of detail? I shall never be an artist; I have no patient love of execution; I am delighted with my sketch, but if I try to finish it, I am chilled. Never was there a great sculptor who did not love to chip the marble." She added sadly, "I have talent and knowledge enought to furnish a dwelling for friendship, but not enough to deck with golden gifts a Delphi for the world."[31]

She had a curious reluctance to submit her own ego to that of her subject. While preparing her life of Goethe in 1839, she wrote to Emerson: "It would make quite a cultivated person of me, if I had four or five years to give to my task. But I intend to content myself with doing it inadequately rather than risk living so long in the shadow of one mind."[32] She evidently feared losing her own mental independence by submerging herself so long in Goethe. She criticized the poet Eckermann for such a submissiveness and seemed to believe that an individual's own growth would be stunted if he or she depended too long on another mind. "Plants dwindle in perpetual shadow, even from the stateliest tree," she said.[33] She might have added that some plants thrive in the shadow of a grander, deep-rooted growth, but obviously she was not one of them.

Fuller's unwillingness or inability to execute a longer work made the essay or some other short form inevitable. Though the essay allows a more personal, less systematized writing, she found it unsatisfying. "What a vulgarity there seems in this writing for the multitude," she once exclaimed. "We know not yet, have not made ourselves known to a single soul, and shall we address those still more unknown? Shall we multiply our connections and thus make them still more superficial?"[34] When she later went to work for the New York *Tribune*, she reversed her views, thinking that form was now less significant than helping others by disseminating her ideas. Horace Greeley helped her to evolve her own journalistic style and to excise the esoteric features of her writing; he was virtually the only person who taught her anything about writing. She said of her *Tribune* pieces, though, that her old friends in New England did not regard them highly:

> They think I ought to produce something excellent, while I am satisfied to aid in the great work of popular education. I never regarded literature merely as a collection of exquisite products, but rather as a means of mutual interpretation. Feeling that many are reached and in some degree helped, the thoughts of every day seem worth noting, though in a form that does not inspire me.[35]

Fuller at that time had broadened her interests beyond the (as she thought) narrowly esthetic cultural life of her New England circle. She had left behind her the endless talk and theorizing and had become actively concerned with politics, poverty, prostitution, mental illness, and industrial exploitation. Although she remained unsatisfied with the form of the journalistic essay, and although she continued to regard inspiration as necessary to produce works of enduring merit, she did produce "something excellent" in her *Tribune* work. The best essays have maturity, breadth of viewpoint, command of subject, and incisiveness of language. Fuller criticized Emerson for being aloof, remote, otherworldly. And although her own writing expressed a deepened understanding of the world and a compassionate involvement in it, she still evaluated it by the elitist criteria of her refined New England literary acquaintances; she lamented the failure of her work to meet standards that she had outgrown. Fuller's severe self-criticism and her disparagement of her work thus encouraged posterity to think of her writings as an inferior footnote to the annals of her life.

Fuller's obvious limitations as a writer should not blind us to her strengths. She had not mastered long written forms, but she commanded the vivid, succinct sentence; she ranks with the best writers of her age as an epigrammatist. Her style was vigorous, forceful, and persuasive, as Poe said. And she exercised her descriptive powers and sense of drama not only in her public writings but in her letters and private journals as well. Her letters and journals have been published only in fragments, often so heavily interpolated (as in the *Memoirs*) that their essential qualities are blurred by editorial judgments. These private writings half-reveal, half-create both her inner life and her sense of the life around her, in all its hidden struggles, its drama and flashes of meaning and moments of exaltation and structurelessness and boredom—the process itself, inescapably personal, not the abstraction from the process.

In the best of Fuller's prose, thought comes alive. Her mind worked in harmony with her emotions and nerves and senses, as well as her abstract reasoning faculties. Rarely does she fail to illuminate her chosen subject. Often she uses the exhortatory mode, a characteristic of most Transcendentalists' style, which probably grew out of their consciousness of being intellectual and cultural missionaries, and out of their pervasive clericalism, which found its proper element in the sermon. But even when exhorting, Fuller's writing is a product of a keenly conscious intelligence, "one of those on whom nothing is lost," in Henry James's famous phrase. When W.H. Channing said of her, "By [her] power to quicken other minds, she showed how living was her own," he unknowingly gave us a good description of her writing.[36]

Fuller's use of the metaphor best reveals her essentially poetic imagination. She had that image-making faculty, the eye for resemblances that Aristotle called the hallmark of the true poet, the one indispensable gift that cannot be imparted by anyone else. Fuller invariably used metaphor to tell her meaning. In her poorer work the metaphors are murky, high-flown, or strained in effect, but in her best writing they are controlled, pointed, and clarifying.

For example, when revolution was brewing in Europe and the United States was convulsed with tensions rising out of slavery and the Mexican War, she wrote:

> Altogether, it looks as if a great time was coming, and that time one of democracy. Our country will play a ruling part. Her eagle will lead the van; but whether to soar upward to the sun or to stoop for helpless prey, who now dares promise? At present she has scarce achieved a Roman nobleness, a Roman liberty; and whether her eagle is less like the vulture, and more like the Phoenix, than was the fierce Roman bird, we dare not say. May the new year give hopes of the latter, even if the bird need first to be purified by fire.[37]

The bird image changes from eagle to vulture to phoenix: because each of these birds is strong, dominating, and impressive, inspiring awe or respect, the image points up America's importance and leadership position among nations. In metamorphosis, the image evokes national pride (the noble, aspiring eagle), anger and disgust (the predatory vulture), and hope for the future after purification by fire, which prophesied the Civil War.

In a lighter mood, Fuller used a metaphor of family life to comment on European opinions of America:

> America cares for shallow blame, just or unjust, because she wants not only self-respect but faith. She has, as the foreigner thinks, the unmannerly tricks and disagreeable obtrusions of an overgrown child. Like children of a rich and energetic nature, prematurely brought forward, she is peculiarly likely to offend the decorum and even the good feelings of uncles and aunts. She makes dirt-pies, kills flies, and oversets the tea-pot. Still she is learning all the while.[38]

The image of the unmannerly, precocious child points to America's misdeeds and crudities, but simultaneously expresses an affectionate conviction that this undisciplined youngster shows great promise. The metaphor grows from the concept of nations as a family.

The images and the subjects they illuminate are varied. Discussing the settling of the western frontier, she wrote, in a passage reminiscent of Thoreau, of "the love of ravage which distinguishes the American settler and which makes the marks of his first passage over this land, like those of a corrosive acid upon the cheek of beauty, rather than that smile of intelligence which would ensue from the touch of an intelligent spirit."[39] When, in Europe, she visited the Chamber of Deputies library in Paris to see the manuscripts of Rousseau, she wrote of his importance as a prophet of the modern age. "Such is the method of genius, to ripen fruit for the crowd by those rays of whose heat they complain."[40]

Like other Transcendentalist writers, Fuller took most of her analogies from nature. Blanchard remarks that Fuller "herself knew she was incapable of any deep, Wordsworthian communion with the natural world," a lack Fuller attributed to her early education that, cramming her mind and neglecting the external senses, deprived her of feeling in response to nature.[41] However, numerous passages in Fuller's writings indicate that she experienced the "Wordsworthian communion" often enough.[42] Of course, sometimes she only wished to experience it and could not, as in the journal passage Blanchard quotes, or in her reaction to Niagara Falls (see Chapter 8); many people would like to experience ecstasy more often than they do. It is a mistake to look to her writing for the Thoreauvian or Wordsworthian style; she neither deifies nature nor embraces it as an escape from social intercourse. But no one who reads *Summer*, her journals, or her poems can miss her awareness and love of nature. She often seemed self-concious when trying to focus *primarily* on nature, and the self-consciousness damages the effect. She wrote best of the natural world seeing it interwoven with human thought, human activity, and human feeling—not as a mere backdrop, but as an essential nourishing and esthetic element of life. Thus, though Emerson made supercilious judgments about Fuller as a nature writer, he did not see how essentially nature entered her writing, as a constant source of metaphor on which she drew to illuminate even the most abstract subjects, such as the philosophical bases for her literary criticism (see Chapter 7).

Occasionally there is a mixing of metaphors, as in the following passage on Carlyle, whom Fuller often visited during her stay in England in 1846:

> I approached him with more reverence after a little experience of England and Scotland had taught me to appreciate the strength and height of that wall of shams and conventions which he more than any man, or thousand men,—indeed, he almost alone,—has begun to throw down. Wherever there was fresh thought, generous hope, the thought of Carlyle has begun the work. He has torn off the veils from hideous facts; he has burnt away foolish illusions; he has awakened thousands to know what it is to be a man,—that we must live, and not merely pretend to others that we live. He has touched the rocks and they have given forth musical answer; little more was wanting to begin to construct the city.[43]

Despite the conflation of tearing veils, making music, and constructing cities, there is neither incongruity in the thought nor ludicrousness in the effect, but rather a powerful perception of what Carlyle had done for his age. The passage captures not only the energetic spirit of Carlyle but also his language, with its juxtaposition of forceful verbs that convey the acts of tearing down, exposing, cutting through, and so on. And because Carlyle saw himself as a latter-day prophet, the image of Carlyle as Moses striking the rocks is apt. Poe, who judged Fuller's merits and defects as a writer more fairly and objectively than any of her other contemporaries, disapproved of her "frequent unjustifiable Carlyleisms, (such as that of writing sentences which are no sentences)."[44] In one sweep of the pen Poe disposed of the literary styles of Emerson, Carlyle, and Fuller as affected and euphuistic. But Poe makes no distinction between Fuller's early style of the New England years, including her *Dial* pieces, and her later style; presumably he had the latter in mind when he said, "It is everything that a style need be."

Poe knew Margaret Fuller during the years she considered herself a writer by profession. As such, she attempted to organize American writers into an association for their own protection against publishers' contractual infringements. She took up the cudgels against literary censorship when Harro Harring, a published novelist in his native Denmark, ran afoul of an American publisher who reneged on his promise to publish Harring's work. Fuller gave several hundred dollars of her own to ensure the private publication of his work, and she wrote for the *Tribune* a vigorous denunciation of publishers' assuming the role of censor. She understood the practical problems of being an independent writer in a new nation, which cared little about its writers. It was not enough to write well. This she had learned from *Tasso*. One also needed the means to write, and the public attitudes and specific business practices (such as protection by copyright) that would allow reasonable security to the profession of writing. For all her belief in inspiration, she knew that writers must eat, and that they do not produce their best work in cowering defensiveness and fear.

Margaret Fuller made important contributions to her profession. Her reputation as a conversationalist and personality, although well deserved, does not do full justice to her achievement. Finish, polish, and well-ordered forms are not the only goals of writing. Fuller was the prophecy of a poet, not a fully realized one, but she did not fail as a writer. Because of its vitality and power to excite, much of her work ranks with the best discursive prose of her age. An important purpose of writing is to communicate interior life, and with the publication of her journals and letters, we will at last be able to balance public statement with private expression and understand what Fuller was trying to tell us. That her writings have lapsed into obscurity is a misfortune they do not deserve. In Margaret Fuller's writings I have found endless illumination, disquiet, and delight, for they show me the world through her eyes, mind, and emotions. What need to seek further justification for the writings of genius? The reader who gives them thoughtful attention will be richly rewarded.

CHAPTER 6

Literary Criticism and the Arts

Once Margaret Fuller turned her attention from trying to write great poetry, her creative nature, extraordinary intelligence, and abiding love for the arts found an outlet in the professions of critic and editor. Of all her enterprises, literary criticism was sustained the longest. As a critic she produced much of her best writing and helped to shape American literary history.

A critic, unless also a novelist or poet, rarely has reputation or influence past his or her own time. The criticism of Coleridge, Poe, Henry James, Pound, and T.S. Eliot has received continued attention because of their accomplishments as artists. But who today outside of small circles of specialists remembers Edwin Whipple or Rufus Griswold? The chief use of criticism is in the age for which it was written. Fuller's criticism, written for her contemporaries, was only part of her life's work, though a substantial part. Some is dated; surprisingly much of it remains fresh, cogent, and illuminating.

Theories about art and the process of its creation usually accompany a lively interest in art. A critic is a theoretician of art as well as a mediator between the artist and the public. "The critic is beneath the maker, but is his needed friend," wrote Fuller of her profession as critic. "Next to invention is the power of interpreting invention; next to beauty the power of appreciating beauty."[1]

Artists sometimes see critics as enemies or parasites, not friends—"lice in the locks of literature" was Tennyson's epithet. To Fuller, criticism complemented art. "Analysis and comparison methodically, with sensitiveness, intelligence, curiosity, intensity of passion, and infinite knowledge: all these are necessary to the great critic," said T.S. Eliot in "Criticism in England." Fuller thought certain moral qualities as necessary to the critic as mental ones, and she explained her calling in this way:

> It is even more rare to meet a great Critic than a great Poet. True criticism . . . supposes a range and equipoise of faculties, and a generosity of soul which have as yet been rarely combined in any one person. The great Critic is not merely the surveyor, but the interpreter of what other minds possess; he must

78

have a standard of excellence, founded on prescience of what man is capable of; he must have, no less, a refined imagination and quick sympathies to enter into each work in its own kind, and examine it by its own law, so that he may understand how certain faults are interwoven, in growth, with certain virtues; he must have a cultivated taste, a calm, large, and deep judgment, and a heart to love everything that is good, in proportion to its goodness.[2]

Women have more often become novelists, poets, and playwrights than critics. One reason is that women in former times seldom had access to the broad education, the cultural and historical knowledge that the critic needs. Virginia Woolf spoke eloquently of these needs, and of women's deprivation, in *A Room of One's Own*. Novelists and poets, on the other hand, must come to terms chiefly with their own experience. Books, even history, may be secondary, may even hinder the confrontation with experience. Critics also must evaluate and judge, and few women have had the necessary confidence in their own intellectual judgments. An effective critic must speak with authority, and that authority must be acknowledged. For women this has seldom been possible.

Thus Margaret Fuller's achievement was all the more extraordinary. She was one of the best critics of her century; some have said she was *the* best critic in America before 1850.[3] Certainly she was far more catholic in scope and taste than most other critics of her day. She helped educate an untutored American public about the importance of the arts; she worked to raise the level of public taste and to free that taste from a spurious moralism; she formulated a critical theory and method that surpassed a merely subjective impressionism; and she helped lay the foundation for a distinctively American literature. An enlightened, international humanism, the nucleus of her critical work, gave her consistent principles. Moreover, her great range of interests helped her understand other writers; she often digressed from some literary subject to discuss children's education or the pleasures of eating or the horrors of lynching. A critic who is interested in nothing but literature, said T.S. Eliot in "The Frontiers of Criticism," has little to tell us, "for his literature is a pure abstraction." Margaret Fuller brought to her criticism not only a broad knowledge but a broad experience of life, which, together with superb literary judgment, equipped her admirably for her profession.

The American public she addressed in the 1830s and 1840s thought little about art. Their attention and exuberance went into building the country. These formative years for the new republic, following the first shaky decades of its life, saw the expanding of territories, increasing population and immigration, and consolidation of political principles and institutions. Americans were still awed by and dependent on Europe in all the fine arts, despite a thriving folk culture in music, decorative art, and crafts that dated from colonial days. In music there were no native composers or performers of distinction, and concerts, though frequent and well attended, were usually presented by Europeans on provincial tour. In sculpture most important commissions went to Europeans. Though the 1830s saw the first notable group of American sculptors, including Horatio Greenough, Hiram Powers, and Thomas Crawford, they studied and worked mostly in Italy, as did painter-sculptor William Wetmore Story, a friend of Margaret Fuller and later of Henry James. American painting had advanced further than sculpture, with the growing Romantic influence especially evident in landscape art. But there were almost no galleries or art museums in America. Painters went abroad for their training, and if they returned at all, painted as they had learned in Europe.

When Americans spoke of the need for cultural independence, they chiefly had literature in mind. The language bound America closely to England's modes and traditions, and even if these seemed inappropriate for their experience, American writers had little clear sense of direction. There was not yet a sufficient intellectual basis for significant literature. More and better schools, universities, libraries, theaters, newspapers, magazines, publishing houses, and copyright laws were needed. In addition, most readers and writers assumed that the Old World was the only real source of serious literature.

Fuller saw her critical mission as educative. First it was necessary to elevate taste and teach a culturally immature public how to value the arts and literature. T.S. Eliot in "The Frontiers of Criticism" spoke of the essential function of literary criticism as "the elucidation of works of art and the correction of taste," or more simply, "to promote the understanding and enjoyment of literature." Both needed promotion in America, for many doubted that the arts would find a home here, thinking that Americans would simply imitate Europe. Fuller knew these difficulties: "There is no poetical ground-work ready for the artist in our country and time," she wrote. "We have no old established faith, no hereditary romance, no such stuff as Catholicism, Chivalry afforded. What is most dignified in the Puritanic modes of thought is not favourable to beauty. The habits of an industrial community are not propitious to delicacy of sentiment."[4]

Change would come gradually, over a long period of time. Fuller applied herself to the task. She began with the most elementary precepts, such as telling her readers why the arts were necessary and desirable, for one could not assume that large numbers of people appreciated the arts. Again and again in her critical essays she pleaded the necessity of the arts:

The arts are no luxury, no mere ornament and stimulus to a civic and complicated existence, as the worldling and the ascetic alike delight in representing
them to be, but the herbarium in which are preserved the fairest flowers of
man's existence, the magic mirror by whose aid all its phases are interpreted,
the circle into which the various spirits of the elements may be invoked and
made to reveal the secret they elsewhere manifest only in large revolutions of
time.[5]

Usually she explained patiently, as though to an unruly inattentive child,
but sometimes she spoke sharply, as in this passage attacking the superficiality of American cultural knowledge:

If New England thinks, it is about money, social reform, and theology. If she
has a way of speaking peculiarly her own, it is the lecture. But the lecture,
though of such banyan growth among us, seems not to bespeak any deep or
permanent tendency.... Lectures upon every possible topic are the short
business way taken by business people to find out what there is to be known,
but to *know* in such ways cannot be hoped, unless the suggestions thus received are followed up by private study, thought, conversation.... Not that it
is unmeaning, something they learn; but it is to be feared just enough to
satisfy, not stimulate the mind. It is an entertainment which leaves the hearer
too passive. One that appealed to the emotions would enter far more deeply
and pervasively into the life, than these addressed to the understanding, a
faculty already developed out of all proportion among this people.[6]

It was the life that needed nourishment, not the understanding.

Sometimes Fuller's enthusiasm betrayed her into making esthetic pronouncements for which she was unqualified. She was particularly weak
on the visual arts. She knew her deficiencies and carefully added that her
comments on painting and drawing were only personal impressions, not
criticism, but she nevertheless overreached herself at times. In a country
of the blind, the one-eyed man is king, and most Americans knew far less
than she about visual art. Her willingness to make pronouncements
about all the arts arose in part from her beliefs that the arts had similar
fundamental principles, and that this concept was generally accepted:

The principles which pervade the Fine Arts are identical, and ... nothing but
partial organization prevents any man who traces them in one form from
tracing them in all. The subject is one of such profound interest that the
discernment of new analogies is always interesting. It pleases us to hear Archi-
tecture called 'frozen music,' [Goethe's phrase] or to know that the dimensions
of a pillar may be estimated by the tension of chords, but it is merely that we
take pleasure in the application of recognized principles; recognized, we mean,
by all the thinking part of the world now."[7]

Clearly Fuller did not intend to limit her range by overspecialization or
intellectual timidity. Frequently in her life exuberance led her onto shaky
ground.

Her widest and soundest knowledge, and the great bulk of her critical writing, was about literature. Next to literature she wrote most about music. Though concerts were popular, the rude habits of American audiences at that time must have been anguishing for the music lover—conversing, noisy flirting, strolling about during the performance, for example. Manners as well as taste had to be formed and educated. As a columnist for the New York *Tribune* she frequently reviewed concerts and used every available opportunity to educate her readers or to scold them for stupidity if she thought they deserved it. Once, when an audience coldly received the world-famous violinist Ole Bull, meeting his selections with utter silence, she indignantly but carefully spelled out why the artist needed a sympathetic audience to elicit a good performance.[8]

Fuller reprimanded audiences for bad manners and criticized the common practice of alternating on a program the works of Beethoven or Mozart with selections intended merely to amuse and divert the audience. Such devices would never raise the public's taste above mediocrity,

> for the performer goes down to them, instead of drawing them up to him. We think they should never do so, and that the need of money is not an excuse. Compromise, always so degrading, is especially so with those beautiful arts which we expect to lift us above everything low and mercenary, and give us light by which to see the harmony destined to subsist between nature and the soul of man.[9]

These explanations, lectures, and reprimands indicate the impoverishment of the American cultural milieu, partly due to the nation's youth, partly to the dominant bourgeois mentality. The Puritan tradition was a formidable obstacle to the arts. For art to thrive in America, Fuller knew it had to overcome what Poe later called "the heresy of the didactic," the tendency of both audience and critics to read or view a work primarily for its moralistic message and to judge it for its moral suitability. She consistently fought for the principle of the autonomy of art and tried to show her readers that art and literature were not the handmaidens of religion and morality. She understood better than anyone else in her New England group the antagonism of the Puritan influence to the arts. One of her *Dial* essays discussed this:

> What would the Puritan fathers say, if they could see our bill of fare here in Boston for the winter? . . . Their fullness of faith and uncompromising spirit show but faint sparks among us now, yet the prejudices with which these were connected from the circumstances of the time, still cast their shadows over us. The poetical side of existence, (and here I do not speak of poetry in its import or ethical significance, but in its essential being, as a recreative spirit that sings to sing, and models for the sake of drawing from the clay the elements of beauty,) the poetical side of existence is tolerated rather than revered, and the

lovers of beauty are regarded rather as frivolous voluptuaries than the conse-
crated servants of the divine Urania. Such is the tendency of the general
mind.[10]

Fuller argued that the esthetic faculty embodied an absolute need of
human nature.

Their action [the Puritan fathers], noble as it was, exhibited but one side of
nature, and was but a *re* action. . . . The desire for amusement, no less than
instruction, is irrepressible in the human breast; . . . The love of the beautiful,
for its own sake simply, is no more to be stifled than the propensity of the
earth to put forth flowers in the spring; and . . . the Power, which in its life
and love, lavishes such loveliness around us, meant that all beings able to
receive and feel should, with recreative energy, keep up the pulse of life and
sing the joy it is to be,—to grow.

She denounced those who disapproved of dancing and acting because
they objected to the personal life of the performer, a point on which
Goethe was found blameworthy. She tried to counter the prevailing
opinion of the immorality of ballet by discussing the art of the dance and
pointing out that the human body was beautiful. This comment seems
elementary until we remember Emerson thought ballet was immoral,
and in Europe, sculptures of the unclothed human body shocked and
disgusted Hawthorne. The public outrage that greeted Hiram Powers's
statue "The Greek Slave" in the 1840s took years to die down.

Fuller's attempts to counter the prevailing moralistic approach to art
took many forms: necessarily, because the moralism took so many forms.
In the essay "Modern Drama" she emphasized the difference between
her way of evaluating literature and that of modern-day Puritans. She
discussed John Sterling's play *Strafford*, indicating *artistic* grounds for
rejecting it, not only *moralistic* grounds. Analyzing the character of Strafford according to the Aristotelian principles of credibility and consistency, she concluded that it failed dramatically, and that the play's language was not natural, lifelike speech. The play is forgotten now, but the
modes of evaluation she detested are not. Fuller attempted to wrest away
from the moralists the whole sphere of dramatic and literary criticism
and to establish esthetic standards by which to measure the success or
failure of a work. She tried to counter the bourgeois Victorian mentality
too, though she did not use those terms.

Whether Puritan, bourgeois, Victorian, or merely immature, a common way of reading literature was to search out its moral, its "message."
In a *Tribune* review Fuller pointed out the distortions that resulted when
a story or poem was read primarily for its "moral":

It is always a mistake to force a meaning from any tale. As long as it is to your
mind a piece of life, it exercises a living influence. A correct picture from

Nature is always instructive in proportion to the power of the mind which looks on it to receive instruction, but the attempt of any one person to get from it a formal moral for all, is distasteful and dissuades from a natural surrender to the charm of the facts. Accordingly, children, those wise readers, always skip the moral; and let not grown-up pedants believe they, on that account, fail of the genuine benefit of the tale![11]

Goethe wrote on the same subject in 1827: "All poetry should be instructive, but unobviously so. It should draw the attention of a reader to the idea which is of value to be imparted; but he himself must draw the lesson out of it, as he does out of life."[12] It is uncertain whether Fuller had read that particular essay, but she had read Goethe's autobiography, which in Book 13 condemns the "old prejudice" that a work of art must have a didactic purpose, and says in Book 12, "A good work of art can, and will indeed, have moral consequences, but to require moral ends of the artist is to destroy his profession."

Throughout the nineteenth century and until World War I, Americans used the criterion of moral utility to justify literature: it provided both a reason for art's existence and a tool for evaluation.[13] Fuller's efforts to establish the independence of art and literature anticipated Poe's. His pronouncements, which have become better known than hers, were more consistently practiced, for Fuller, while attacking moralism in literary criticism, was not always free from it herself. Only someone entirely outside the New England religious-intellectual tradition could articulate a convincing criticism of its esthetic. Poe established the principle of the autonomy of art more uncompromisingly than Fuller. He completely separated the realm of beauty and art from that of morality. However, Poe went to the other extreme and divorced art from truth, claiming that the truth or value of an author's opinions were of no interest to the critic. But he tended to equate truth with moral preaching or with logic and syllogisms, a truncated concept of truth, to say the least. Unlike Poe, Margaret Fuller never thought that art should be entirely unconnected with morality or truth. She went further than most critics of her day, except Poe, in establishing the right of works of art to be read, viewed, and judged for themselves and not for their moral posture or message. But she was not unaffected by moral and religious considerations, and occasionally these swayed her judgments. Freer of moralistic bias than most of her contemporaries, she had not vanquished it entirely. The conflict in her between Puritan and esthete sometimes surfaced in her criticism, for criticism inevitably reflects the characters and biases of critics, that is, unless they can function in a complete vacuum, in which case their criticism is lifeless and utterly useless.

Before looking at some examples of Fuller's biases, it is necessary to clarify her fundamental critical position and to explore the standards on which she based her judgments. She distinguished between critics who evaluated works on the basis of their impressions and feelings and critics who evaluated according to fixed principles. She once said, after viewing an exhibition of paintings, "Seeing so many of them together, I can no longer be content merely to feel, but must judge these works. I must try to find the centre, to measure the circumference.[14] This statement describes the critic's motivation. Criticism, for Fuller, was not only a process of evaluating but of knowing, a way of giving form to her esthetic experience. To feel was not enough. Creative genius organized experience, she said, and criticism understood that organization.[15] Like art itself, criticism arose out of the fundamental human impulse toward form.

Fuller thought there were three classes of critics. The first was the *subjective*, who recorded impressions and personal feelings about a work, thereby revealing more about himself or herself than about the work. This type of critic sought no permanent law or standard beyond his or her own taste as it had been shaped by a particular time, age, nation, family, or religion. Here Fuller recognized the necessity for principles and standards that transcended the particular and parochial. Nearly every age produces impressionistic critics. James Russell Lowell was such a critic in Fuller's time, and Virginia Woolf was one in the twentieth century. The literary opinions of these critics, despite superb taste and perceptions, often fail to survive the generation for which they speak so eloquently. Thus Fuller sought a more universal criticism.

The next class of critics she called the *apprehensive:* these enter imaginatively into the existence of the work. They live within it, so to speak, and tell what it means. She adopted this method from Goethe, who, following his teacher Herder, suggested that the most fruitful approach to a work of art was to penetrate the work, to discern the artist's aim and the methods chosen to accomplish it, in short, to enter intuitively and sympathetically the creative mind that produced the work. This criticism characterizes the Romantic school of critics and is valuable for understanding a work. Yet Fuller cautioned that it is necessary to explain not only what a work is but what it is not. The apprehensive critic does not classify the work, and tends toward critical relativism, in which all works are treated alike.

The third class of critics, which Fuller called the *comprehensive*, are also apprehensive, for they must first enter into the intrinsic law of the work. After having done this, the comprehensive critic then judges the work, places it, estimates its relations. James Clarke said that for every writer Fuller studied, she knew his relation to other writers, to the world, to life, to nature, and to herself.[16] She set forth these relations in her criticism. Comprehensive criticism requires a coherent philosophical position, as well as the extensive knowledge and experience of life that T.S. Eliot insisted on.

Though she was a comprehensive critic, in practice Fuller often used the second method, the apprehensive, especially when a particular book was not important enough for a full-scale treatment of all its relationships. She thought the method of the apprehensive critic was sufficient to acquaint her readers with a book or author who fell short of universal significance. W.H. Auden once said that the conscientious critic who has only limited space for reviews of poetry knows that the fairest method is to give a series of quotations without comment, and many of Fuller's reviews for the *Tribune* do just that. This method encourages readers to make their own judgments (though it may abrogate the critic's function of evaluation).

The next important distinction in her critical system was among kinds of works. The great works of highest excellence and permanent value—those of Homer, Milton, Shakespeare, Dante, Goethe—constituted a small part of literature. A far larger part spoke to the people of its day, literature being "the great mutual system of interpretation between all kinds and classes of men."[17] Such writings were important because they revealed the life of people to each other and had some share in perfection of form. These two kinds of works should not be judged in the same way, nor do they serve the same purpose. Fuller at times believed the first class of works were more significant; at other times she believed the second kind took precedence. The more she became involved in the active life of her age, the more she tended to think that "the common and daily purposes of literature are the most important."[18]

Sometimes she added a third category of literary works, that of scholars, which does not enjoy extensive fame but is nonetheless valuable and necessary. But her essential distinction is between ageless works of superlative merit and those that express the lives, thoughts, souls, and aspirations of a specific era to other people in that same era.

What was her standard of excellence in evaluating a particular work? In her early criticism, and occasionally later, the greatest poetry was the touchstone of excellence by which she judged other work. Sometimes she used the ideal of perfection in her own mind and judged each work by how close it came to meeting that ideal.

A recent study of Fuller by Henry L. Golemba pointed out that her criticism evolved through stages. The first, during which she formulated her standards, roughly coincided with her work for James Freeman Clarke's journal the *Western Messenger*, 1835–40; the second period was during her work for the *Dial* and her close association with Emerson and the Transcendentalists; the third was that of her work in New York, 1844–46. (Her essays to the *Tribune* from Europe contained some noteworthy comments on art and literature, but the bulk of her critical work was done in America.) Generally Fuller's early criticism measured a work against the standards of the best poets.[19] During the second period, when Transcendentalist ideas dominated her thinking, she applied the standard of "ideal perfection" in measuring a work. In her third phase she became gradually more interested in literature that communicated to those in its own time; she was less concerned with applying ideal standards. Fuller's criticism, reflecting the growth of her mind and the maturing of her ideas, makes many distinctions among works, a criticism of great flexibility and range.

Her practical judgment of writers and books was shrewd and usually accurate. As a reviewer for the *Tribune*, she maintained consistently high standards of evaluation under the day-to-day pressure of deadlines. She discerned the shortcomings of extremely popular writers. All wise readers know that contemporary fame is not necessarily a hallmark of excellence. One of the critic's most difficult tasks is to estimate new writers, without the advantages of time's perspective and the accumulated commentary of intelligent readers. One of Fuller's special talents was balancing overinflated reputations, Lowell's, for instance, or that of P.J. Bailey, author of the Faustian "epic" *Festus*, as famous then as it is forgotten now. Lowell was hailed as a first-rate poet, but Fuller said that his work was stereotyped, shallow, mechanical, lacking in vitality; it would not sustain its high reputation. Time corroborated those judgments. She called Emerson's poems too philosophical, lacking "the simple force of nature and passion," and said the revered Dr. Channing knew no more than Emerson about the emotional and passionate side of human nature.[20] She also discerned merits in writers who were unjustly ignored. Robert Browning's poems were virtually unknown in America when she reviewed them in 1846, or if known, were thought to be obscure and difficult. Fuller saw the value of his work and accurately predicted that he would be one of England's major poets.

Her criticism had its weaknesses. Some were stylistic mannerisms that flawed but did not invalidate her basic perceptions and ideas. For example, she used apostrophe excessively. Often employed with effusive flourishes, it probably came from an overflow of enthusiasm. Still, the device rings of exaggerated rhetoric and grates on the ear of the modern reader, attuned to simpler expression. And the euphuisms that Poe disapproved of still make us flinch. Another flaw is Fuller's tendency toward preachiness, difficult to avoid for those who believe fervently in their Mission to Educate the Unenlightened. However noble her intent, the condescension in this attitude is sometimes annoying. It annoyed some of Fuller's contemporaries too: Lowell derided her I-turn-the-crank-of-the-universe air, and others mocked her for her high-priestess-of-culture attitude.

Time has not verified all her judgments. For example, she rated the works of Henry Taylor, Ellery Channing, and Cornelius Mathews as far better than we rate them today. Occasionally the bias of her day blinded her to the value of certain writers and modes of writing. Balzac's novels contained too strong a dose of reality for her. Admitting a distaste for literary realism, she found little to praise about him. Novels had only recently claimed the status of art, and even if accepted as art, they were thought an inferior form. Like many of her contemporaries, Fuller dismally failed to do justice to Balzac, primarily because she needed moral uplift in works of art and did not find it in Balzac. She did not, with Emerson, find the French intellect sick, but she preferred art that showed human beings as they might be rather than in the squalor of what they often are. The Ideal continued to haunt her criticism, as moralism haunted American criticism. Even when novels and realistic techniques gained greater acceptance as art forms later in the century, Henry James still found that Balzac's lack of a "natural sense of morality" was a serious fault in a novelist.[21]

Religious criteria often played a part in Fuller's literary evaluations. This is clear from her treatment of Goethe's *Elective Affinities* and *Iphigenia in Tauris*. First she established the right of *Elective Affinities* to serious critical discussion:

"Not Werther, not the Nouvelle Héloise, have been assailed with such a storm of indignation as [Elective Affinities] on the score of gross immorality. The reason probably is the subject; any discussion of the validity of the marriage vow making society tremble to its foundation; and, secondly, the cold manner in which it is done. All that is in the book would be bearable to most minds if the writer had had less the air of a spectator, and had larded his work here and there with ejaculations of horror and surprise.[22]

Fuller attempted to show why the book was not only a work of art but moral in the widest sense, even pious ultimately, as it will seem to most readers today.

Others, it would seem, on closing the book, exclaim, "What an immoral book!" I well remember my own thought, "It is a work of art!" At last I understood that world within a world, that ripest fruit of human nature, which is called art. With each perusal of the book my surprise and delight at this wonderful fulfilment of design grew. I understood why Goethe was well content to be called Artist, and his works, works of Art, rather than revelations."

Despite her exalted response to *Elective Affinities* and her admiration for it, Fuller devoted much more space to *Iphigenia* and declared it a better work, "a work beyond the possibility of negation; a work where a religious meaning not only pierces but enfolds the whole; a work as admirable in art, still higher in significance, more single in expression." Fuller did not feel it necessary to define "religious"—one measure of the difference between her age and ours. I conjecture that she meant by the term not myopic piety or clericalism, but whatever pertains to a supreme Being and to those transcendent, immutable powers and principles known by intuition or faith.

Perhaps Fuller was trying to defang the hostility of her readers toward Goethe by praising *Iphigenia* so extensively.[23] Goethe's works were art; she knew the public wanted revelations. No one could possibly object to *Iphigenia* on moral grounds. If the public could be shown Goethe's loftiness and moral nobility, they might be more receptive to his other works. There is no reason to suspect her critique of insincerity, however. She actually did believe *Iphigenia* to be the superior work. Despite Fuller's efforts to establish the esthetic faculty as valid and to separate it from narrow moralism, she did not care for art that left unsatisfied her own moral and spiritual needs. Not many modern readers will sympathize with the recurrent religious note in her criticism.

Questions of morality in literature are always troublesome, and perhaps Fuller loved music partly because it beautifully left all such questions behind. Goethe wrote:

> Music, like all the arts, has little power directly to influence morality, and it is always wrong to demand such results from them. Philosophy and Religion alone can accomplish this. If piety and duty must be stimulated, the arts can only casually effect this stimulation. What they can accomplish, however, is a softening of crude manners and morals; yet even this may, on the other hand, soon degenerate into effeminacy.[24]

Goethe decisively influenced Fuller's humanistic esthetic creed, and her desire to affirm the validity of art arose from this humanism. "If we only knew how to look around us, we should not need to look above," she said.[25] Though she sometimes referred to the "divinity" of art or artists, most of her statements about the nature of art described it as a human activity, as in the passages in which she called art "the ripest fruit of human nature" or "the fairest flowers of man's existence." Literature, she said in "Poets of the People," is "an epistolary correspondence between brethren of one family, subject to many and wide separations, and anxious to remain in spiritual presence one of another."[26] This analogy of the human family appeared in her writings on society and politics as well as in her literary criticism—a sign of the unifying tendency of her mind. The analogy became for her a more and more compelling image and fact. It is a commonplace of our times that the world has grown smaller and people closer together; Fuller knew this in her bones a century and a half ago. In one of her most decisive humanist statements about art, she wrote:

> Poetry is not a superhuman or supernatural gift. It is, on the contrary, the fullest and therefore most completely natural expression of what is human. It is that of which the rudiments lie in every human breast, but developed to a more complete existence than the obstructions of daily life permit ... Our definition of poetry is large enough to include all kinds of excellence. It includes not only the great bards, but the humblest minstrels. The great bards bring to light the more concealed treasures, gems which centuries have been employed in forming and which it is their office to reveal, polish, and set for the royal purposes of man; the wandering minstrel with his lighter but beautiful office calls the attention of men to the meaning of the flowers, which also is hidden from the careless eye, though they have grown and bloomed in full sight of all who chose to look. All the poets are the priests of Nature, though the greatest are also the prophets of the manhood of man.[27]

Since, for her, art was "the fullest and most completely natural expression of what is human," Margaret Fuller preferred the kind of literature that reflected her own deep and sure humanity. She loved continental literature for its wide range of strong, vivid portrayals of individual and national greatness. A little-known passage on humor shows how her humanist criteria helped form her literary taste:

> The sort of wit that consists in making a single person the representative of an opinion or a whim, and making it comic by its excess, and its consequent unbearable clashing with the whims of other men, was carried to perfection by the old English dramatists, where each man stood behind his "humor" as behind a waxen mask. You longed to melt it, and see whether the man's natural face, if it made you laugh less, would not also tire you less. Give us comedy like that of Cervantes and Moliere, where the men, with all their oddities and follies, were really men, and the nose two feet long had behind it a real body of average size. Caricature will only bear a glance.[28]

She disliked distortion, caricature, or abstraction, but she knew that the depiction of human nature's comic side was a valid purpose of literature. This refreshingly contradicted the prevailing notion, in Victorian England and America, that humor was unworthy of consideration as literature. "True" art, for most of the Victorians, was supposed to be lofty, dignified, ennobling, and deadly serious. Dickens, for example, was thought to be a mere entertainer; and Fuller's own writing seldom reveals the keen wit and sense of humor that delighted those she conversed with.

Music, to Margaret Fuller, was the art with the greatest power to unite people. As the most universal art, music surpassed language; it communicated most perfectly among human beings. "We look upon music as the great modern teacher of the world, the universal language which should bring nations and men together in the noblest and best way."[29] Other art forms of the past were dissolving, she wrote, but music showed the most promise for the future.[30]

> Music is the great art of the time. Its dominion is constantly widening, its powers are more profoundly recognized. In the forms it has already evolved, it is equal to representing any subject, can address the entire range of thoughts and emotions. These forms have not yet attained their completeness, and already we discern many others hovering in the vast distances of the Tone-world.[31]

Fuller's comments on music do not have the same authority or breadth of knowledge as her literary criticism. She knew literature better, though she loved music more, not only for its unsurpassed power to unite and communicate but also because more than any other art, music lent to humankind—and to her—a "winged existence."[32] In music she experienced more perfection, freedom, fulfillment, and harmony than in anything else. Beethoven's music embodied her strongest passions and highest aspirations. Her love for Beethoven, which linked her with the Romantic movement, had a political aspect as well: she admired his "uncompromising democracy,"[33] in which he contrasted so favorably with Goethe. She repeated with relish Beethoven's account of walking with Goethe on the streets of Töplitz. As the imperial family passed in a procession, Goethe stepped to one side and waited, hat in hand, bowing ceremoniously. Beethoven kept his hat jammed firmly on his head, ignored the greetings of archduke and empress, and pushed on through the crowd. After the procession had passed, he scolded Goethe roundly for his reverence toward all those "princes and parasites."[34] Beethoven's kingdom was that of art and the nobility of the heart. Fuller recognized this and revered him for being as fervent a democrat as she.

One important question posed by Fuller's humanism and respect for art has touched most American critics and artists, native or expatriate, in her century and ours: What is an authentically American work of art, and how is it created? In her time American literature was almost nonexistent, yet the ferment of creation had begun. The American Romantic movement and Transcendentalism manifested that ferment. Emerson's landmark 1837 lecture, "The American Scholar," proclaimed the birth of a national culture. The *Dial*, the Transcendentalists' most famous journal, began as a forum for the new American voice. Its writers and thinkers sought to break out of the mold of the past, to explore American experience, to search for new ways to articulate that experience. Fuller, the *Dial*'s first editor from 1840 to 1842, was also one of its principal writers during its four-year existence.[35] Much heralded, laughed at, criticized and bemoaned, but avidly read at home and abroad, the *Dial* marked the beginning of a vital new epoch in American thought and letters. As editor, Fuller insisted that it be free of partisan spirit or dogmatism, and that it express many points of view. When Emerson assumed the editorship, she chided him for letting his personal tastes and friendships determine his selection of pieces. She thought the role of journals and reviews in American life was so important that she discussed it at length in her essay "American Literature."

In her career as a critic, Margaret Fuller gave considerable thought to the creation of a native literature. She understood the link between uniquely American art and national development and character. The outlines of all three were just beginning to appear when she wrote, but they were not yet clearly perceived or well developed. She spoke to W.H. Channing of American literature, "contrasting its boyish crudity, half boastful, half timid, with the tempered, manly equipoise of thorough-bred European writers."[36] She wrote in the *Dial:*

> We have nothing of our own [in art], for the same reason that in literature, a few pale buds is [sic] all that we yet can boast of native growth, because we have no national character of sufficient fulness and simplicity to demand it. There is nothing particular to be said, as yet, but everything to be done and observed. Why should we be babbling? let us see, let us help the plant to grow; when it is once grown, then paint it, then describe it. We earn our brown bread, but we beg our cake; yet we want some, for we are children still.[37]

A section in her *Memoirs* (2:26–31) explained in detail the connection between the physical and political conditions of the young American nation and its lack of cultural development. She had great hopes for women's part in that development.

One condition that made America unique was its mixture of races and peoples. The fulfillment of the national character would not come, she believed, "till the fusion of races among us is more complete."[38] She named two other conditions: that the nation learn to prize moral and intellectual freedom as much as political, and that the nation be explored and settled, giving rise to the necessary leisure "to turn its energies upon the higher department of man's existence." Only when the national character had formed and matured, and not until then, she believed, would national ideas emerge, and from those a national literature. Goethe had had similar thoughts on the development of literature in the new German nation, and Fuller's ideas about America's development remind us of Whitman's, later in the century. She knew that she was witnessing only the beginning of the nation's evolution, nothing near its zenith. "Our thoughts anticipate with eager foresight the race that may grow up from this amalgamation of all races of the world which our situation induces. It was the pride and greatness of ancient nations to keep their blood unmixed, but it must be ours to be willing to mingle, to accept in a generous spirit what each clime and race has to offer us."[39] She knew there might be failures as dismal as the original hopes had been high.

In actuality, a great national literature did emerge before the fulfillment of the three conditions Fuller enumerated. But the conditions have not been wholly fulfilled even now, except for the third. If she was right—and she was often right about the future—then American literature is still young. The fusion of the races and the valuing of moral and intellectual freedom have not yet been realized in American life as she envisioned. Margaret Fuller did not foresee the chaos of the twentieth century. She shared with most other American thinkers of her age an expansive optimism about the nation's potential for greatness. Although events of the middle 1840s in America—the growing menace of slavery, the sordid Mexican war, increasing materialism—shook her faith in America's lofty mission, she never abandoned her belief that America would still fulfill "the great destiny whose promise rose like a star only some half a century ago upon the hopes of the world."

Many nineteenth-century American critics all too willingly allowed art to wait, however. W.D. Howells, for example, impressed by an exhibition of machinery during the first American centennial, could not refrain from boasting that America made better machines than other nations. "The superior elegance, aptness, and ingenuity of our machinery is observable at a glance," he wrote in his *Atlantic Monthly* in July 1876. "Yes, it is still in these things of iron and steel that the national genius most freely speaks; by and by the inspired marbles, the breathing canvases, the great literature; for the present America is voluble in the strong metals and their infinite uses." As the second centennial passes, this has hardly changed, except for the addition of plastic to the list of materials. The national spirit still finds expression more in machinery and feats of engineering than in artistic achievements.

Few questions in American literary history have been so much discussed as that of the artistic and symbolic relationship of America to Europe. Fuller thought, like Emerson and Poe, that the American writer should no longer imitate the forms and subject matter of Europe, although she saw no contradiction between a national art and a cosmopolitan one. Literature could only arise out of our unique national experience; this idea repeatedly appears in her *Tribune* reviews. She praised Brockden Brown, for example, because he disdained sham and imitation (she also liked his novels because of their intelligent and psychologically perceptive treatment of women). Commenting on a book of poems about the Indians, she admired their use of the materials of people's actual lives in this country. "It is thus that an American literature may grow up," she said, "if men will write of what is rooted in their real lives, instead of copies from foreign models or ideals which rest only on the clouds above them."[40] She preferred writers whose art grew from their own experience; on this account she criticized both Lowell and Longfellow, whose poetry reflected second-hand experiences. She also applied this criterion to poets other than Americans: she faulted Elizabeth Barrett's poems because her wide learning and culture stemmed more from books and other minds than from her actual experiences of life.

Fuller encouraged and praised American writers who deserved it. She called Hawthorne the best American writer of the day, even before he had written his major novels. She discerned in Poe one of the most talented and promising American writers. Her critique of James Fenimore Cooper mentioned thinness of character, shallowness of thought, and baldness of plot, but she praised his books for preserving the beauties of the wilderness, which, even as she wrote, was succumbing to "the corrosive acid of a semi-civilized invasion."[41]

Margaret Fuller foresaw the problem of the emergence of a popular culture and its destructive effect on literature. Few other American critics of that time, except for Poe, were so aware of the potential of democracy for the corruption of esthetic standards. Goethe had foreseen this phenomenon in modern life and knew it boded ill for the truly creative artist, his or her work, and its reception. Fuller denounced those who catered to the lowest, most vulgar popular tastes, flattering the public's mental indolence for financial gain. Inevitably, she said, such a phenomenon would degrade and demoralize the arts, reducing artists to a "troop of mercenaries."[42] She knew of democracy's inherent problem of the tyranny of the majority, particularly in the life of art and thought. Yet she distinguished between a genuine popular or folk culture and a factitious one. She was keenly interested in the former: from it came art, indeed, it often *was* art. From a manufactured and meretricious popular culture came only degraded taste, blunted sensibilities, and a thicker layer of philistinism. Often she was optimistic, even exuberant, about the survival of excellence in a mass culture, believing that the wide practice of an art increased the chances that work of high quality would emerge. A broad popular culture could make, she thought, a solid foundation for the houses of art:

> The larger the wave and the more fish it sweeps along, the likelier that some fine ones should enrich the net. It has always been so. The great efforts of art belong to artistic regions, where the boys in the street draw sketches on the wall and torment melodies on rude flutes; shoals of sonneteers follow in the wake of the great poet.[43]

She also saw that if artists were not to become solely a troop of hireling entertainers, their financial needs had to be met. Contributors to the *Dial*, for example, received no money for their pieces, nor did she ever have a salary as its editor. After printing costs were met, there was simply no money to pay the writers. "Pitiful" was her summation of the American writer's financial condition. It would have to change, she said firmly.

> No man of genius writes for money; but it is essential to the free use of his powers, that he should be able to disembarrass his life from care and perplexity. This is very difficult here; and the state of things gets worse and worse, as less and less is offered in pecuniary meed for works demanding great devotion of time and labour ... The publisher, obliged to regard the transaction as a matter of business, demands of the author to give him only what will find an immediate market, for he cannot afford to take anything else.[44]

Art would not be paid for if art was not valued, another reason she believed in her mission to elevate the public's taste. If it demanded and needed works of high quality, it would be willing to pay for them, she thought. But the lives of many American artists in her century and this one bear eloquent witness that the problem is more grimly evident than the solution.

The effect of such efforts to improve the American intellectual and artistic milieu has no tangible measure. Margaret Fuller saw her work as a critic as preparation, a humbler role than that of artist. Aware of this, she nevertheless accepted her place as "unhonoured servant to the grand purposes of Destiny."[45] "There is through all art a filiation," said Goethe. "If you see a great master, you will always find that he used what was good in his predecessors, and that it was this made him great. Men like Raphael do not spring out of the ground. They took root in the antique, and the best which had been done before them."[46] Paradoxically, though the history of art largely omitted and ignored women, it was this same sense of tradition and continuity that imparted meaning to Fuller's efforts. She regretted that she would not see America's national genius flower, yet she gladly helped it along. She saw herself as an instrument of an emerging national greatness, struggling to realize itself, to find a form and a voice. "The future is glorious with certainties for those who do their duty in the present, and, lark-like, seeking the sun, challenge its eagles to an earthward flight."[47] Nowhere more keenly than here do we feel the gulf between Margaret Fuller's era and our own. Whatever her disappointments about America, her faith in its future sustained her and made her work worthwhile. Her exultant optimism finds few echoes today, and where such faith in America's future still exists, it is far more cautious and subdued. Yet the sense of continuity that strengthened Fuller can do the same for us. Her legacy still holds out the hope for a national life rich in human and artistic fulfillment and points the way toward its achievement.

CHAPTER 7

The True Eclectic

By any measure, Margaret Fuller's achievements as a critic are superlative. At its best, her criticism successfully fused theory and practice, the cosmopolitan outlook and the nationalistic, Romanticism and classicism. The best of it also blended a concern for art and poetry with a concern for the life of people in society. "Judgment of art is unavoidably both an aesthetic and a social act," F.O. Matthiessen said, "and the critic's sense of social responsibility gives him a deeper thirst for meaning."[1] Without that sense of responsibility, criticism quickly becomes sterile and lifeless.

The nucleus of Fuller's critical thought at the zenith of its development appeared in an essay of 1846, "Poets of the People." The key passage from that essay is an extended metaphor of a garden, here quoted in full because of its importance:

> There are two ways of considering Poems, or the products of literature in general. We may tolerate only what is excellent, and demand that whatever is consigned to print for the benefit of the human race should exhibit fruits perfect in shape, colour, and flavour, enclosing kernels of permanent value.
>
> Those who demand this will be content only with the Iliads and Odysseys of the mind's endeavour.—They can feed no where but at rich men's tables; in the wildest recess of nature roots and berries will not content them. They say, "If you can thus satiate your appetite it is degrading; we, the highly refined in taste and the tissue of the mind, can nowhere be appeased, unless by golden apples, served up on silver dishes."
>
> But, on the other hand, literature may be regarded as the great mutual system of interpretation between all kinds of classes of men. It is an epistolary correspondence between brethren of one family, subject to many and wide separations, and anxious to remain in spiritual presence one of another. These letters may be written by the prisoner in soot and water, illustrated by rude sketches in charcoal;—by nature's nobleman, free to use his inheritance, in letters of gold, with the fair margin filled with exquisite miniatures;—to the true man each will have value, *first*, in proportion to the degree of its revelation as to the life of the human soul, *second*, in proportion to the perfection of form in which that revelation is expressed.
>
> In like manner are there two modes of criticism. One which tries, by the

highest standard of literary perfection the critic is capable of conceiving, each work which comes in his way; rejecting all that it is possible to reject, and reserving for toleration only what is capable of standing the severest test. It crushes to earth without mercy all the humble buds of Phantasy, all the plants that, though green and fruitful, are also prey to insects, or have suffered by drouth. It weeds well the garden, and cannot believe, that the weed in its native soil, may be a pretty, graceful plant.

There is another mode which enters into the natural history of every thing that breathes and lives, which believes no impulse to be entirely in vain, which scrutinizes circumstances, motive and object before it condemns, and believes there is a beauty in each natural form, if its law and purpose be understood. It does not consider literature merely as the garden of the nation, but as the growth of the entire region, with all its variety of mountain, forest, pasture, and tillage lands. Those who observe in this spirit will often experience, from some humble offering to the Muses, the delight felt by the naturalist in the grasses and lichens of some otherwise barren spot. These are the earliest and humblest efforts of nature, but to a discerning eye they indicate the entire range of her energies.

These two schools each have their dangers. The first tends to hypercriticism and pedantry, to a cold restriction on the unstudied action of a large and flowing life. In demanding that the stream should always flow transparent over golden sands, it tends to repress its careless majesty, its vigour, and its fertilizing power.

The other shares the usual perils of the genial and affectionate; it tends to indiscriminate indulgence and a leveling of the beautiful with what is merely tolerable. For indeed the vines need judicious pruning if they are to bring us the ruby wine.

In the golden age to which we are ever looking forward, these two tendencies will be harmonized. *The highest sense of fulfilled excellence will be found to consist with the largest appreciation of every sign of life.* The eye of man is fitted to range all around no less than to be lifted on high.[2]

This metaphor of the garden is the central and most recurrent image in Fuller's criticism, and the essay is an essential document of American literary criticism. Fuller proposes art as a growth and flowering, an organic concept she shared with the Romantic school. But a garden is impossible without planning, effort, and cultivation, so the image also suggests how much conscious human shaping is necessary for art. Order, classification, and distinction are implied in the garden metaphor; all these are classical qualities. The metaphor implies a dual function for art: beauty and usefulness, neither excluding the other. Gradually the metaphor expands from a single garden to the varied geography of an entire region; this evokes the idea of a national literature, and the critic's role as cultivator and co-creator of that national literature.

The metaphor makes concrete and lucid many of the abstractions of Fuller's critical theory. The stream that waters the garden symbolizes the life that nourishes art. (Later in the same essay Fuller used a metaphor of a stream to signify thought.) She borrowed the image of the golden apples from Goethe,[3] and the modern reader may recall Yeats's golden birds on golden boughs, in "Sailing to Byzantium." Both Goethe and Yeats used such images to symbolize the separateness, greater permanence, and greater perfection of art over nature. A similar ideality is implied in the golden sands and golden fruit of Fuller's metaphorical garden, as well as in the "golden letters" used by "nature's nobleman." She develops the basic distinction between critics and readers who insist on perfection of form, the highest excellence in literature ("fruits perfect in shape, colour and flavour"), and those for whom literature is less exalted but more immediately useful and responsive to present life. These critics and readers demand that art serve a functional purpose, as does food for the body ("roots and berries," "pasture," "tillage"). Some, then, will seek ideal forms in literature, and some are attentive to each form as it exists; even a lichen or weed is not without value for those who have eyes to see. Thus, like a garden with its fruit, flowers wild or cultivated, buds, boughs, and grasses, literature encompasses a nearly infinite range of forms and degrees of perfection. The metaphor suggests that literaure may and must be as complete, self-contained, and varied as the forms of nature. Elsewhere Fuller said explicitly: "Nature is ever various, ever new, and so should be her daughters, art and literature."[4]

The passage also makes graphic her views about the condition of American literature. Much can be inferred from phrases like "humble offerings" in "barren spots," or the weed that "in its native soil" is a "graceful plant"—what is a weed in a garden may be a wildflower in field or woods. Such references point to the chronic American inferiority complex about European culture and art. Fuller suggests that literature's proper concern is the unique spirit of America, that "spirit of place" that D.H. Lawrence, William Carlos Williams, Constance Rourke, and others have emphasized.[5] It is the critic's business to recognize and encourage such a spirit, however insignificant its manifestations seem beside more full-blown and glorious achievements of art.

Yeats's golden birds sang to emperor and courtiers, and Fuller's metaphor points to existing distinctions of social classes. Some think literature should be produced by an elite for an elite, "the highly refined," and some think it should exist to benefit "all kinds and classes of men." Though she recognized that the two tendencies were opposed, she looked toward an age when they would be harmonized. This concept of a golden age of the future she absorbed from Goethe and the German Romantics.[6] But for the present, the "genial and generous tendency shall have the lead."[7] Elitism can be found in Fuller's literary criticism, yet her critical theory shows a decisive trend toward a more populist view. This essay, "Poets of the People," probably expresses most fully that populist view.

Most of the Transcendentalists sensed the need for strong mutual connections between writers and the people. Though some of them were suspicious of society, no group of thinkers in the entire nineteenth century reflected more earnestly about the relation of literature to the vast energies at work in the new American nation. In 1838 George Ripley, the founder of Brook Farm, wrote:

> There is nothing more dangerous to correctness of thought or to clearness of expression, than for the literary men of a nation to withdraw from the sympathies of the common mind, and thus to lose the benefit of comparing the abstractions of speculation with the natural good sense of the body of the people. The most sublime contemplations of the philosopher can be translated into the language of the market; and unless they find a response in the native feelings of humanity, there is probably some error in the doctrine, or some defect in its exposition.[8]

Orestes Brownson spoke out forcefully on behalf of a proletarian literature that would reflect the needs of the people and serve their social aims, and Emerson's criticism too had a strongly democratic strain. It remained for Whitman, later in the century, to articulate a fully developed theory of an American literature based on a democratic faith.

But Transcendentalism, whether its primary interest was religion and the Platonic ideal (like Emerson), or democracy and social problems (like Brownson), or nature and the individual conscience (like Thoreau), or utopia for the select few (like Ripley), was perpetually in danger of denying art by making it subservient to something else. Margaret Fuller was the only Transcendentalist who respected art enough to insist on its being a separate entity with a purpose, laws, and a value of its own not to be subordinated to any other.

Too often the popular mind confuses an art not subservient to anything else with an art cut off and isolated from everything else. Margaret Fuller never thought art and literature were created or experienced in a vacuum. "Poets of the People" explored the relationship of literature to the masses of people in society. Actually, her later socialism is implicit in this essay. For example, she describes a flood tide of change, after which "there may still be many low and mean men, but *no lower classes; for it* will be understood that it is the glory of a man to labour, and that all kinds of labour have their poetry, and that there is really no more a lower and higher among the world of men with their various spheres, than in the world of stars."[9] The signs of her time led Fuller to perceive that a new leveling, democratizing force was at work in people and nations and in their forms of expression. Though she could not call their work great

100

or lasting literature, she found vitality and eloquence in the new poets of the people, men of the working classes. "The genius of the time is working through myriad organs, speaking through myriad mouths, but condescends chiefly to men of low estate. She is spelling a new and sublime spell; its first word we know is *brotherhood*, but that must be well pronounced and learnt *by heart* before we shall hear another so clearly. One thing is obvious, we must cease to worship princes even in genius."

Though she became more interested in poets of the people, Fuller never reduced art to a tool of the people's social or material needs, no matter how urgent these were. Gradually she gave her energies to those needs, for, as Edmund Wilson said of the 1930s, if society couldn't work, then enjoyment of literature hardly mattered. Yet Fuller never espoused the theory so prominent in this century, that art must directly serve revolution or the needs of the masses. Art could express those needs, as well as other human experiences and aspirations; it was not to be an instrument of social policy, nor propaganda for any cause, however righteous. The distinction is subtle, but where it has been lost, art and literature have deteriorated grievously. Fuller knew that art must remain free. She was never deceived into betraying the principle she fought for so long, the autonomy of art, the integrity of the esthetic faculty in human nature. She moved into socialism, she even took part in a revolution, but she did not push art to serve political ends. Wise enough to know that art was sometimes irrelevant to human concerns, she abandoned it rather than distort or falsify it. Art exploited by the demands of ideology loses its vitality, its creative force, its liberating and regenerative powers. Fuller's clearsighted ability to distinguish between kinds of human activity, and to accord each its own validity and place, kept her from yoking them together in an unwholesome confusion.

There are still further implications of Fuller's analogy of the garden. Discussing the development of the drama, for example, she speculated:

> There is, perhaps, a correspondence between the successions of literary vegetation with those of the earth's surface, where, if you burn or cut down an ancient wood, the next offering of the soil will not be in the same kind, but raspberries and purple flowers will succeed the oak, poplars and pine. Thus, beneath the roots of the drama, lay seeds of the historic novel, the romantic epic, which were to take its place to the reader, and for the scene, the oratorios, the opera, and ballet.[10]

The forms of art, seemingly eternal and endemic to the psyche, do change, deteriorate, and yield to newer forms. Sometimes Fuller used the garden image to suggest time in literature: for each plant or fruit there is

101

a proper season, and in the life of the garden a succession of seasons. About discerning true poetry from false, she said:

> There will always be a good deal of mock poetry in the market with the genuine; it grows up naturally as tares among the wheat, and, while there is a fair proportion preserved, we abstain from severe weeding lest the two come up together; but when the tares have almost usurped the field, it is time to begin and see if the field cannot be freed from them and made ready for a new seed-time.[11]

Many literary critics have used organic and garden metaphors. Words like soil, roots, branches, and seeds enter the language of criticism easily, and though I have not yet encountered bulbs, mulch, or manure, they are possible in criticism. Historic critics often use the metaphor of the stream or river of literature. They like to speak of currents, channels, tributaries, and backwaters to convey their meaning.[12] Henry James used organic metaphors to illuminate the creative processes of artists. He often spoke of their ideas as a germ or seed or fruit, springing out of the soil of the artist's sensibility. His organic metaphors contrast with Fuller's, for unlike hers, they refer primarily to the growth of the work itself, its genesis and development in the artist's mind. The Jamesian critical images lead us to meditate on the process of creation, but not on the relation of the work of art to anything outside itself, as do Fuller's images.

Fuller's garden metaphor has great flexibility, scope, and suggestiveness. Since the Book of Genesis, a garden has symbolized paradise, the golden age that human beings dream of, past or future. Yet a garden not only symbolizes an imaginary ideal, it is a real existing thing as well. A garden unites the real, the ideal, the mythic and the historic, labor and fruition; thus it is an appropriate symbol for art. One has only to recall Baudelaire's *Fleurs du Mal*, or the sinister and fantastic garden of Hawthorne's Dr. Rappaccini, to perceive a dark side to the garden image, which Fuller did not develop. Her own love of flowers and their symbolism may even have personally expressed her sense of identity with art and artists.

Fuller's metaphor of the garden leaves unclear the artist's nature and method of producing works. These subjects interested her. Although her criticism generally moved toward a more explicit humanism, her ideas about artists did not. She spoke of them alternately as divine, human, or natural, sometimes even using these terms interchangeably. Though she recognized the artist's importance, she never consistently defined his or her role. Sometimes, borrowing from Emerson, Fuller referred to the artist as a high priest or a liberating god. This view implies that art was a religion, whose priests served to initiate the laity into its mysteries.

Another time she said, "All the poets are the priests of Nature, though the greatest are also the prophets of the manhood of man," and at least once she conferred divinity on the artist: "The maker is divine."[13]

Frequently she inclined toward thinking the artist was like other people. In the essay "Lives of the Great Composers" she explored this point:

> Like the hero, the statesman, the martyr, the artist differs from other men only in this, that the voice of the demon within the breast speaks louder, or is more early and steadily obeyed than by men in general. But colors, and marble, and paper scores are more easily found to use, and more under command, than the occasions of life or the wills of other men, so that we see in the poet's work, if not a higher sentiment, or a deeper meaning, a more frequent and more perfect fulfilment than in him who builds his temple from the world day by day, or makes a nation his canvass and his pallette [sic].[14]

Yet artists, though so closely akin, were not entirely like others, she recognized. "The artists too are the young children of our sickly manhood, or wearied out old age," she said. "On us life has pressed till the form is marred and bowed down, but their youth is immortal, invincible, to us the inexhaustible prophecy of a second birth." The essay emphasized the artist's identity with, rather than differences from, humankind.

She spoke of artists as unself-conscious geniuses driven by forces no more subject to their control than those that cause a flower or tree to grow. She found three distinctive charcteristics of all artists:

> Clear decision. The intuitive faculty speaks clear in those devoted to the worship of Beauty. They are not subject to mental conflict, they ask not counsel of experience. They take what they want as simply as the bird goes in search of its proper food, so soon as its wings are grown.
>
> Like nature they love to work for its own sake. The philosopher is ever seeking the thought through the symbol, but the artist is happy at the implication of the thought in his work. He does not reason about "religion or thorough bass." His answer is Haydn's "I thought it best so." From each achievement grows up a still higher ideal, and when his work is finished, it is nothing to the artist who has made of it the step by which he ascended, but while he was engaged in it, it was all to him, and filled his soul with a parental joy.
>
> They do not criticise, but affirm. They have no need to deny aught, much less one another. All excellence to them was genial; imperfection only left room for new creative power to display itself. An everlasting yes breathes from the life, from the work of the artist. Nature echoes it, and leaves to society the work of saying no, if it will.

All three characteristics, in that Carlylean passage, stress the artist's affirmation of existence and oneness with nature. Fuller often returned to these ideas, particularly when discussing musicians.

She had an avid interest in the relationship of artists' work to their

personal lives and to the life of society that they either shared or re-
nounced. She liked the idea that artists' lives should be as praiseworthy
as their works, and the compromise in Goethe's life at Weimar always
disappointed her. The uncompromising Beethoven was for Fuller the
prototypical genius whom the vulgar crowd misunderstood and thought
a madman. She agreed that Milton was a great and noble human being;
admitting her propensity for hero worship, she praised Milton's life for
combining grandeur, virtue, and constancy with great poetic gifts. Still,
she saw that such artistic gifts could leave their possessors incomplete
rather than fully developed human beings. She said, for example, that
Mozart was "not a whole man," but, as "the exquisite organ of a divine
inspiration," he remained a child, with the virtues of a child. "Any art
tends to usurp the whole of a man's existence, and music most of all to
unfit for other modes of life, both from its stimulus to the senses and
exaltation of the soul." The remarkable point to her was that any artist
attained "severe and manlike lives," as so many did. She did not discuss
in this essay the separate problem of the woman artist, though she personally struggled with it.

Fuller knew that total devotion to art often precluded the fullest life
and the most harmonious personal development. In the artist's work we
must look for knowledge about the artist's life: "The biography of the
artist is a scanty gloss upon the grand text of his works." She understood
well the dichotomy expressed by Yeats: perfection of the life or of the
work. She said simply, "There is a medium somewhere. Philip Sidney
found it; others had it found for them by fate."[15] She sought this medium
for herself, as she characteristically did with many extremes presented to
her as mutually exclusive.

The relation of the artist's life and works interested the nineteenth-
century Romantics. Fuller has usually been regarded as a Romantic,[16]
though her biographer, Paula Blanchard, found the classical and the
Romantic inextricably mixed in her character. Certainly her copious use
of organic metaphors and concepts links her with that movement. The
Romantics, rediscovering intimate connections between human creativity
and the creativity of nature, typically employ such images when discussing literature and art. From the beginning, Romantic concepts and the
growth of native American culture have been intertwined, a truth that
Emerson and Whitman expressed. Classicism has always been a somewhat alien mode or style in this country,[17] and its weak hold here has
probably impoverished American art and thought. The richest cultural
traditions fuse many elements, are fertilized from many sources, arise out
of the interplay of a variety of modes. Possibly the lack of a sturdy native

classicism has prevented recognition of the classical element in Fuller's criticism.[18] At any rate, there is unquestionably a synthesis of Romantic and classical traditions in her thought.

In one of her earliest critical essays, Fuller defined classicism and expressed her preference for its characteristic restraint and concentration.[19] She loved order and form, a trait that required her to classify works of literature and to make clear distinctions among them. She also respected the ancient cultures of Greece and Rome, from which she benefited so greatly through her own education. She defended those cultures when she saw the older education, based on the classics, dissolving because of pressures for a modernized curriculum. Although she recognized the need for change and advocated an education specifically designed for American life, she did not want to throw out what she saw as the nucleus of a civilized life.

> There is a beautiful propriety in referring back to the Greeks and Romans, could this but be done with intelligence and in harmony with the other branches of culture. It is only pedantry and indolence that makes this dangerous. . . . Those nations brought some things to a perfection that the world will probably never see again. We must not lose the sense of their greatness because our practice is in a different sphere. For this it is that marks the true eclectic, that he need not cling to the form because he reveres the spirit that informed it.[20]

Fuller's classical bent is evident in this advice she gave to a young artist:

> Avoid details so directly personal, as to emotion. A young and generous mind, seeing the deceit and cold reserve which so often palsy men who write, no less than those who act, may run into the opposite extreme. But frankness must be tempered by delicacy, or elevated into the region of poetry. You may tell the world at large what you please, if you make it of universal importance by transporting it into the field of general human interest. But your private griefs, merely as yours, belong to yourself, your nearest friends, to Heaven and to nature. There is a limit set by good taste, or the sense of beauty, on such subjects, which each who seeks may find for himself.[21]

The emphasis here on universality, objectivity, restraint, and taste reveals her classicism, as does her love of tradition. She also recognized the limitations of the human mind, a thoroughly anti-Faustian admission. Of Robert Browning's youthful Shelleyan poem *Paracelsus*, she wrote:

> It is one of those attempts, that illustrate the self-consciousness of this age, to represent the fever of the soul pining to embrace the secret of the universe in a single trance. Men who are once seized with this fever, carry thought upon the heart as a cross, instead of finding themselves daily warmed and enlightened to more life and joy by the sacred fire to which their lives daily bring fresh fuel.

Sometimes their martyrdoms greatly avail, as to positive achievements of knowledge for their own good and that of all men; but, oftener, they only enrich us by experience of the temporary limitations of the mind, and the inutility of seeking to transcend, instead of working within them.[22]

The qualifying adjective "temporary" here is an intriguing variation on the age-old classical dictum about human limitations. It suggests that Fuller's acceptance stopped short of absolute assent. In practice, one must accept limitation and work within it, but never discount the possibility that these limitations may suddenly dissolve or disappear, thus opening new vistas of infinite possibility and aspiration. The passage hints at her impatience with the dogmas of both Romantic and classical thought and suggests a new synthesis of the two.

Balance, moderation, and a striving for unity are hallmarks of Fuller's thought. One might easily add objectivity, sense of hierarchy, and organizing power—all associated with classicism. That these could coexist happily with so many Romantic traits is evidence of a high degree of intellectual and personal harmony. She sought and found a new synthesis, applied it in her criticism, and embodied it in her life.

This synthesis of Romanticism and classicism is nowhere more evident than in Fuller's concept of form in literature, specifically meter in poetry. Here the superiority of her concept over Emerson's and Poe's better-known concepts becomes evident. She often took a critical position midway between the two polarities those men represented. Emerson believed that meter was negligible: "It is not metre," he said in "The Poet," "but a metre-making argument that makes a poem." Emerson never cared as much about the forms of poetry as its ideas, content, and meaning ("argument"). His poems, however, were conventionally metrical, so his theory does not mesh with his practice. Poe, however, paid meticulous attention to the meters and forms of poems and tales, but he tended to divorce form from content and make the rules of literary art mechanical and arbitrary. Poe—possibly the first of the great American literary manipulators, a class brought to consummate perfection in our time— gauged the success of a literary form by the extent to which it manipulated the reader's emotions through its "effect."

Fuller understood that the form of a work of literature was intrinsic to it, not mechanical or irrelevant. "No form of art will succeed with him to whom it is the object of deliberate choice," she wrote in the *Dial*. "It must grow from his nature in a certain position . . . and be no garment taken from the shining store to be worn at a banquet, but a real body gradually woven and assimilated from the earth and sky which environed the poet in his youthful years."[23] This passage is reminiscent of some of

106

Goethe's statements about form, for example, in Book 12 of his autobiography. Goethe insisted that both works of art and living beings were organized by an interior principle. This Transcendentalist and Romantic doctrine implies that form is not subject to the conscious will or shaping faculty; it is a thing that "grows" as inevitably and naturally as the subject. In her later essays for the *Tribune*, Fuller further modified her concept of poetic form and moved toward Poe's position. Taking exception to Lowell's discussion of meter, she wrote:

> It is true, as he says, that the mind rises from prose into poetic measure quite naturally, as from speech to song, when it has something to express above the level of the lower necessities of life. It is true that rhythm cannot more easily be disengaged from the poetic thought expressed in it than the skin from the pulp of the grape. But this is not merely because it holds it together "in a compact and beautiful form." Metres themselves are actually *something* apart from the thought they are destined to convey. They are the music of that thought; its more or less perfect organization.
>
> Madame de Stael was not wrong in receiving a high delight from the mere cadence of verses that she did not understand. As the same thought is expressed in all Gothic Cathedrals, but with peculiar force in that at Cologne, so may the same thought be expressed with equal distinctness in two metres, but with more force in one than the other. Just so two faces may look on you with love ... but one will be full fraught with soul, and will express the beauty of love, the other not. The charms of metres are subtle and more deeply grounded than the obvious meaning of the words; their analysis is not impossible, but it requires as clear a knowledge of the laws of harmony, i.e. of proportion, as delicate a sense of the subtle efficacy of thoughts, i.e. of spiritual gradation, as the analysis of what are more strictly styled musical compositions does; therefore, while many men are too dully organized to feel their power, a larger proportion of those who feel cannot render a reason. Let us put from us, once for all, the vulgar frivolity of assuming that that does not exist for us which *we* cannot yet render a reason.[24]

Poe defined poetry as "the rhythmical creation of beauty" and emphasized the music of a poem, as Fuller does here. But Poe, in his own words in "The Poetic Principle," was "inspired by an ecstatic prescience of the glories beyond the grave." He was perpetually reaching through the beauty of poetry and music to the "Beauty above," struggling "to attain a portion of that Loveliness whose very elements, perhaps, appertain to eternity alone." Fuller, on the other hand, perceived in poetic rhythm the manifestation of inner harmony and universal harmony. In another essay of this period, she linked the meters and forms of poetry with the explicit character of a nation.

> The metres, the methods of verse that grow up in a nation are one of the highest expressions of its spirit, one of the finest organizations of its life. The rules which are derived from them give the science of life as far as it can be

understood *from without*. . . . To make verse according to rule will enable no man to write one word of poetry, but it may make him more deeply familiar with the sense in which poetry has been written, by refining the taste and cultivating the ear. . . . The boy learns how the great poets wrote in measure, and copies the cadence of their feet, but neither by his tutor is he taught, nor of his seeking does he learn, that metres are nothing except the harmonious movements of a mind deeply conscious of the universal harmony, and that only by adoring and studying *that* can he really emulate them.[25]

The poetics of both Poe and Emerson always draw us into some ideal, extraterrestrial realm. Fuller draws us more deeply into the real poetry of earth and its inexhaustible variety.

Meters, then, are not mechanical, not mere outward forms, not exercises in ingenuity. They express, she believed, the poet's own sense of harmony, an expression at once unique, individual, and universal. Fuller used these principles actively in discussing and judging a poet's work, though often she emphasized content more than form. She wrote of Elizabeth Barrett's poems, for example, that "great variety of metres are used, and with force and facility. But they have not that deep music which belongs to metres which are the native growth of the poet's mind. In that case, others may have used them, but we feel that, if they had not, he must have invented them; that they are original with him."[26]

Fuller did not share Poe's interest in extensive technical analysis of meter, nor did she share Emerson's (theoretical) disregard for meter. It is not a question here of absolute rules for poetry, for there are none. Goethe mentioned the absence of objective laws for the internal and external construction of a poem. Madame de Staël likewise spoke of the rules of art as a calculus of the probable means to success.[27] This does not mean there are no criteria by which to construct or evaluate a poem. But Emerson, by dismissing form, and Poe, by making it contrived and artificial, have both distorted the understanding of an essential element in poetry. When Emerson said in "The Poet" that "there is no doctrine of forms in our philosophy," he was subverting poetry and all art. Without form there is no art, as Emerson must have known. Perhaps he intended the pronouncement to counter the prevailing doctrinaire esthetic. For the Platonist, the only forms that matter are eternal, preexisting ones.

Both Emerson and Poe believed they were liberating poetry from stultifying and worn-out modes of expression. Historically, their critical pronouncements served necessary purposes, though they now seem unsatisfying. Emerson in particular betrayed the inadequacies of his critical theory by his pronounced inability to judge and evaluate specific writers—his early recognition of Whitman's greatness being the one shining exception. By contrast, Poe's theory fused with his practice, resulting in a much more effective practical criticism. But Fuller's understanding of poetic form was subtler and more mature than that of either, if less easily reduced to simple formulas.

Fuller's place among the most penetrating and farsighted critics of her century is indisputable. Apart from the few best critics, nineteenth-century American criticism was generally burdened by an encrusted moralism, a dreary utilitarianism, and later an effete gentility that she probably would have abhorred, had she lived to see it. The contributions of Poe and Henry James toward freeing art from that excess baggage and establishing its autonomy and independence can hardly be overestimated. The nineteenth century also produced the theory and practice of literature as escape, as refuge, a literature connected to nothing outside itself, responsible to nothing outside itself. Historically, this too may have been necessary, though it increased the fragmentation of the human psyche, that peculiar sickness of the nineteenth and twentieth centuries. Such an art had no way to avoid the fearful narcissism, isolation, and ultimate disintegration that Poe portrayed so starkly in the poem "The Haunted Palace" in his tale of the House of Usher. However fervently Margaret Fuller wished to free art from its subservience to moral didacticism, she was too much Goethe's disciple ever to espouse any concept of art divorced from nature and reality. She always insisted on the close relation of art to both, and we may hazard a guess that she would not have cared for these developments.

Through much of the twentieth century, the same issues that preoccupied her have still been debated. One example is America's paradoxical artistic relationship to Europe. At least until World War II, discussion continued about whether any genuine American literature or culture existed, and if it did, what it was precisely, what it should be, whether it should use an American language or an international one. Our century has seen the same mixture of attitudes as in Fuller's day: the wish to conform to European standards, a snobbish condescension toward American art as inferior or immature, a belligerent or braggart defensiveness about art of native origin and character. Cultural provincialism still prevails in the literature departments of many American universities, with their exclusive emphasis on English-language literatures, though this is beginning to change. Perhaps the most eloquent statement of all has been the escape of artists and writers from America to Europe—though since World War II, there has been much reverse movement from Europe to America. Even now it is by no means clear whether such issues have been decided or only temporarily suspended under the pressures of urgent global realities: world wars, sinister concentrations of unchecked power, the threat of nuclear holocaust, the dehumanization of a technological age, racial enmity, social change too disjointed and rapid to be absorbed. These dangers to human survival and well-being cast their shadow over the creation and enjoyment of art.

In that shadow have grown the pessimism and the apocalyptic mood that pervade so much twentieth-century American writing about literature. The century began as H.G. Wells questioned, in *The Future of America*, whether the nation was a "giant childhood or a gigantic futility." The latter possibility never occurred to the optimistic and hopeful Margaret Fuller. Even now, much of what she worked for in her criticism is imperfectly realized, if at all. One does not have to look far to see the myopic utilitarianism she fought against (often called "relevance" today), the Puritan suspicion of the arts, the mushrooming of a cheap and vulgar mass culture. Perhaps Wells's question is still to be answered.

In the twentieth century, American literary criticism has coalesced around certain philosophies or movements, and the most heated debates have been over values—how they are determined, established, tested, and applied.[28] Too often these schools of criticism have been marked by a doctrinaire rigidity of approach and a truculent insistence on their own correctness and validity, to the exclusion of all others. Of these schools and movements—neohumanism, New Criticism, neo-Aristotelianism, Marxism, Freudianism, the mythological and archetypal methods— Margaret Fuller would perhaps have shared a common viewpoint with the neohumanists, although she would certainly have found incomprehensible their hostility to the future and their insensitivity to human lives and needs. In any case, as a generous-minded, free-wheeling eclectic, she probably would have disliked the partisan spirit of all these groups and found them all too confining.[29]

The critical spirit represented by Margaret Fuller, her flexibility, moderation, and dislike for dogma, together with "the largest appreciation of every sign of life," is all too rarely encountered in twentieth-century criticism. The intellectual breadth and tolerance she advocated and practiced are notably absent. The rationality and essential sanity of her critical thought contrast to the apotheosis of incoherence that has become more and more prominent in literature, art, and criticism since midcentury. The study of Fuller's criticism is thus all the more worthwhile, for it restores to us the conviction that what has been lost is still of great value and needs to be rediscovered. At its best, Fuller's criticism excites us by renewing our sense of the living truth of our heritage. It suggests that, far from being exhausted, the full possibilities of American art and cultural life have yet to be realized.

This is not to say that all her work retains its interest and immediacy. Much of her criticism is outdated: her position as reviewer of current books made a certain amount of obsolescence inevitable. A few writers and issues that she waxed eloquent about make us yawn today. The main value of her criticism lies in her philosophy of literature, her penetrating approach to works of art, the completeness of her response to what was good or excellent in them. A great mind at work on a great human question—the nature and value of art—compels our interest still.

Margaret Fuller's best criticism reveals a sensibility poised on that precarious center between love of order and form, and love of human beings and their actual life in the world. A balance between these two often incompatible loves, such as she achieved, can rarely be sustained for long. "We seek to know, to act, and to be what is possible to Man," she wrote.[30] This was ultimately the meaning of her critical achievement and of her life-long involvement with art and literature. The power of art in human lives is continually demonstrated in our time by attempts to squelch, channel, exploit, castrate, or ostracize it, or failing all else, to exile artists, or execute them. Margaret Fuller knew the power of art, how human potential is realized through it, and how necessary courage is to artistic and intellectual leadership. She speaks to our age as eloquently as she spoke to her own.

CHAPTER 8

Margaret Fuller's America

If Margaret Fuller had never written a word about literature and art, she would still have been a significant social thinker and leader. Her books *Summer on the Lakes* and *Woman in the Nineteenth Century*, together with her *Tribune* essays, retain much of their interest and importance today. These works, together with her letters and journals, bear witness to her continual efforts to understand society and improve it. They are the product of keen observation, incisive thought, and dedication to principle. A powerful mind is at work here, probing, questioning, analyzing, synthesizing. The variety of tone and mood in these writings is striking. She could be whimsical, mildly persuasive, meditative, playful, puzzled, sweetly reasonable, oracular, cryptic. She could also lash out with savage anger, Swiftian contempt, devastating irony, for this sphere of life roused in her passions that art—for all her devotion to it—did not.

Fuller's social awareness and commitment came relatively late. Despite her father's career in law and government, she was, as a young girl, indifferent to politics and repelled by politicians. Her father's associates bored, even disgusted her, and after he retired from public life she said of them:

> The violent antipathies,—the result of an exaggerated love for, shall I call it by so big a name as the "poetry of being?"—and the natural distrust arising from being forced to hear the conversation of half-bred men, all whose petty feelings were roused to awkward life by the paltry game of local politics,—are yielding to reason and calmer knowledge. . . . I hope to feel no more that sometimes despairing, sometimes insolently contemptuous, feeling of incongeniality with my time and place.[1]

Though she disdained it, politics stayed in her blood, and she once described a Whig convention in Providence as the most exciting event of her two-year teaching stint in that city.

As a young New England bluestocking avidly pursuing learning and artistic cultivation, Fuller was almost oblivious to social and political issues. At the age of thirty-one she wrote: "Others have looked at society with far deeper consideration than I. I have felt so unrelated to this sphere, that it has not been hard for me to be true. Also, I do not believe in Society."[2] The transformation from political innocent to dedicated activist came gradually over the last decade of her life, a process begun in America and accelerated by the conditions of her life in Europe.

The American society Fuller felt unrelated to provided too little comfort and nourishment for either body or spirit. Her longing for Europe was a measure of her cultural and educational deprivation at home. In the early decades of the nineteenth century, life was often crude and difficult, at least by present standards.[3] Northern society was being transformed by the beginnings of the Industrial Revolution. New roads, railroads, and canals were being built, yet travel, usually by stagecoach, was still arduous. The spirit of hard work was everywhere dominant. Most people knew little of the uses of leisure, and the absence of parks, resorts, games, and sports surprised European visitors. People suffered because of rudimentary or nonexistent medical care, poor health, and frequent epidemics and plagues like typhus and yellow fever. Plumbing, heating, and sanitation were primitive, and Dickens in the 1840s was surprised to see pigs running in the streets of New York.

This time of rapid physical growth saw successive, ever-larger waves of immigration throughout the 1830s and 1840s, the addition of new territories, and at least one imperialistic venture, the Mexican war. Migration to the midwest had begun, but it did not extend much beyond the prairies until midcentury. The new immigrants swelled the population of eastern cities, inevitably causing social tensions. Though the immigrants provided cheap labor, they were targets of virulent antagonism, especially toward the Catholic Irish. (Another Transcendentalist, Orestes Brownson, after his conversion to Catholicism, tried to educate Irish Catholics about American thought, but his efforts were largely unsuccessful.) The immigrants and the urban political machines like Tammany Hall established mutually profitable arrangements that affected American politics for decades. Racial and religious riots erupted often in cities like Philadelphia and Baltimore.

Social reform was in the air. Temperance societies thrived, and new humanitarian impulses led to prison and asylum reform. Utopian communities like Brook Farm, Ripon, and New Harmony were begun, and the feminist movement grew in numbers and strength, culminating in the Seneca Falls convention of 1848. The Abolition movement sprang up in response to the nation's worst problem, slavery. Yet in the 1830s and 1840s few in either the North or South foresaw slavery's terrible consequences.

On the contrary, problems seemed soluble. America's future looked unlimited. Great leaps of growth gave new impetus to the concept of a distinctive American mission among the world's nations. Ideas about human and social perfectibility abounded—the utopian communities were one manifestation. In this intellectually vigorous atmosphere Transcendentalism flourished. Few disputed the dominant belief that the law of progress was a universal law of history, supremely favoring America. It was truly America's Age of Innocence.

A product of this society, Margaret Fuller became its critic and one of its intellectual leaders. She was not indifferent to America's growth, hope, promise, and problems. American to the core, she shared the belief in her country's unique and sacred destiny among nations, never imagining what crimes would be committed in the name of that belief in future ages. To the end of her life she loved America, believed in its principles and its greatness.

Fuller absorbed much of her patriotism from her study of Jefferson, the only political thinker who interested her during the formative years of her self-education. Her admiration for Jefferson was in part a paternal legacy, Timothy Fuller's politics being Jeffersonian. The study gave her a welcome common meeting ground with her father, from whom she often felt estranged. She also saw in Jefferson a mind kindred to her own and was highly receptive to his ideas on religion, education, and government.[4] Her later writings from Italy reflected Jefferson's conviction that the ancient monarchies and ecclesiastical structures of the Old World were hopelessly corrupt, beyond remedy. As they developed over the years, her convictions about human equality and America's destiny in the world bore the Jeffersonian imprint.

She learned from him that pettiness and politics were not necessarily synonymous, that American citizenship could be reconciled with high cultural aspirations:

> He has given me a higher idea of what a genuine citizen of this republick may become. He may become a *genuine man*. He need not stoop to be a demagogue, he need not swagger his Demosthenian thunders on every petty local question, he need not despise, nay he ought not to disregard general literature, nor elegant pursuits. The ideas I got from the conversations of those persons I have been obliged to hear, are in a great measure false, and I love my country better.[5]

One of the first social questions that touched Fuller personally was the establishment of Brook Farm, the best known of the nineteenth-century American utopian communities. Many fellow Transcendentalists committed themselves to the experiment, but in spite of keen interest in Brook Farm, she, like Emerson, could never be induced to join. She often visited the farm and conducted conversations on education and

114

self-improvement, but she could not wholeheartedly assent to the community's goals and methods. In fact, she was amused to find herself taking the part of the conservative in those earnest discussions with the Brook Farmers. She shared their repugnance for a vulgar, materialistic, spiritually unsatisfying society, but a skeptical, practical turn of mind prevented her from being seduced by visions of perfect or perfectible communities. She outlined her ideas in a letter to W.H. Channing: "Utopia it is impossible to build up. At least, my hopes for our race on this one planet are more limited than those of most of my friends. I accept the limitations of human nature, and believe a wise acknowledgement of them one of the best conditions of progress. Yet every noble scheme, every poetic manifestation, prophesies to man his eventual destiny."[6]

She knew that her talents were not suited to farm work, and she may have felt it beneath her. Weeding onions was not the best way to link the self with nature, she told Emerson.[7] Intent on guarding her independence, Fuller, like Thoreau, simply could not believe in group solutions for social ills. "Why bind oneself to a central or any doctrine?" she asked. "How much nobler stands a man entirely unpledged, unbound."[8] She feared that communal schemes would only paralyze individual energies, character, and heroism. "Man is not made for society," she wrote to Channing, "but society is made for man. No institution can be good which does not tend to improve the individual." At this time Fuller believed that only individual effort could remedy the world's moral flaws, which she thought were a constant of history. She told Channing:

> I feel that every man must struggle with these enormous ills, in some way, in every age, in that of Moses, or Plato, or Angelo, as in our own. So it has not moved me much to see my time so corrupt, but it would if I were in a false position. . . . I do not know what their scheme will ripen to; at present it does not deeply engage my hopes. It is thus far only a little way better than others. I doubt if they will get free from all they deprecate in society.

Goethe's influence was still strong at this period in her life, and Goethe taught individual self-cultivation: "He vindicates the individual against the mass, seeks for help to the world in private culture rather than public measures, and would educate the people indirectly through the influence of the Beautiful, refining and elevating the whole nature, rather than through direct legal or moral stress in any one or two directions."[9]

What Henry James called "the stamp of provincialism" may also have made Fuller hold back from the Brook Farm enterprise. With her usually unerring instinct for distinguishing the local and ephemeral from the universal and enduring, she perhaps sensed that Brook Farm would not amount to much more than an interesting eccentricity, however good and generous its hopes. "It was a beginning without a fruition," said

James, "a dawn without a noon; and it produced, with a single exception [Hawthorne], no great talents."[10] For all its earnest commitment to fundamental social change, not one radical or militant reformer emerged from its innovative school and communal arrangement.[11]

Her critics have seen in Fuller's attitude toward Brook Farm a self-assertive egotism. Possibly she was also reluctant to submit herself to the discipline and the rewards of moral commitment. During these insular New England years many thought her an intellectual snob. Gross social injustices had scarcely touched her yet. She had seen too little human wretchedness to awaken her social conscience.

Fuller has also been criticized for obtuseness to the urgency of the slavery question and for holding aloof from the Abolitionists. Like Hawthorne, she had little use for them, partly because of their excesses of zeal and rhetoric. She found them too partisan, fanatic, tedious, and narrow. Her skepticism about the efficacy of group efforts also kept her from joining or actively supporting them. Harriet Martineau severely criticized Fuller on this score. In her autobiography Martineau described Fuller as frivolous and supercilious, and her Boston Conversations as a circle of well-dressed, spoiled women who sat around pretentiously discussing literature and Greek mythology while others devoted themselves to purging the nation of the fatal poison of slavery.[12]

The criticism may not have been wholly disinterested. Fuller and Martineau had once been close friends, and when Martineau's *Society in America* appeared in 1837, Fuller bluntly expressed her displeasure with the book. But more than a piqued literary ego was at stake here. The two women differed fundamentally about what was necessary to American society and what required the most loyalty. Fuller believed that her role was unique and no less necessary in its subtler way than that of the Abolitionists. She believed that by disseminating ideas among the women of her milieu, she provided an essential leaven for the transformation of society. Martineau's criticism ignored the fact that the Boston women whom Fuller influenced—whom she helped toward boldness of mind, personal courage, and the sense of their own potential as free beings—were the women in the vanguard of the movement for social change, especially for Abolition. To picture them as idle dreamers or self-indulgent upper-class exotics was grossly misleading. As Chevigny notes, "Fuller's premise that women should nurture their serious responses to each other . . . was trail-blazing," and the insistence on women's right to think "was subtly subversive."[13]

Fuller later learned that there is a moment when self-cultivation must be abandoned for wholehearted commitment to social change. That moment came for her in Rome rather than Boston. There, in the throes of the Roman revolution, Fuller admitted that she had not formerly appreciated Garrison and the Abolitionists enough. But she followed her own lights. Conscious of "a natural and acquired aloofness from many, if not most popular tendencies of my time and place," she thought her best course was "the free pursuit of truth," rather than to be "permanently ensnared in the meshes of sect or party."[14] She believed, as Robert Browning said of Shelley, that the best way to remove abuses was to stand fast by truth.

She sympathized with the Abolitionists' cause and abhorred slavery and slavery's defenders. She devoted many *Tribune* columns to the subject,[15] and she saw the growth of slavery as one of the two or three cardinal signs that the nation had shamefully betrayed the principles on which it was founded. Her distaste for the rabid invective of the Abolitionists never prevented her from wielding her "lightning pen" toward the goal of slavery's destruction.

Fuller's opposition to slavery arose out of principle. But the condition of the blacks, individually or collectively, never touched and awakened her imagination as much as the plight of the Indians. At that time the Indians had far fewer defenders than the black slaves. There was not much awareness that abominable injustices had been committed against the Indians and were still being committed. Very few others in her time saw so clearly and condemned so fearlessly the crimes done to the Indians in the name of civilization. More than a century passed before Americans widely recognized the victimization of the Indians.

She had never seen an Indian until 1840. In that year she wrote to Emerson describing a man named Forest, an Indian traveling in the East. He was "a nobly formed man," she wrote, who "seemed much nearer one's ideal than Cooper's or Miss Sedgwick's fancy sketches. . . . There was something tragic in the contrast between him and the [white] people around him . . . like rats and weazels round a lion. . . . I should like very much to visit one of the tribes. I am sure I could face the dirt, and discomfort and melancholy to see somewhat of the stately gesture and concentred mood."[16]

Fuller observed Indians firsthand when she traveled to Niagara and the Great Lakes region in 1843. Out of that trip came *Summer on the Lakes*, a travel book of the genre then popular, consisting of descriptions, anecdotes, and observations. On her trip, Fuller wanted not only to learn something about the Indians and their culture but also to see what the Easterners and immigrant European settlers were making of the new land. She wanted to see a nation in the making.

In tone and intent, *Summer on the Lakes* is reminiscent of Thoreau's *A Week on the Concord and Merrimack*.[17] Written before their authors' mature style had developed, both books are self-consciously literary, episodic, and rambling. Though uneven, both contain vivid, memorable passages and incipient ideas that are developed in later works. The richly ironical *Summer* reveals Fuller's keen interest in language and her concern with the literary vocation. Its play of moods and lightness of tone seldom appear in her other writings, and it remains one of the most penetrating and intelligent of the nineteenth-century commentaries of frontier life. *Summer* has the quality of travel itself—scenes glimpsed in passing, bits of lore quickly learned, sudden insights into people's lives, instant like or instant dislike of people and places, even the moments of tedium and discomfort, all accurately observed, felt, and recorded.

Those who look for superficial unity in *Summer* will be disappointed, yet there is an underlying unity. The theme of *Summer* is nature and civilization, and their interaction. This fundamental theme unifies the book's seemingly random anecdotes and descriptions. The Indians represented nature to Fuller, the whites civilization. The Indians fascinated her for the very differences that many white people loathed and attempted to eradicate.

Much romantic myth clustered around the Indians. Fuller, surveying the existing literature about the Indians, deplored the false pictures purveyed by popular writers like Mrs. Jameson, though she knew they had formed her own ideas of Indians. She herself tried to avoid sentimentality, but she tended to overidealize them, to see in them Rousseau's noble savages.

In *Summer on the Lakes* she wanted to counter the prevailing idea that the Indian was a fiend or at best a low, vicious barbarian, impervious to "higher" civilizing influence. The early Puritan settlers despised the Indians because they worshiped other gods and rejected Christianity; later Americans despised them because they refused to progress, to "better themselves," unable to comprehend that the Indians were already as "good" as they cared to be. Fuller thus realized the inevitability of the collision between the European and Indian peoples. "Had they [Europeans] been truly civilized or Christianized, the conflicts which sprang from the collision of the two races might have been avoided; but this cannot be expected in movements made by masses of men. The mass has never yet been humanized, though the age may develop a human thought."[18] History could not be reversed. Yet the whites had so grievously injured the Indians that hatred and contempt of each for the other was inevitable. Fuller began to see the futility of individual good will when two alien civilizations collided, as they had on the North American continent. Even the kindest of white men, she wrote, feel "the aversion of the injurer for him he has degraded." The European felt justified by a "superior" civilization, and the Indian bowed to it: "The power of fate is with the white man, and the Indian feels it." Later she simply called it power.

Fuller did not argue with fate or history in *Summer*. She mainly wished to dispel the stereotypes of the Indians as bloodthirsty, ignorant savages by portraying them as human beings, and by showing that they had their own standards of belief and conduct, to which they were far more faithful than the whites were to theirs. She described the courtesy with which the Pottawattamie tribe received her as a stranger, though they themselves, driven from their land, were utterly destitute: "They seemed, indeed, to have neither food, utensils, clothes, nor bedding; nothing but the ground, the sky, and their own strength." She told of the Indian women's decorum and their delicate manners, timid yet self-possessed. She wrote of the Indians' religion and their virtuousness, "if virtue be allowed to consist in a man's acting up to his own ideas of right."

White European civilization, on the other hand, meant "might makes right," a code veiled with evasion and deceit to hide its true nature. She had no illusions about the future of the Indians: "I have no hope of liberalizing the missionary, of humanizing the sharks of trade, of infusing the conscientious drop into the flinty bosom of policy, of saving the Indian from immediate degradation and speedy death." She knew that if the whites allowed themselves to regard the Indians as fellow human beings, this would have severely impeded their policy of degradation and extermination. Twentieth-century history has showed us all what Fuller knew, that one's enemies must be seen as subhuman in order to carry out an extensive campaign of treachery and brutality upon them.

The European's religion had aided him in his policy of conquest, Fuller saw. She leveled her severest criticism, in *Summer* and later in two *Tribune* essays about the Indians, at the hypocrisy of Christians and the ineptness of Christian missionaries. The whites felt justified, she explained, by their sense of having not only a superior civilization to that of the Indian but also a superior religion. Yet the missionaries wrought only havoc in their attempts to Christianize the Indians. What would have happened, she wondered, if the Indians had been approached with love and intelligence? No one tried it: if some of the missionaries had love, they had not the intelligence to understand the Indians and so did them more harm by interfering. She found it perfectly just and natural when a group of Indians replied scornfully to the missionary who preached to them the religious benefit of becoming Christian: "Christians! Why, the white men are Christians!"[19] How could it be otherwise, she asked, when the Indians knew their teachers as powerful robbers?[20]

Once a Cherokee chief named Lowry sent out an appeal to the Christian community, that very community, wrote Fuller, "which today has been dozing in the churches over texts of scripture which they apply only to the bygone day, while there is before them at this moment such a mighty appeal for sympathy, for justice, such wrong to be set right, such service to be done to the commands of Christ, Love one another—Feed my lambs."[21] She excoriated religious hypocrisy against the black people too, and she pointed out how often the clergy used religion as another tool of domination by commanding slaves "to obey a gospel which they will not allow them to read."[22]

In her reflective, philosophical analysis of the Indians' plight in *Summer on the Lakes*, Fuller generally seems to view the collision of the white and red races as inevitable. As her social conscience awakened more in the 1840s, she grew angrier. The two *Tribune* essays about the Indians make no attempt to hide that anger. She attacked the popular myths and fictions about the Indians that she, like others, had been brought up to believe. Contrary to myth, she discovered "that the white man had no desire to make the red owner of the land his fellow citizen there, but to intoxicate, plunder, and then destroy and exile him."[23] She made her strongest statement in her last essay on the Indians, written shortly before she left for Europe:

> Spoliation, aggression, falsehood of the blackest character, a hundred times repeated, each time with increased shamelessness, mark every step of this intercourse. If good men have sometimes interposed, it is but as a single human arm might strive to stay the torrent. The sense of the [American] nation has been throughout, Might makes Right. We will get what we want at any rate. What does it signify what becomes of the Indians? They are red. They are unlike us in character and person.—Let them save themselves if they can, the Indian dogs.[24]

It was not only the damage inflicted on the Indians that evoked Fuller's interest and sympathy. She journeyed to the West to search for the roots of the American experience, and she intuitively sensed how much that experience had to do with the land itself. Her interest in the Indians arose partly from her awareness of their ancient connection with the land now being settled by white European immigrants. This may explain why the Indian captured her imagination as the blacks did not. To Africans, brought to this continent in bondage, the land was as alien and strange as it was to the Europeans; thus the black slaves were doubly degraded here. Only the Indians, of the three races in America, could have any long-established sense of relationship to the land. This was a theme Faulkner explored a century later in *The Bear*. For Americans today, the most visible signs of the original Indian presence are the ubiquitous Indian place names in nearly every region of the country, those constant ghostly reminders that the Indians first conferred identity, through human language, on the rivers and valleys and mountains of the continent. In Fuller's day, the Indian presence was much more visible, particularly in the frontier territory of Illinois and Wisconsin. She saw traces everywhere of the recently evicted Indians—their burial mounds, settlements, arrowheads, tomahawk marks. "Kishwaukie is, according to tradition, the scene of a famous battle, and its many grassy mounds contain the bones of the valiant. On these waved thickly the mysterious purple flower, of which I have spoken before. I think it springs from the blood of Indians."[25]

A hill in one western state poignantly symbolized to Fuller the new order on the continent. It contained the bones of one of the tribes. The whites drove the Indians away, but they often stole quietly back to the hill, a ritual of reverence to their dead. The whites complained of this nuisance, especially the hunters, angered that the Indians came back and drove away "*our* game."

Fuller saw in the North American Indians a primitive harmony of person forever lost to civilized whites. The white, she wrote, has two natures: "One, like that of the plants and animals, adapted to the uses and enjoyments of this planet, another which presages and demands a higher sphere." The mental nature is forever forging ahead and breaking away from the instinctive. "As yet, he loses in harmony of being what he gains in height and extension; the civilized man is a larger mind, but a more imperfect nature, than the savage." Some Indians understood this too. One reportedly said that "the white man no sooner came here, than he thought of preparing the way for his posterity; the red man never thought of this." Whites triumphed because of their ability to "look before and after," the same quality that made them "pine for what is not." Indians were thoroughly happy, when they were happy, and thoroughly good, but not conscious of being good. Fuller's continual search for wholeness, for unity of being, drew her to the Indians, who had once possessed such a wholeness.

Her understanding of this contrast between the white Europeans and the red Indians prevented her from sentimentalizing the Indians. She knew that some intelligent comprehension of them, even in their present demoralized condition, was essential to understanding America: "There *was* a greatness, unique and precious, which he who does not feel will never duly appreciate the majesty of nature in this American continent." In one especially memorable passage, she went to the heart (or the jugular) of the American frontier experience: "Wherever the hog comes, the rattlesnake disappears; the omnivorous traveller, safe in its stupidity, willingly and easily makes a meal of the most dangerous of reptiles, and one which the Indian looks on with a mystic awe. Even so the white settler pursues the Indian, and is victor in the chase."

The primitive's instinctive unself-conscious response to experience was not, could not be, hers. She felt its absence, but had no replacement yet. Her reaction to Niagara Falls illustrates this imperfect assimilation. Already this marvel of nature had been so much written about that the danger of banality, the conventional response, was hard to avoid. Knowledge of others' reaction to the falls did not hinder Fuller's enjoyment of it nor blunt her sense of wonder; but it did make her more self-conscious, aware of another dimension of Niagara than the spectacle itself. Because so many others had seen and marveled at it, painted, and written of it, all this accumulation inevitably must be part of her experience. "Happy were the first discoverers of Niagara, those who could come unawares upon this view and upon that, whose feelings were entirely their own," she exclaimed. Fuller searched for an authentic reaction to a stupendous natural phenomenon. In her account of the falls, nature and civilization, or spontaneity and art, play out a miniature drama within her own mind, part of the larger drama of the American continent.

The dilemma Fuller recorded in *Summer on the Lakes*, then, was a response to nature that could no longer be instinctive and uncomplicated, but was not yet humanized by the long, gradual growth of many generations of human associations with it. Americans have been ignorant and exploitative of nature at worst, only semicivilized at best. Fuller explored other possible relations to the vast new continent than those known and practiced by the white settlers she observed. When she wrote of nature, she invariably perceived it in the context of some human relation—to others, or to herself.

Everywhere in the West she observed that the white settlers barely noticed and seldom respected the majesty of nature. The new residents of the frontier territory were rapacious. In the same areas she visited, many New Englanders had resettled hoping to find more fertile land; German and Scandinavian immigrants were also prominent among the newcomers. Fuller knew the New England character well. She wrote of its caution, calculation, love of polemics, and acquisitiveness. As settlers, such people wanted chiefly "more ease and larger accumulation." They rushed into an area heedlessly, cut down trees everywhere, threw up crude, hasty dwellings, all with the intent to "use" the land, to "get" something from it. They were with almost no exceptions insensitive to its mystery and beauty. This to Fuller contrasted to the settlements of the Indians, "who chose the most beautiful sites for their dwellings, and whose habits do not break in on that aspect of Nature under which they were born. We feel as if they were the rightful lords of a beauty they forbore to deform. But most of these settlers do not see it at all; it breathes, it speaks in vain to those who are rushing into its sphere." Ironically, these same white Europeans who prided themselves on their "superior" civilization seemed to her as barbaric in their way as the native tribes they despised: "Their progress is Gothic, not Roman. . . . The march of peaceful is scarce less wanton than that of warlike invasion."

An episode at Niagara typified the usual American response to nature. A white man strode up to the falls, looked at it a moment "as if thinking how he could appropriate it to his own use," then spat in it and walked away. This is the attitude of the modern "developer," who, looking at a green and pleasant meadow, sees forty acres of parking pavement and a hundred rentable shops.

The "mushroom growth" of the West dismayed rather than pleased her: "Where 'go ahead' is the only motto, the village cannot grow into the gentle proportions that successive lives and gradations of experience involuntarily give." Everywhere she looked for some sign that the new settlers were aware of the need for continuity. Occasionally she found it, as in one new prairie home in Illinois.

> Near the door grew a Provence rose, then in blossom. Other families we saw had brought with them and planted the locust. It was pleasant to see their old home loves, brought into connection with their new splendors. Wherever there were traces of this tenderness of feeling, only too rare among Americans, other things bore signs also of prosperity and intelligence, as if the ordering mind of man had some idea of home beyond a mere shelter beneath which to eat and sleep.

Particularly in *Summer*, but not exclusively there, Fuller's thinking on nature and civilization reveals her fundamental respect for all forms of life. She was always sensitive to whatever destroyed or disfigured it, however much that mutilation was rationalized as necessary for some desirable immediate end. She had as keen a sense of the harmony that should exist between human beings and the natural world as Thoreau, whose reverence for nature she shared, if not his passions for precision, detail, and solitude. The dominant attitude of that day was an exuberant, careless expansionism. Few spoke out, as she did, against "the love of ravage which distinguishes the American settler and which makes the marks of his first passage over this land, like those of corrosive acid upon the cheek of beauty, rather than that smile of intelligence which would ensue from the touch of an intelligent spirit."[26]

One form of this "corrosive acid" of progress particularly appalled her. The wanton cutting of trees and destruction of forests everywhere seemed all out of proportion to the settlers' need for lumber, fuel, or cleared land for farming. She offered this explanation a year or so after her western trip: "We suppose that the hatred of our people for trees is from a feeling that they are symbols of wilderness to be conquered; and inherited from a time when each was a shield or hiding place for an Indian face." Wilderness and Indian alike were there to be conquered. What was needed, she suggested, was more of the ancient Druidical veneration for trees, and even more, care for *all* forms of life. To defend and protect only one form was not enough: "We have often marvelled to see the Reformers who weary everyone by their protest against violence done to life in the animal kingdom, coolly hewing down and heaping on the hearth trunks that half a century had been required to rear, trunks of trees, the home of birds, and the fairest monuments of earth's devotion."

Fuller was equally sensitive to human cruelty to animals. She wrote of seeing, on the western trip, an eagle chained for a plaything:

When a child, I used often to stand at a window from which I could see an eagle chained in the balcony of a museum. The people used to poke at it with sticks, and my childish heart would swell with indignation as I saw their insults, and the mien with which they were borne by the monarch-bird. Its eye was dull, and its plumage soiled and shabby, yet, in its form and attitude, all the king was visible, though sorrowful and dethroned. I never saw another of the family till, when passing through the Notch of the White Mountains, at that moment glowing before us in all the panoply of sunset, the driver shouted, "Look there!" and following with our eyes his upward-pointing finger, we saw, soaring in majestic poise above the highest summit, the bird of Jove. It was a glorious sight, yet I know not that I felt more on seeing the bird in all its natural freedom and royalty, than when, imprisoned and insulted, he had filled my early thoughts with the Byronic "silent rages" of misanthropy.

Now, again, I saw him a captive, and addressed by the vulgar with the language they seem to find most appropriate to such occasions,—that of thrusts and blows. Silently, his head averted, he ignored their existence, as Plotinus or Sophocles might that of a modern reviewer. Probably he listened to the voice of the cataract, and felt that congenial powers flowed free, and was consoled, though his own wing was broken.[27]

Gratuitous cruelty often condemns itself. When cruelty masqueraded as necessity, sport, or virility, subtler weapons were necessary to unmask it. One ironic passage in *Summer* alludes to the hunter who was irritated that the Indians drove away "*our* game."

Showing us some antlers, he said: "This one belonged to a majestic creature. But this other was the beauty. I had been lying a long time at watch, when at last I heard them come crackling along. I lifted my head cautiously, as they burst through the trees. The first was a magnificent fellow; but then I saw coming one, the prettiest, the most graceful I ever beheld,—there was something so soft and beseeching in its look. I chose him at once, took aim, and shot him dead. You see the antlers are not very large; it was young, but the prettiest creature!"

Fuller knew that that eloquent esthetic needed no further commentary. She remarked only that the hunter showed "the true spirit of a sportsman, or perhaps I might say of Man, when engaged in any kind of chase."

Generally she was reluctant, though, to fully endorse those who condemned *all* killing of animals, such as vegetarians. Their tendency toward fanaticism repelled her, as did their moral rigorism, a characteristic of the incorruptible Thoreau. (Who, on reading *Walden*, has not wondered if he could have held out longer there if his diet had not been so sparse and tasteless?) The Greeleys, Horace and his wife Molly, were health food enthusiasts, and Molly had strong convictions against the killing of animals. One day the two women met on the street, and when Molly Greeley touched the kid-gloved hand of Margaret Fuller, she drew back shuddering, "Skin of a beast, skin of a beast." Surprised, Margaret asked, "Why, what do you wear?" "Silk," came the reply. It was Margaret's turn to shudder, perhaps mockingly: "Entrails of a worm!"[28]

Fuller never thought as long or deeply about human beings' relations to the animal world as she did about some other subjects, but she once pointed out that in hunting and fishing for sport, moderation, "the beautiful law," was called for. "There may be excess . . . in hunting, in angling," she wrote in a review of books on those topics. "There is deeper objection to [them] because pain is given to living things, and violence done in the world by the ministers of a higher dispensation. This is done in earnest all the time, but one would think it need not for pleasure."[29]

For all the shortcomings of the new settlers in the West, Fuller was not uniformly disheartened by what she saw among them. Though sometimes they had unrealistic expectations about their new surroundings—for instance, they brought their pianos, where no one could tune them or find leisure to enjoy them—they often possessed much simplicity, gaiety, modesty, generosity, and cheerfulness. In spite of wanton disregard for nature, it still seemed expansive and genial there:

> To me, too, used to the feelings which haunt a society of struggling men, it was delightful to look upon a scene where Nature still wore her motherly smile, and seemed to promise room, not only for those favored or cursed with the qualities best adapting for the strifes of competition, but for the delicate, the thoughtful, even the indolent or eccentric. She did not say, Fight or starve; nor even, Work or cease to exist; but, merely showing that the apple was a finer fruit than the wild crab, gave both room to grow in the garden.[30]

This expansiveness, geniality, apparent tolerance, and promise of room enough for all seemed to create new scope and freedom in the West. Yet

125

this much-touted freedom was more illusion than reality, for nature in itself could not bestow it: "It is from the position of men's lives, not the state of their minds. So soon as they have time, unless they grow better meanwhile, they will cavil and criticise, and judge other men by their own standard, and outrage the law of love every way, just as they do with us."

Many other thoughtful persons in the nineteenth century observed America in the making and reflected on the disparity between promise and fulfillment. Both the disparity and the promise were underlying motifs of almost everything Fuller wrote about society in America. She would see yet another face of that society during her years in New York.

Fuller had long felt restive in her New England milieu, and when in 1844 she accepted Greeley's offer to become the *Tribune*'s chief reviewer-critic, her move to New York decisively changed her life. She entered a new and different phase than that of high priestess of culture. Her New York experiences intensified her social awareness and social conscience. She visited prisons and hospitals; she talked and corresponded with prostitutes, convicts, and the mentally ill; and she wrote about them in her reviews and editorials. She was deeply moved by their sufferings. Her columns reflected an implicit belief that knowledge of wrongs or evils led to their correction: her readers had only to be told of injustice and misery and inevitably the ills would be eradicated. If capital punishment was demolished in print, it must soon be demolished in the penal system.

Fuller rejected the Brook Farm idea because she believed more in individual than in collective solutions to social problems. In her *Tribune* columns she still urged the need for a private change of heart. "We want individuals to whom all eyes may turn as examples of the practicability of virtue. . . . Let men feel that in private lives, more than in public measures, must the salvation of the country lie."[31] Like Carlyle and Ruskin, she sometimes envisioned an enlightened plutocracy assuming the role of educators and protectors of society's unfortunates, its outcasts. Fuller's political outlook, like her literary, always contained classical and Romantic elements; belief in an elite coexisted with populism. In her *Tribune* columns, the elitist viewpoint is more prominent. She argued for an aristocracy of merit rather than one resting on mere externals of clothes, carriages, possessions. "Our nation is not silly in striving for an aristocracy," she wrote. "Humanity longs for its upper classes."[32] It seemed to Fuller entirely possible that wealthy persons might use their wealth responsibly, though she had no illusions that most of them did so.

Her urgent pleas for individual and private improvement came from the realization that reform measures were the sport of political change. In New York City, Tammany Hall was the dominant political mechanism, and men in charge of public asylums and institutions were usually political appointees with no qualifications whatever for their posts. It was still unthinkable for women to be active in politics, and the appeal to the individual thus seemed Fuller's chief recourse. Poverty, for example, she once described as a regrettable condition that the poor man himself could and should cope with. "He must accept his lot, while he is in it. If he can change for the better, let his energies be exerted to do so. But if he cannot, there is none that will not yield an opening to Eden, to the glories of Zion, and even to the subterranean enchantments of our strange estate. There is none that may not be used with nobleness."[33] Today this sounds naive at best, patronizing at worst. Whether or not she knew it, she echoed the social rationale of laissez-faire capitalism.

In the 1840s problems seemed approachable through individualism, conscientiously applied. Europe had gone further, as she soon discovered. But in America she contemplated social and urban ills believing that individual will was the source of all moral or mental disorder, and that every individual had the potential for health. Once she wrote, after a visit to an asylum where amazing cures had been effected, "For the mentally or morally insane, there is no irreparable ill if the principle of life can but be aroused. And it can never be finally benumbed, except by our own will."[34] There is much psychological truth here, but she later recognized that grievous social ills required more drastic solutions.

Fuller's humanism, combined with her Transcendentalism, informed her writing and her philanthropy. Dignity, spiritual aspiration, the right of choice, free development of one's abilities and potential—these rightfully belonged to human life, and she spoke out or took action against their suppression as best she could. She asserted again and again in her columns "the right of every man to justice,"[35] but sometimes her editorials were merely pious or pleading. She did not connect poverty to systematic exploitation; she did not yet contemplate restructuring society by eliminating the abuses of excessive power and privilege. True, the worst abuses, apart from slavery and the Indians' wretchedness, had not yet appeared on the American scene, but the refractoriness of the social ills she saw baffled her. They yielded scarcely at all to any theoretical solution she proffered. Alternately she advocated paternalism, noblesse oblige, individual change of heart, monetary contributions, better education, or religious acceptance and devout hope that God would bring good somehow out of all these evils. Not surprisingly, poverty, squalor, vice, and degradation persisted. Her discouragement became evident, but she did not abandon her efforts.

Fuller's *Tribune* columns reveal her steadily widening consciousness of social conditions in nations other than America. Her literary cosmopolitanism, almost unique in the middle 1840s, now acquired a social dimension as well. Her position in New York helped her to this awakening, for "New York is the focus, the point where American and European interests converge."[36] In "First of January 1846," one of her best social essays and surely one of the most poetic editorials ever to appear in an American newspaper, she wrote of Europe's sickness, of the terrible gap there between rich and poor, of conditions so grave they must come to a head. "The caldron simmers, and so great is the fire that we expect it soon to boil over, and new fates appear for Europe."[37]

As alive to the life or death of nations as to that of individuals or nature, she perceived the waning of historic Europe. Monarchy was everywhere dead or dying; the democratic tide was spreading; communist principles were on the rise. Fuller preceded most of her contemporaries in seeing the importance communism would have in the world's future. The development of new and more rapid communications and transportation systems portended the breaking down of barriers among peoples and nations. She foresaw a new era in which human beings would more and more feel that all must be provided for, or all would suffer the consequences. She prophesied that the great sleeping Russian bear would one day awaken.

No power is in the ascending course except the Russian; and that has such a condensation of brute force, animated by despotic will, that it seems sometimes as if it might by and by stride over Europe and face us across the water. Then would be opposed to one another the two extremes of Autocracy and Democracy, and a trial of strength would ensue between the two principles more grand and full than any ever seen on this planet, and of which the result must be to bind mankind by one chain of convictions. Should, indeed, Despotism and Democracy meet as the two slaveholding powers of the world, the result can hardly be predicted.

It took a century for this prediction to evolve into the harsh reality that today affects most of the globe.

In the 1840s Fuller focused her attention principally on Europe because there the most dramatic events were taking place. But Europe and America, with all their problems and promise, did not occupy her exclusively. She wrote of Mexico and Argentina, for example, and the effects of their despotic governments on the lives of the people there. She wrote sympathetically of China, praising its highly developed society, its people's adroit good breeding and civilized serenity. The Chinese, she suggested, lived up to their own standards far better than the Westerners, who disdained the Chinese as barbarians. Like the American Indians, they possessed a tranquil unity of existence. "They are all opposite to us, who have made ships, and balloons, and magnetic telegraphs, as symbolic expressions of our wants, and the means of gratifying them."[38]

Fuller's international viewpoint never conflicted with or lessened her belief in America's greatness. Her compassionate concern for other peoples and nations grew alongside her concept of America's potential and its destiny of moral leadership. "The whole history of its discovery and early progress indicates too clearly the purposes of Heaven with regard to it," she wrote. "We too [like the Chosen People] have been chosen, and plain indications have been given, by a wonderful conjunction of auspicious influences, that the ark of human hopes has been placed for the present in our charge."[39] She admonished the American nation to live up to the principles of its revolution, its founding. Her high expectations of America led to dismay at its failures:

> We doubt not the destiny of our country—that she is to accomplish great things for human nature, and be the mother of a nobler race than the world has yet known. But she has been so false to the scheme made out at her nativity, that it is now hard to say which way that destiny points.... One thing is certain; we live in a large place, no less morally than physically: woe to him who lives meanly here, and knows the exhibitions of selfishness and vanity as the only American facts.[40]

In the mid-1840s three facts of national life seemed to her clear evidence of the nation's betrayal of its fundamental principles: the spread of slavery, the crass and shameless pursuit of material wealth, and imperialistic expansion. Fuller wrote of greed and idolatry of money: "Our nation has indeed shown that the lust of gain is at present her ruling passion. She is not only resolute, but shameless, about it, and has no doubt or scruple as to laying aside the glorious office, assigned her by fate, of herald of freedom, light, and peace to the civilized world."[41] She condemned the imperialism of the United States in Mexico, and her global awareness led her to condemn it wherever it was practiced, whether by Napoleon in Europe, Cromwell in Ireland, or England in India. At a time when the *Tribune* was full of jubilant headlines announcing American victories in Mexican territories, Fuller wrote a savage denunciation of the whole sordid undertaking:

> "It was a famous victory," sighs the songster after abashing and affrighting the unsophisticated mind of his hearer with details of the horrors of a battle.
>
> We, too, are called to rejoice over bloodshed and burning, and these in vindication of a most unrighteous act. Vain have been the hopes that the victories of this nation would be over wrong and ignorance, not mere conquest of bodies of other men to obtain their possessions or guard our own. Our Stars have lighted us only to the ancient heathen—the vulgar path of national ag-

grandizement; and our Eagle, like the Roman, loves better to snatch its prey from the field than to soar to the purer regions near the source of light. . . .

All omens marked out [this country] as the dominion where the hopes of the Prince of Peace might be realized. But aversion to his precepts and disbelief in his mission died not with the contemporaries of Pilate. A Church is to be dedicated today. But the flames of burning towns rise higher than those of the altar, and tell to the departed Friend of Man, that at the end of eighteen centuries, his simple precepts, "Love one another," and "Feed my lambs," are as far as ever from being obeyed. If the lion lies down with the lamb for an hour of slumber, it is only to get an appetite for breakfast, and the wolves of war rage abroad without the slightest excuse from hunger.[42]

Despite the betrayals, Fuller believed that America's health and strength were so remarkable that it must be only superficially, not deeply, diseased.

She had some misgivings about democratic society. We have already seen her doubts about the survival of artistic excellence in a democracy. She also saw the nihilism of democracy, when it took the form of "that fierce vulgar radicalism which assumes that the rich and great *must* be bad."[43] In other words, she saw how close Jacobinism was to despotism. Napoleon, for example, far from being regarded as a despot in this country, was a hero to many Americans. "The spirit of our popular oratory, our public press, inclines far more to justify and laud than to blacken and defame Napoleon. . . . Napoleon, as Emerson has well said, is the hero of Democracy—that is, of the Democracy which exalts the supremacy of the numerical majority and the preponderating physical force regardless of intellectual or moral power."[44] Despotism and Jacobinism had much in common: "A Jacobin is a powerless despot; a despot is a Jacobin invested with power."

The swelling of the population by the immigration of the 1840s increased her disquiet about America's democratic society, for the purposes that impelled the immigrants were often incongruous with the nation's avowed principles. Many people, she wrote in *Summer on the Lakes* and in her *Tribune* columns, emigrated to America hoping chiefly for material gain, though the first ones came for conscience's sake.

We must believe that the pure blood shown in the time of our revolution still glows in the heart; but the body of our nation is full of foreign elements. A large portion of our citizens, or their parents, came here for worldly advantage, and have never raised their minds to any idea or destiny or duty. More money—more land! are all the watchwords they know. They have received the inheritance earned by the fathers of the revolution, without their wisdom and virtue to use it.[45]

She thought that the new immigrants would not be assimilated into American life without prodigious and selfless efforts by those already comfortably established here. Instead of these efforts she saw resentment, hate, and discrimination against the newcomers. She devoted one of her longest *Tribune* essays to the problems of the Irish immigrants and their maltreatment by their employers. The chief remedy, she thought, lay in education:

> "We cannot blame—we must not reject them; but let us teach them, in giving them bread, to prize that salt, too, without which all on earth must lose its savor. Yes! let us teach them, not rail at their inevitable ignorance and unenlightened action, but teach them and their children as our own; if we do so, their children and ours may yet act as one body obedient to one soul; and if we act rightly now, that soul a pure soul."[46]

Fuller's recognition of America's failures, in a self-congratulatory era, was one of the main achievements of her pioneering journalistic career. She had more difficulty recognizing the deficiency in her own thinking. But she had the courage to change. Confronting in New York a variety of social ills, she realized the inadequacy of her former beliefs to effect a cure. She began to sense that individual response, individual effort, and good will could not solve grave social problems. She came to see that self-culture, the beautiful goal of a harmonious development, was an ideal not to be achieved in a world in which deprivation, exploitation, and misery were the common lot of humankind. "To no man in this brief earthly sojourn is permitted a harmonious development," she wrote sadly, a few weeks before she left America. "To many a full chance is not granted on any side."[47]

Those quiet words signaled the end of an era in Fuller's life and thought. They mark the transition to another phase, which would take place in Europe. She began to understand the limits of individualism, to sense that the humanist standards she had long striven after could not be reached by the single individual, unaided. But she never forgot the standards, never compromised with them. Whether confronted by prostitutes, convicts, or mentally retarded children in New York, or the factory workers in Europe's industrial cities, or the Italian peoples struggling for the right to shape their own political destiny, she unfailingly held people and societies accountable to those principles. Time, fear, or the burden of experience never dulled her capacity to perceive the deviation between standard and actuality. Fuller refused to accept that deviation, and her refusal made her choice of radical political action inevitable. Seeing the enormous unrest in Europe, she sensed that the world stood on the brink of a new era, a great new time for democracy. "The caldron simmers," and her destiny plunged her into that caldron, into revolution.

CHAPTER 9

Feminism

"A man's ambition with a woman's heart, is an evil lot," said Margaret Fuller of herself.[1] She tried all her life to resolve this conflict. Her society regarded the "masculine" and the "feminine" as opposed and irreconcilable. Thus, having a generous share of both attributes, she could either straitjacket half of her nature or do battle with the society that relegated women to second-class status and so forbade her the development and rewards that her mind, talents, and powers required. She chose to fight rather than submit.

During her life, Fuller's reputation as a feminist equaled or surpassed her reputation as a critic. She was one of the first American feminists to provide a reasoned basis by which the condition of women might be improved. Like her literary and social criticism, her feminism was grounded firmly in principles, informed by a knowledge of history and a sense of tradition, vitalized by her personal experience. Fuller's achievement as a feminist involved both public and private efforts. Her public endeavors, her bold, uncompromising challenge to society, made her an acknowledged leader of the fledgling feminist movement. Her private life too, that long, exciting, difficult search to discover and create her own selfhood, was shaped by her struggle against the virulent antifeminism of her society and her century. Her efforts grew from her conviction that the honored American principle "all men born free and equal" must be expanded to "all men and women born free and equal."

The nineteenth-century woman lived from cradle to grave under restrictions and humiliations that we can scarcely imagine today. In the United States and England the law accurately reflected her condition: a woman after marriage was "dead in law," a chattel. Her husband had absolute rights over her person, her children, her property, and her earnings. Napoleon told one of his ministers, "Nature has made women our slaves," then framed a legal code to support that concept. Since a woman existed solely to enter the state of marriage and then motherhood, it might be said that women were born and bred for quasi-death and legal slavery—in a century that prided itself on its unparalleled progress and saw only a bright future for *man*kind.

An inadvertent commentary on the situation of women in Victoria's age appeared in an 1841 medical journal, at the birth of one of the queen's male children:

> The medical attendants in waiting at the palace, at the birth of the prince, were Drs. Clark and Ferguson, to be consulted in case of necessity. Dr. Locock, the royal accoucheur, is the luckiest man in England, and therefore quite an object of envy to the less fortunate professionals. His fee, on this occasion, will be immensely superior to the one received on the birth of a princess.[2]

Even royal females were not worth as much as males.

The battle against the innate, unspoken sense of her own worthlessness was only one of Margaret Fuller's battles. From earliest childhood she felt alienated from her surroundings, "a changeling," she said. She fantasized in childhood that she was not her parents' child but a European princess stolen away at birth and abandoned in an alien land. Such a fantasy might have many sources in the psyche. Most obviously it expressed her feeling of being undervalued in proportion to what she was. In adult life, the fantasy gave way to the sensation of absolute confinement she expressed repeatedly to her friends. "The circumstances in which Margaret lived appeared to her life a prison," wrote James Freeman Clarke. "She had no room for utterance, no sphere adequate; her powers were unemployed. With what eloquence she described this want of a field!"[3] Clarke added that he was sure she exaggerated the evil, but he could not refute her. Perhaps that was because he had ample scope to exercise his powers, and not enough imagination to comprehend what limitations women, especially gifted women, were subject to.

The American ethos has always placed great value on education, yet most women of Fuller's era had almost no education. Education for women was looked on with apprehension and suspicion, principally for three reasons: it would allow women to compete intellectually with men; it would distract them from their household duties; and it would make them freethinkers and thus (the logic went) immoral.[4] The foundations of Victorian society depended on keeping women ignorant. Eleanor Flexner, in *A Century of Struggle*, has shown the parallel between the ignorance of women and that of the slaves. "An educated Negro was not only an anachronism but a threat. To educate him was to disprove the premise of racial inferiority on which slavery was founded, and to arm him for the struggle for freedom."[5] Blackstone's classification of wives with minors and idiots, as without responsibility under the law, possessed a certain precision.

As we have seen, Margaret Fuller would never have been educated had her father not tutored her like a first-born son. Without that education—her sister Ellen received nothing remotely like it—her extraordinary mind would have developed erratically, if at all. Though unusual, her education was haphazard and incomplete, as she knew only too well. Yet she never voiced resentment of the impossibility of a university education for women, while she worked and worried for years to send her brothers to Harvard. It was bold even for Fuller to request the use of the Harvard library; she was the first woman ever to receive that privilege. It is tempting, though unwise, to speculate on the relation between the intellectual mediocrity of the Fuller brothers and their education. Conversely, literary genius can develop without a university education— Whitman, Twain, Melville, Dickinson, Sand, Flaubert, Baudelaire, George Eliot, Robert and Elizabeth Browning, Dickens, and countless others come to mind. Nevertheless, one cannot help suspecting that Margaret Fuller would have made much better use of such an education than the brothers for whom she sacrificed herself.

In Fuller's society, the peculiar tragedy of the intelligent, spirited woman was that she understood the unjust restrictions that bound her and her lack of power to break them. The same spirited intelligence led to ambitions that alienated her from all the men and women who saw in her an intolerable threat to the status quo. In the early nineteenth century, even women who wrote favorably of women were confused about women's minds and the spheres in which mind could be exercised, such as law, commerce, or public life. The accepted view was that women's minds could not assimilate what men's minds could. Because of their intellectual deficiency, then, the home was their sphere of influence and activity.[6] Harriet Martineau remarked, "The sum and substance of female education in America, as in England, is training women to consider marriage as the sole object in life, and to pretend that they do not think so."[7] To be adventurous, independent, ambitious, strong, capable of wielding authority, and proud of one's worldly achievement was to be masculine. A woman who exhibited such qualities aroused the implacable hostility of society and made bitter enemies among those she threatened. Yet Fuller dared, almost alone in her time, to consider women the intellectual equals of men. This defied centuries of tradition and custom that ranked women as mentally, socially, and physically inferior to men. Further, she lived by that belief, to the bewilderment and disapproval of others and at enormous cost to herself.

Fuller's friends and acquaintances thought she possessed a "masculine" mind. F.H. Hedge explained what this meant: "Its action was determined by ideas rather than by sentiments. And yet, with this masculine trait, she combined a woman's appreciation of the beautiful in sentiment and the beautiful in action."[8] W.H. Channing wrote that her genius resulted from a combining of opposite qualities: "To her might have been well applied the words first used as describing George Sand: 'Thou large-brained Woman, and large-hearted Man.' She blended in closest union and swift interplay feminine receptiveness with masculine energy."[9] The line Channing quoted was from a sonnet by Elizabeth Browning in praise of Sand. But it misfires as a compliment and seems grotesque instead. The stereotypes of language often constricted even the best minds and most articulate thinkers.

This was true of Fuller too. Nineteenth-century society, with few exceptions, had rigid ideas about what traits and activities were male, which were female. The man or woman who crossed those barriers, in wish or deed, became a deviant, an affront to God and nature. Lydia Maria Child, the New England abolitionist and author, pointed out that the feminine ideal approached the Christian gospel standard much more than masculine ideals, for Jesus is presented as mild and meek. "None speak of the bravery, the might, or the intellect of Jesus; but the devil is always imagined as a being of acute intellect, political cunning, and the fiercest courage."[10] Because Fuller had internalized many of the imperatives of her society, as we all must, she thought she had some "masculine" qualities—a philosophical mind, love of learning, self-reliance, ambition, love of command. To some extent she acquiesced in the use of rigid sexual categories, so many of which passed for accepted and time-hallowed wisdom. Men had minds, women had hearts. Men were abstract, logical thinkers, women were intuitive and emotional. Women were the inspirers of deeds and poems, men the doers and creators. Men were active, aggressive, bold, courageous; women were passive, receptive, modest, timid. And if no one said that men were born to kill and wound, they all said that women were born to nurture and heal. Men's place was in the "world" and women's was in the kitchen, nursery, and drawing room, the two spheres being eternally and unalterably opposed. Thus in private journals and letters Fuller often spoke of the man or the woman in her. She was groping toward some sense of identity in a world that had no categories for the particular mixture she embodied, a world that could not even comprehend the desire to blend them.

Though she always conscientiously performed the so-called women's duties that fell to her, Margaret Fuller was no fool. She clearly saw the lot of women in her society: as childbearers, drudges, slaves, ornaments, bodiless ideals, superfluities, or some combination of those. To be sure, they were often loved, provided for, and protected from life's harsh and sordid realities. (Harriet Martineau stated it more bluntly: "Indulgence is

135

given her [woman] as a substitute for justice."[11] When Fuller was twenty-nine, she said in a letter to F.H. Hedge, "From a very early age I have felt that I was not born to the common womanly lot."[12] She was ambivalent about this womanly lot, for it was not without real benefits. She continued:

> I knew I should never find a being who could keep the key of my character; that there would be none on whom I could always lean, from whom I could always learn; that I should be a pilgrim and sojourner on earth, and that the birds and foxes would be surer of a place to lay the head than I. You understand me, of course; such beings can only find their homes in hearts. All material luxuries, all the arrangements of society, are mere conveniences to them.
>
> This thought, all whose bearings I did not, indeed, understand, affected me sometimes with sadness, sometimes with pride. I mourned that I should never have a thorough experience of life, never know the full riches of my being; I was proud that I was to test myself in the sternest way, that I was always to return to myself, to be my own priest, pupil, parent, child, husband, and wife. All this I did not understand as I do now; but this destiny of the thinker, and (shall I dare to say it?) of the poetic priestess, sibylline . . . lay yet enfolded in my mind. Accordingly, I did not look on any of the persons, brought into relation with me, with common womanly eyes.

There is an unmistakable tone of deep regret here, a sense of renunciation and loss and loneliness, as well as pride. The next words reveal her emotional vulnerability:

> Yet, as my character is, after all, still more feminine than masculine, it would sometimes happen that I put more emotion into a state than I myself knew. I really was capable of attachment, though it never seemed so till the hour of separation. And if a connexion was torn up by the roots, the soil of my existence showed an unsightly wound, which long refused to clothe itself in verdure.

She may have thought like a man, but she hurt like a woman.

To love, to need love, to have feeling—these were "feminine," and this is what Fuller meant by lamenting that her woman's heart was incompatible with her manly ambition. Obviously, men too have been grievously deprived and stunted by society's restrictive roles. Taught to scorn feeling as feminine, too many men have denied themselves the richly varied possibilities of feeling. The result has often been truncated emotional lives, an unbalanced emphasis on power, and disaster in personal relationships. When a man allows himself to feel, his universe, including his ideas, changes drastically, and his humanity gains dimension and depth. But if men were not permitted to have and express emotions as women were, Fuller observed that their prerogatives amply compensated: "Early

I perceived that men never, in any extreme of despair, wished to be women."[13]

She partially accepted the conventions of women's and men's distinct roles. To the extent that she did so, her friends and family praised her as a "true" woman. "I do think that the vocations of men and women differ," she said, "and that those who are forced to act out of their sphere are shorn of inward and outward brightness."[14] Partly accepting, partly rejecting the tenacious sexual stereotypes, she experienced great confusion and turmoil about her identity and goals. Self-doubt dragged at every step she took in the male-dominated worlds of ideas, art, and politics, and her interior conflicts often made her physically ill. What is surprising is how much she achieved despite the conflicts.

Margaret Fuller believed herself destined for greatness. She once wrote to a woman friend, enclosing her translation of Goethe's "Prometheus,"

> Does it not seem, were we gods, or could steal their fire, we would make men not only happier, but free,—glorious? Yes, my life is strange, thine is strange. We are, we shall be, in this life, mutilated beings, but there is in my bosom a faith, that I shall see the reason. . . . But I take my natural position always: and the more I see, the more I feel that it is regal. Without throne, sceptre, or guards, still a queen.[15]

The person of unusual powers often appears arrogant when acknowledging or using those powers. But Fuller knew herself, knew her powers of leadership in a world that forbade women to lead. It was more acceptable for women to write than to command, despite formidable obstacles to authorship. Some of Fuller's dissatisfaction with the literary vocation surely had its roots in this knowledge that her temperament fitted her for a more active life than that of careful artisan of written words.

Fuller's contemporaries recognized her talent for leadership, to which the success and fame of her Boston Conversations attested. Fuller knew women well. She loved them, and they loved, trusted, and talked to her freely. The Conversations grew out of her desire to help remedy the ignorance of women: she knew that they lacked education, that they needed to feel their own mental strength and to respect the minds of other women before their situation could change. She hoped to awaken women's awareness of innate intellectual and imaginative powers and to provide an opportunity for their exercise. The women of Boston eagerly cooperated. Fuller's proposal touched an ardently felt need. This series of liberal arts courses, conducted in the Socratic manner, was the women's only access to anything like higher education. With her flair for the dramatic, she transformed them into high adventure. Adventures of the spirit they undoubtedly were, for most women grappled seldom with ideas. A number of them said later that the Conversations had been turning points in their lives.

Fuller's introductory remarks at the first meeting in 1839 focused on the difference between female and male education. She said that although women were taught all that men were in school (by school she meant primary education), from an early age men had to reproduce and use what they learned in professional studies, college work, and political life. Women, by contrast, learned only for display. Harriet Martineau made a similar and more explicit observation:

> The intellect of woman is confined by an unjustifiable restriction of both methods of education,—by express teaching, and by the discipline of circumstance. . . . As women have none of the objects in life for which an enlarged education is considered requisite, the education is not given. Female education in America is much what it is in England. There is a profession of some things being taught which are supposed necessary because everybody learns them. They serve to fill up time, to occupy attention harmlessly, to improve conversation, and to make women something like companions to their husbands, and able to teach their children somewhat. But what is given is, for the most part, passively received; and what is obtained is, chiefly, by means of the memory. There is rarely or never a careful ordering of influences for the promotion of clear intellectual activity. Such activity, when it exceeds that which is necessary to make the work of the teacher easy, is feared and repressed. This is natural enough, as long as women are excluded from the objects for which men are trained. While there are natural rights which women may not use, just claims which are not to be listened to, large objects which may not be approached, even in imagination, intellectual activity is dangerous: or, as the phrase is, unfit. Accordingly, marriage is the only object left open to woman. Philosophy she may pursue only fancifully, and under pain of ridicule; science only as a pastime, and under a similar penalty. Art is declared to be left open: but the necessary learning, and, yet more, the indispensable experience of reality, are denied to her.[16]

The black educator Anna Julia Cooper described the disappointment she felt as a girl at Oberlin College, on discovering that the young men received ministerial training, but the highest goal for the young women was to marry a minister. Subsequent generations, battling for equal education for women, often lost sight of the disparity in the utilization of that education.

"The progress or emancipation of any class usually, if not always, takes place through the efforts of individuals of that class," wrote Martineau,

> and so it must be here. All women should inform themselves of the condition of their sex, and of their own position. It must necessarily follow that the

noblest of them will, sooner or later, put forth a moral power which shall prostrate cant, and burst asunder the bonds, (silken to some, but cold iron to others,) of feudal prejudices and usages.[17]

American women in the 1830s and 1840s were beginning to burst those bonds. More and more they spoke out against "feudal prejudices and usages." Women industrial workers became organized, particularly in the textile mills. Emma Willard, Mary Lyon, and others widened and reshaped female education. Lydia Maria Child, who, as Lydia Maria Francis, had been Margaret's girlhood friend, Frances Wright, Catharine Beecher, Maria Stewart, the Grimké sisters, and many others articulated a vigorous feminist viewpoint.

Margaret Fuller's Conversations and the book that grew out of them, *Woman in the Nineteenth Century*, were her major public contributions to the progress and emancipation of women.

> By her conversations and her writings she touched the women she knew, or who knew her through her work, and told them there was more in themselves than they had ever known, and they should dream dreams even as men did. She told them to know more, do more, expect more than their mothers had, and to take pleasure in their accomplishments. As an antidote to so much of the mentor literature of the period, preaching submission and resignation, she gave women egos and told them to enjoy them.[18]

Both book and Conversations were imbued with her humanist belief in education, her humanist love of tradition and art and Graeco-Roman civilization, her power to awaken immortal aspirations and impart the unshakable conviction that they are attainable. She influenced her contemporaries enormously. Elizabeth Cady Stanton and Susan B. Anthony said of Margaret Fuller that she "possessed more influence upon the thought of American women than any women previous to her time."[19]

In the 1840s American feminism was only beginning. During the nineteenth century, it dealt with a wide range of legal, educational, and labor issues. The right to control property and earnings, guardianship of children, the right to divorce, opportunity for education, lessening of exploitation in the labor market, and attainment of legal status came about as a result of hard-fought battles.[20] But though the nineteenth-century feminists attacked the concept of female inferiority as perpetuated by established religion, they did not otherwise explore psychological questions nor probe the basic social structures that kept women in servitude.

Thus, when Fuller in *Woman in the Nineteenth Century* boldly dared to write of sex, prostitution, marriage, the double standard of morality, women's concepts of themselves, and men's concepts of them, she astounded her contemporaries. The book is her most radical surviving work because it examines and criticizes the root of the social and personal relations that affect women's lives.

Fuller did not stress the legal, political, and economical issues of the women's rights movement. Paradoxically, one of the first American women to earn an independent living through journalism did not discuss economic independence or legal rights, nor did she speak of organizing groups to effect change. Her intention was twofold: to show that women need and have the same right to freedom for their inner and outer development as men, and to set forth, as a goal for women's aspirations, an ideal of womanhood fundamentally different from that imposed by the culture of the time. Ranging freely if unsystematically over history, mythology, and religion, she tried to show that in all ages and societies there had been some "witness of the equality of the sexes in function, duty and hope."[21] In other words, sexual equality was not some new and dangerous notion but an old and venerable human ideal. Knowing the power of myths over the consciousness of humankind, she explored the meaning of mythological creations like Minerva or the Muse. She looked to history, to Elizabeth of England, Isabella of Spain, and Mary Stuart. Such women showed others what a women might become.

Though every age has had its stellar examples of heroic women rewarded by their societies, she protested that any woman who has heroic courage, energy, or creative genius is called "manly." When she achieves something, she is told "you have *surpassed your sex*." Women's interior and exterior development has been tragically crippled by social roles. When women like Mary Wollstonecraft or George Sand broke the bonds of the intolerably narrow place they were born into, they became outlaws. For "self-dependence . . . is deprecated as a fault in most women. They are taught to learn their rule from without, not to unfold it from within." Fuller objected strenuously to the rigid spheres and occupations assigned to one sex or the other, and she was one of the first to argue that sexual stereotyping restricted personal freedom.

Artistic creativity was one example of the divisive assigning of roles (man the poet, woman the inspiration) that Fuller questioned. Alluding to the poet Manzoni, who dedicated a poem to his wife, Fuller asked: cannot the position be reversed? the woman singing the deeds, giving voice to man's life, creating great poetic beauty? The idea was undreamed of then. She argued that women were gifted in that "unimpeded clearness of the intuitive powers" that often appeared as prophecy or poetry, and "should these faculties have free play, I believe they will open new, deeper and purer sources of joyous inspiration than have as yet refreshed the earth."

Women need as wide a range of occupations as men, instead of the dull, stifling circle of routine duties to which they were consigned. Girls who loved carpentry, she wrote, became sullen and mischievous when denied that exercise for their talents. "We would have every arbitrary

140

barrier thrown down," she wrote. "We would have every path laid open to Woman as freely as to Man." Further, this freedom must "be acknowledged as a *right*, not yielded as a concession."

In their struggle to win this dignity, Fuller recognized that women needed self-respect and self-help. She once thought more men would help in this emancipation, since so many were unhappy with weak women. But most men simply could not comprehend woman as an independent being; not one man in a hundred million could rise above the belief that woman was made for man, she said. How then could he possibly do her justice, even when he wished to be generous? On the whole, men did not really want *women*, they wanted girls, because of their vanity, which required them to be the lord over at least one being, and because they found it impossible to feel superior to a strong woman.

The question of superiority is allied to the question of power. Fuller knew the devices used to keep women out of public life, such as the widespread assumption of their weak physical constitution. To this charge she retorted that the same persons who voiced it most loudly were those who expected pregnant black slaves to work in the fields, or washwomen and seamstresses to perform their drudgery whatever their state of health. Black leader Maria Stewart also pointed out the absurdity of that position. Fuller attacked this anomaly even more vigorously several years later:

> The rhetorical gentlemen and silken dames . . . , quite forgetting their washerwomen, their seamstresses, and the poor hirelings for the sensual pleasures of man that jostle them daily in the streets, talk as if Woman need to be fitted for no other chance than that of growing like a cherished flower in the garden of domestic love . . . I would point out as a primary source of incalculable mischief, the contradiction between her assumed and her real position, between what is called her proper sphere by the laws of God and Nature, and what has become her real sphere by the law of necessity, and through the complex relations of artificial existence. In the strong language of Carlyle I would say that 'here is a LIE, standing up in the midst of society'—I would say 'down with it, even to the ground' . . . if she be liable to be thrust from the sanctuary of home to provide for herself through the exercise of such faculties as God has given her, let her at least have fair play; let it not be avowed in the same breath that protection is necessary to her, and that it is refused to her; and while we send her forth into the desert, and bind the burthen on her back, and put the staff in her hand—let not her steps be beset, her limbs fettered, and her eyes blindfolded.[22]

Fuller was learning much about exploitation, but on the issue of power she was strangely indecisive. Several times in *Woman* she implied that woman's nature and destiny were not the public ones of power and rule, although she rejected the truism that women were satisfied to exercise power indirectly through their influence on a particular man. Anticipating John Stuart Mill's later argument that power over one man was small compensation for women's loss of freedom, Fuller said that women in their present condition of servitude too often used their power meanly and frivolously. A prey to childish vanity, ignorant of life's important purposes, women were trained to selfish coquetry and the love of petty power, the pleasure of exerting a momentary influence. Deprived of equality and freedom, "they made use of the arms of the servile,— cunning, blandishment, and unreasonable emotion."[23]

Yet Fuller did not explore how women might use power if they were freer. In fact, she thought that free women would not want public power. But her own confession, "I aspired to wield the sceptre or the lyre; for I loved with wise design and irresistible command to mould many to one purpose,"[24] admitted the desire for power over others. And, in *Woman:* "If you ask me what offices they may fill, I reply—any. . . . Let them be sea-captains if you will. I do not doubt there are women well fitted for such an office, and, if so, I should be . . . glad to see them in it."[25] Women sea captains were obviously women in positions of command, and thus at best her position is contradictory. However, our age is acutely power conscious; hers was not; and so the issue interests us more than it interested her, evidently. The fact that she used the pronouns "they . . . them" instead of "we . . . us" in the above passage suggests that Fuller did not think this problem pertained to her, further evidence that she had not resolved the issue of women and power. This ambivalence, I believe, had its roots in a deeply felt though ill-defined personal need to yield to superior masculine authority. The submissiveness bred into nineteenth-century women had not been wholly bred out of her. Tragically, she discovered over and over through her life that masculine authority was too often *not* superior. "The best are so unripe, the wisest so ignoble, the truest so cold," she lamented.[26] Acknowledging this fact intellectually, however, did not obliterate the psychological need.

Fuller throughout her book prepared the way for women to use their minds and talents in domains other than the home. For example, she forcefully attacked the idea so deeply embedded in conventional thinking that women were creatures who existed primarily for relations, for affections. Why should a woman any more than a man be born only for personal love? Was she not also born for truth, asked Fuller, for universal love, to use her talents? Even when she was educated, the purpose was only to make her a better companion for men and a better mother for men. The summit of ambition held out to an American woman was to be the mother of a George Washington. Fuller insisted that women's talents and intellect be allowed to develop not for a relationship but because they existed. "It is not Woman, but the law of right, the law of growth that speaks in us, and demands the perfection of each being in its kind—apple as apple, Woman as Woman."[27]

Because Fuller recognized how much women presently needed to find the sources of their own being, she advocated celibacy, at least temporarily. Women's lives have always belonged to others, to their parents or husbands or children or guests. Therefore women needed to withdraw from relations and particularly needed to put aside all thought of being led and taught by men, said Fuller. Only truth should lead a woman. "Men do *not* look at both sides, and women must leave off asking them and being influenced by them, but retire within themselves, and explore the ground-work of life till they find their peculiar secret."[28] This call to celibacy, which was not likely to find many receptive hearers, needs to be seen in the context of nineteenth-century Puritanism. Fuller may have been partly led to that assertion by her repugnance for the degradation that sex, or rather the double standard, caused for women.

In the Victorian age women were thought to have no sexual passion. Frequently women thought so too. Queen Victoria, the mother of nine children, abhorred as "too dreadful" what she called "the animal side of our nature,"[29] and is said to have advised one of her daughters to "think of England" during the miserable business of conception.

Women were not supposed to have passion; nor were they supposed to speak of it. When Fuller dared openly to discuss sex in a book meant for both men and women, she overstepped the bounds of propriety. She questioned why men should be less pure than women, attacked men for the existence of prostitution, and pointed out the countless contradictions in society's codes of sexual morals, so different for men and women. Women have been told for centuries that men's passions are stronger, she said, and though women were not supposed to understand those passions, they were obliged to submit to them in marriage or else wickedly risk turning their husbands' thoughts to illicit relations, "for a man is so constituted that he must indulge his passions or die!"[30] Consequently, women came to regard men as a species of wild beast, she said, and married women told the unmarried not to expect continence or self-restraint from men.

Fuller answered the double standard by expressing the wish that men might become more virtuous, not women less. She greatly admired men of pure lives, like Beethoven. Her advice about female celibacy and male purity had a practical basis, Barbara Welter points out. "Until better means of birth control were devised, the ability of a woman to achieve her goals was at least partially dependent on her ability to limit the size of her family. To do this it was necessary either to be celibate or to live with a man who accepted the principle of self-control."[31]

Fuller made herself vulnerable by advocating standards of purity and celibacy—for women and men both—that she herself later did not live up to. Perhaps this discrepancy between what she first advocated and later lived led Hawthorne to chortle over her "moral collapse" in Europe. However, at the time she wrote *Woman in the Nineteenth Century* she *was* practicing what she preached; and, during her liaison with Ossoli, she no longer discussed personal morals. At no time did she recommend chastity and live unchastely. She may have been inconsistent in not meeting her own high standards. But excessive idealism is not the same thing as hypocrisy, though it may lead to it, and at least she was not guilty of hypocrisy.

Fuller wrote:

> Those who would reform the world must show that they do not speak in the heat of wild impulse; their lives must be unstained by passionate error; they must be severe lawgivers to themselves. They must be religious students of the divine purpose with regard to man, if they would not confound the fancies of a day with the requisitions of eternal good. Their liberty must be the liberty of law and knowledge.[32]

She knew the potency of the mixture she served up in this remarkable book. She was challenging some of the most deep-rooted and fanatically held ideas on the relation of the sexes, and she was advocating action that would change one of society's most fundamental structures, marriage. "We cannot rectify marriage because it would introduce such carnage in our social relations," Emerson once wrote. "And it seems, the most rabid radical is a good Whig in relation to the theory of marriage."[33] Fuller aimed to rectify marriage, but she understood that her ideas had no chance of being heard unless people knew that her motives were pure and lofty. If they suspected the slightest breath of self-interest or self-indulgence, they would regard her pages as tainted and every argument in the book void. Change had to be based on some higher moral imperative. Many nineteenth-century feminists—particularly American feminists like Lucretia Mott, Sarah Grimké, or Sojourner Truth—expressed their pleas for reform in religious and pious language. Feminists today use a different rhetoric, but the underlying desire for justice is the same.

Woman in the Nineteenth Century, like its author, was shaped by an era. The book exuded optimism and hope, born out of American ideals and the conditions of American life. Fuller believed that America's destiny was to elucidate a great moral law, and like no other thinker of her time, she envisioned women's part in that great unfolding. The book's "value to the women to whom it was addressed was not so much the specific means it advised but the fact that it postulated as a desirable and possible end, a human being, equal to the glories and demands of the nation, who was a woman."[34] She thought American women were more fortunate than European women; they had more time to think and reflect, fewer conventions and time-hardened customs to enchain them. In America women were better situated than men, for they were less pressured to achieve success. She felt they were generally exempt from the materialism so characteristic of American life, although "its existence, among the men, has a tendency to repress their [women's] impulses and make them doubt their instincts, thus often paralyzing their action during the best years."[35]

The better liberty is understood, wrote Fuller, the broader the protest for the rights of women. The development of men and that of women are always closely linked. Thus a new era of fulfillment for all of humanity lay close at hand: "The highest ideal Man can form of his own powers is that which he is destined to attain. Whatever the soul knows how to seek, it cannot fail to obtain. . . . Man no longer paints his proper nature in some form, and says 'Prometheus had it; it is God-like; but 'Man must have it; it is human'." But for humanity to approach its golden age at last, self-dependence must be established, the weakening habit of dependence on others must be broken. Note that Fuller is not preaching a splendid isolation; always her context is that of community. "When the same community of life and consciousness of mind begin among men, humanity will have, positively and finally, subjugated its brute elements and Titanic childhood; criticism will have perished; arbitrary limits and ignorant censure be impossible; all will have entered upon the liberty of law, and the harmony of common growth." Whitman, in *Democratic Vistas*, also envisioned law internalized in perfect freedom. Fuller had no fear of widespread misuse of freedom, should it come suddenly to women (which it was not likely to do, she knew). Though individuals might indulge in excesses, women possessed "a reverence for decorums and limits," a native love of proportion, a Greek moderation that would inherently restrain, and "would gradually establish such rules as are needed to guard, without impeding, life."

Woman in the Nineteenth Century ranges over an astonishing variety of subjects: the peculiar opposition met by women of intellect; the legal inequalities and personal abuses of women under the present system; the repulsiveness of artificial devices like corsets; the stigmas society attached to the "old maid"; the hypocrisy of much American Christianity; the merits and flaws of leading writers on the situation of women; the defects of marriage as presently constituted; and the education and psychology of women.

Infused with an internationalist consciousness, this uniquely American book is bold in its challenge, exuberant in its optimism. It does contain flaws—the hedging on the question of power, the overzealous moralism, the lack of structure, the air of improvisation that probably reflects the book's origin in the conversation classes. The pearls are flung randomly on a table, not matched and strung carefully into a necklace that might better set off their luster. Still, the book is a classic of feminist literature—and a classic of American literature as well, though an unacknowledged one.

For the rest of the century in America, Fuller was regarded as the philosopher of feminism. She had enunciated the principles on which women's emancipation could move forward and argued the urgent need for change in existing relations between men and women. Though not immediately practical, the book was (as she had said of De Staël's work) useful on liberalizing, regenerating principles. No feminist statement in America before it had been so comprehensive, so eloquent, so uncompromising in its application of fundamental American principles, so unflinching in its examination of the position of women in American life, and so fearless in speaking openly of hitherto forbidden subjects.

Today, when no topic seems taboo, it is difficult to understand the shock waves created by the publication of the book in 1845. It was so popular, and immediately so controversial, that the first edition sold out within a week. Even favorable reviews, like that of Lydia M. Child in the *Boston Courier*, commented on Fuller's audacity.:

> Portions of the book will be considered very bold; for it speaks somewhat plainly on subjects which men generally do not wish to have spoken of, and of which women dare not speak. Every body of any knowledge or experience of life is aware of the terrible pit of pollution which everywhere lies under our feet, covered with the thinnest crust of decorum. We all know what an immense proportion of young men fall through. An innocent savage, looking on our high civilization, might almost imagine that it was the deliberate intention of society to entrap as many human souls, and degrade as many human bodies as possible. But, by universal consent, it is agreed to be vulgar and injurious to allude to the existence of this pity or to venture even a glance through the thin veil that covers it. Because the author does this, she will be considered by many as unpardonably bold. But . . . the spirit in which she does it is pure, and her motive is the ennobling of human character. It is a cheaper effort for me to praise the heroism which I should not have had the courage to practice.[36]

The attacks on Fuller took many forms. She was called deficient in femininity by prominent New York literary men like Lewis Gaylord Clark. The *Broadway Journal* attacked her morals: "Her most direct writing is on a subject no virtuous woman can treat justly. No woman is a true woman who is not wife and mother."[37] Orestes Brownson thought that "no person has appeared among us whose conversation and morals have done more to corrupt the minds and hearts of our Boston community."[38] Rufus Griswold, in his influential *Prose Writers of America*, deprecated Fuller as a writer and claimed to be unable to understand what the book was about, other than "an eloquent expression of her discontent at having been created female."[39] Barrett Wendell, in his *Literary History of America*, called Fuller "an unsexed version of Plato's Socrates" and an intellectual monstrosity.[40] Poe thought the book was suggestive, brilliant, and forcible, although its author did not sufficiently take into account "the intention of the Deity as regards sexual differences," and further, "she judges *woman* by the heart and intellect of Miss Fuller, but there are not more than one or two dozen Miss Fullers on the whole face of the earth."[41]

English reviewers were just as vitriolic. The *New Quarterly* castigated Fuller as "a he-woman," an "intellectual Bloomer," arrogant, aggressive, strong-minded. Grateful that she was not an English woman, the reviewer called the book "false in style and sentiment . . . not a nice book for English ladies" and assuredly not recommended for English family reading.[42] Dickens's journal, *Household Words*, expressed revulsion at Fuller's conceit and her "unwomanly sentiments" in the book.[43]

Private reactions among women differed. Many simply dismissed book and author as unworthy of serious attention. Sophia Peabody (Mrs. Nathaniel Hawthorne) wrote to her mother:

> What do you think of the speech which Queen Margaret Fuller has made from the throne? It seems to me that if she were married truly, she would no longer be puzzled about the rights of woman. This is the revelation of woman's true destiny and place, which never can be *imagined* by those who do not experience the relation . . . Even before I was married, however, I could never feel the slightest interest in this movement. It then seemed to me that each woman could make her own sphere quietly, and also it was always a shock to me to have women mount the rostrum. Home, I think, is the great arena for women, and there, I am sure, she can wield a power which no king or conqueror can cope with.[44]

Mrs. Peabody, replying, spoke of the book's language as "offensive to delicacy," too personal, and obscure. Yet she acknowledged that Margaret Fuller had strongly presented the case for rights that belonged to women. Mrs. Peabody, who unlike her daughter had some intellectual gifts, having once translated Goethe's poetic novel *Hermann and Dorothea*, nevertheless concluded bleakly:

> Woman must wait till the lion shall lie down with the lamb, before she can hope to be the friend and companion of man. He has the physical power, as well as conventional, to treat her like a plaything or a slave, and will exercise that power till his own soul is elevated to the standard set up by Him who spake as never man spoke . . . I wish it [the book] may do good; but I believe little that is high and ennobling can have other foundation than genuine Christianity.[45]

The younger Peabody refused to acknowledge the existence of any problem; the older recognized a problem but left it vaguely to religion to solve. These attitudes, typically encountered by the early feminists, have not entirely vanished in the late twentieth century.

Woman in the Nineteenth Century was not Fuller's only feminist writing. Her feminist consciousness is a continual undercurrent in her writings, surfacing sometimes in her letters, in *Summer on the Lakes*, and in her *Tribune* essays in New York and Europe. After *Woman*, her boldest feminist statement, she tended to see the problems of women's servitude and degradation as part of a larger pattern of social exploitation. Later the cause of women's emancipation became submerged for her in a wider social concern. At the same time, she personally became more conventional in her thinking about marriage and its duties. Whether as a result of social pressures, or the opinions of friends or family, or the innate conservatism that was always one facet of her temperament, Fuller in several later essays retrenched somewhat and acquiesced (was it acceptance or resignation?) in the concept of married woman as helpmate to man and guardian angel of the home. In that far narrower context, she merely suggested small ways in which the wife's mind might be improved and her limited horizons broadened.

Woman in the Nineteenth Century kindled the feminist movement emerging in America, and many hoped that on her return from Europe Margaret Fuller would take a leading role in the movement. But her Transcendentalist suspicion of organizing and of causes kept her from being active in any movement. Her brother Arthur said that she preferred not to speak for any clique or sect, thinking she could accomplish more by remaining independent. She thought that by following her path of thinker-writer-critic, she could best aid women's emancipation. She aimed to succeed, on her own terms, in a profession dominated by men, thereby proving that women *could* do all the things that both men and women alike thought impossible for women. She thought she represented many women who aspired to similar achievements. Like some women today who feel compelled to prove a point by never appearing to be ill, Fuller was determined to refute the charge of women's weakness and unfitness for the world's work. Once, in a letter, she said of her recurrent crippling headaches, "I think the black jailer laughs now, hoping that while I want to show that Woman can have the free, full action of intellect, he will prove in my own self that she has not physical force to bear it. Indeed, I am too poor an example, and do wish I was bodily strong and fair. Yet, I will not be turned from the deeper convictions."[46]

Though women then turned increasingly to writing as a way of earn-ing a living,[47] they faced mountainous prejudice. When Charlotte Brontë in 1837 wrote to Robert Southey, then poet laureate of England, asking his opinion of her poetry, he replied that although it showed talent, she should give up wanting to be a poet. "Literature cannot be the business of a woman's life and it ought not to be. The more she is engaged in her proper duties, the less leisure will she have for it, even as an accomplishment and a recreation."[48] George Eliot and Elizabeth Browning approved of feminism in theory, but did not think the Victorian woman could assume the responsibilities of equality. Mrs. Browning wrote: "I believe that, considering men and women in the mass, there *is* an *inequality* of intellect, and it is proved by the very state of things of which gifted women complain."[49] Not everyone in England concurred in the notion of female literary inferiority. George H. Lewes, in an essay entitled "The Lady Novelists," wrote that the sexes have separate but equal literary abilities. He then repeated the cliché of the masculine spirit being intellectual, the feminine spirit emotional. Whether he changed these ideas during the many years he lived with George Eliot, whose intellect was one of the best of that age, I cannot say; but Charlotte Brontë was angry with Lewes for discussing her work on the irrelevant basis of its "femininity."

In America there was much debate about women and authorship in the first half of the nineteenth century. Many critics blamed women authors for the steady deterioration of the profession. In 1838 James Freeman Clarke's *Western Messenger* recommended that women writers confine themselves to areas for which they were well suited: "All productions, whether poetic, fictitious, or didactic, that concern the affections, the social nature and the social world."[50] A critic in the *Southern Quarterly Review* in 1852 denied that women could reason philosophically or abstractly. In 1841 Poe's *Southern Literary Messenger* contained an open letter to young women contemplating writing, advising them to content themselves with sewing, cooking, nursing, and managing the household, but to stay away from poetry. Several years later in the same journal, a male writer addressed all female writers as "dear Aunts" and admonished them, "If you have nothing to say, do not write 'Poetry.' No: knit stockings—knit stockings in all such cases."[51] Some critics, such as Francis P. Greenwood and Horace Wallace, defended women writers, but their opponents soon silenced them. The increasing female competition alarmed literary men, and they fought back.

As the paramount purpose of a woman's existence, motherhood was thought to convey some mystical wisdom and moral infallibility, and thus critics generally respected women writers more if they were also mothers.[52] Margaret Fuller, after she adopted the "true" role of women, that is, marriage and maternity, was much more favorably reviewed in the British press. (It was Britain that rose to its cultural and imperial zenith under The Great Mother, Victoria.) The *Prospective Review* said that after her "aggressive spinsterhood" had terminated in marriage, "the change is instant and beautiful. She becomes a new creature, a thorough woman, living in and from the heart. She blooms, and softens, and flowers like a rhododendron, or an azalea taken from a clay soil . . . and set in rich bog and warm exposures,"[53] possibly some bog similar to that inhabited by the reviewer. Even Harriet Martineau, strong-minded feminist that she was, spoke of

> that remarkable regeneration which transformed her from the dreaming and haughty pedant into the true woman. . . . How interesting and beautiful was the closing period of her life, when husband and child concentrated the powers and affections which had so long run to waste in intellectual and moral eccentricity, the concluding period of her memoirs has shown to us all.[54]

Martineau was quite decisive on this point: Fuller had utterly wasted her powers pursuing an unsound "metaphysical idealism"; but all this might have been avoided "if she had found her heart a dozen years sooner, and in America instead of Italy."[55] These were typical views, the "love conquers all" school of thought (or un-thought), which assumes that whatever a woman might do or think or become by herself, it is somehow empty, sterile, and worthless until the magic miracle of marriage and motherhood redeems all. But we must remember that a married man with a family was also more likely to be regarded by the Victorians as normal, respectable, responsible, and therefore more worthy of serious literary attention.

There was, we see, little chance for Fuller's work to be accepted for its own intrinsic value in the age in which she wrote. Her century generally preferred to praise not her thought or her work but her motherhood and wifehood. Horace Greeley once remarked, "Noble and great as she was, a good husband and two or three bouncing babies would have emancipated her from a good deal of cant and nonsense."[56] Or silenced her altogether. Poe, angry at Fuller's omission of him in her survey of American writers, called her a "disagreeable old maid." Even in the twentieth century, one of Fuller's most respected biographers said that her varied experiences of friendship prevented her from fulfilling the "true nature of a woman," that those friendships were a "twist in her nature," and that her mystic pieces are visions that "clearly stem from a disordered sexuality."[57]

When Fuller had borne a son and written a book in Italy, her friend Rebecca Spring wrote her congratulations about the baby. In thanking her, Margaret replied: "Yet in answer to what you say, that it is still better to give the world this living soul than a portion of my life in a printed book; it is true; and yet of my book I could know whether it would be of some worth or not, of my child I must wait to see what his worth will be."[58] There is something poignant and unnatural about having to weigh and judge the relative value of books and babies. The assumption of Fuller's time was that God, society, men, and female biology meant women for the production and nurture of babies, not of books. No one then noticed that men never had to make a similar choice. They have had freedom to create both or neither, without enduring the stigma of being thought perverted or antisocial or wickedly blasphemous to the Creator's plan. All Margaret Fuller wanted was a similar freedom for women.

Such freedom had not even begun to exist in her lifetime. A fable in her notebooks, published years after her death, told what it was like to be a woman then. "Woman is the flower, man the bee. She sighs out melodious fragrance, and invited the winged laborer. He drains her cup, and carries off the honey. She dies on the stalk; he returns to the hive, well fed, and praised as an active member of the community."[59]

But she did not want the situations reversed. She never wanted to be a man, never advised other women to imitate men. "Were they free, were they wise fully to develop the strength and beauty of Woman, they would never wish to be men, or man-like," she said.[60] She only wanted to be herself, to help other women find their own selfhood, and to see justice done. "My history presents much superficial, temporary tragedy," she wrote. "The Woman in me kneels and weeps in tender rapture; the Man in me rushes forth, but only to be baffled. Yet the time will come when, from the union of this tragic king and queen, shall be born a radiant sovereign self."[61] For Fuller, the answer to tragedy lay enfolded in time, in a future that would rectify present wrongs. Never content to passively await the great changes of history, she labored long and earnestly to help bring them about.

CHAPTER 10

Triumph and Defeat

Margaret Fuller crossed the Atlantic in August 1846. Few Americans of her century were better prepared than she for such an odyssey, and few undertook it with such sympathy, openness, intelligence, and grace. She went as a tourist and as a journalist and sent back to the *Tribune* a series of reports that proved her a skillful political analyst. As the first American woman war correspondent, she wrote her history of the Italian revolution while it happened. But she did not remain a mere observer, a detached recorder of scenes and events. Arriving as a tourist, she stayed to share in the life of Europe. The hopes and aspirations of Italy became her own, and her most intimate personal experiences there were so inextricably linked with public life and politics that one cannot be spoken of without the other.

Ultimately she was caught up in forces too powerful for her to control, under conditions that made escape impossible. She found in Italy the most unalloyed personal happiness of her life, but she also knew there the naked face of brutal power and watched helplessly while it crushed her hopes and her future. At the end, most of the fruits of her European experience were lost—her book, many of her papers, her child. In Italy, the distinction between public and private achievement virtually vanished for Fuller. She was simultaneously more engrossed in her personal life and thrust closer to the center of public and political action than at any time in her life. Her culminating achievements were personal and moral as well as intellectual. The loss of her book, however, means that a complete estimation of her intellectual achievements remains impossible.

Europe in the late 1840s was a continent in ferment. Britain was the foremost industrial nation of the world, but the appalling condition of its working people served as a horrible example to nations like France and Italy, who in striving toward modernization wanted to avoid such degradation at all costs. In France, under Louis Philippe, the middle classes wanted electoral reforms (only a tiny percentage of men could vote); the poor wanted food. The years 1846 and 1847 were among the worst of the century economically. Crops failed—grain and potatoes in 1845, 1846, and 1848. Wheat and rye doubled in price. The poor harvest of 1846 meant famine and starvation for many, especially in Ireland, Flanders, and Germany. Misery stalked the countryside and the cities. Food riots broke out in Berlin, Vienna, and Paris. There was business depression and financial crisis.

Europe tried to feed itself and, following Britain, to advance into the industrial age. Social problems were often linked to nationalist problems. The vast Austrian empire, not an enlightened despotism, ruled a large part of Poland and many of the Italian states. The nationalist fever burned, and the desire for political self-determination fueled the flames. The old despotisms were on the defensive, but their stubborn hold on the life of Europe surprised many young revolutionaries who felt that the march of history was on *their* side. In 1848 revolutions broke out all over Europe.

Fuller knew of these brewing storms while still in New York. But when she arrived in England in early autumn of 1846, she put aside such concerns for a time. She had always lived impatiently, but her pace of life in Europe quickened even more. With her companions Marcus and Rebecca Spring and their young son Eddie, Margaret plunged into a whirl of travel, sightseeing, theater, and social life. She loved it all, and she wrote to Emerson, "I find myself much in my element in European society. It does not, indeed, come up to my ideal, but so many of the encumbrances are cleared away that used to weary me in America, that I can enjoy a freer play of faculty, and feel, if not like a bird in the air, at least as easy as a fish in water."[1]

In England she met Wordsworth, De Quincey, Joanna Baillie; she visited Harriet Martineau in an unsuccessful attempt at reconciliation. She saw the Carlyles several times, and they introduced her to Mazzini, a favorite of Mrs. Carlyle. In France Fuller met Sand, Chopin, Pierre-Jean de Béranger, Felicité-Robert de Lamennais, Adam Mickiewicz; in Italy Alessandro Manzoni, the Princess Belgiogioso, Goethe's daughter-in-law Ottilia, and Byron's former mistress Countess Guiccioli. She described these meetings either in her dispatches to the *Tribune* or in letters to family and friends. The most memorable and vivid are her accounts of Carlyle and Sand; but of all the persons she met, Mazzini and Mickiewicz became associated most closely with her personal destiny.

In Europe she had the heartache of realizing she would not see James Nathan again, but the pain soon changed into annoyance when he repeatedly refused to return her letters. There were other insults too. In Paris, at the Sorbonne with a male companion, she was told that he could attend a lecture, but she could not. The lecture was, presumably, "too good for female ears."[2] And there was adventure. Making the four-mile climb up Ben Lomond with Marcus Spring, she became separated from him and could not find her way back down amid the treacherous bogs. She spent the night on the mountain, never hearing the shouts of the search parties of shepherds. It was only the first of many times in Europe that her life was in danger.

Fuller's first year in Europe was a time of gaiety, a time of exhilarating social and artistic contacts, but she was not yet deeply engaged by anything she found there. This lent a certain superficiality to her first dispatches to the *Tribune*. Even as travel literature, they are much less successful than her American travel book, *Summer on the Lakes*, although they do contain flashes of brilliant observation, penetrating insight, and felicitous expression. For Fuller to write well, she had to form a strong attachment to place, person, or idea. Her best writing always came out of thorough knowledge of and involvement in her subject, which is why *Summer* and *Woman in the Nineteenth Century* were so successful.

Fuller cared about the same things at home and abroad. She wrote enthusiastically about the schools Mazzini had established in London for poor boys. She had tart words for the commercialism of book publishers and others who made a handsome profit circulating trash. She was interested in day-care centers for workers' children, in schools for the mentally retarded, in the English and French prostitutes. She spent time among the weavers of Lyons and was outraged at the sufferings they endured.

The human degradation in Europe stunned her. Conditions were especially bad in London, Edinburgh, and Glasgow, which seemed to her like Dante's Inferno. "Poverty in England has terrors of which I never dreamed at home," she told her *Tribune* readers.[3] Never in America had she seen such extremes, "all that pomp and parade of wealth and luxury in contrast with the misery, squalid, agonizing, ruffianly, which stares one in the face in every street in London, and hoots at the gates of her palaces more ominous a note than ever was that of owl or raven in the portentous times when empires and races have crumbled and fallen from inward decay."[4] In supposedly prosperous France, she saw how "the poorer classes have suffered from hunger this winter. All signs of this are kept out of sight in Paris. A pamphlet called 'The Voice of Famine,' stating facts, though in a tone of vulgar and exaggerated declamation, was suppressed as soon as published."[5]

Fuller and the Springs left Paris for Italy in February 1847. Her first glimpse of Italy at Naples fulfilled a long-cherished hope, and when she arrived in Rome she knew she had at last found her true spiritual home. "Italy receives me as a long lost child," she wrote to a friend in America, "and I feel myself at home here."[6] Like Madame de Staël's Corinne, Margaret felt in Italy a freedom to be herself that she had never known elsewhere. Goethe had found in Rome a balance for his Germanic seriousness and the springs of renewal for his life as a man and an artist; like him, Fuller discovered in Italy a joy that balanced her Puritan-Transcendentalist moral earnestness. She had been forced to grow up too soon, to think and to assume heavy responsibilities too early. In Italy she recaptured some of that lost childhood. Moreover, women in Italy had and exercised a freedom and responsibility in public affairs—while retaining all their respectability—that the Americans and the English could not understand.[7] The friends Fuller made among the Italian nobility, such as Princess Belgiogioso and Madame Arconati, were living proof of this. In Bologna, Fuller saw monuments to women scholars and professors of Greek, anatomy, and mathematics. The works of women artists were prominently displayed, and she observed that women had a prominent place in society. "A woman should love Bologna," she said, "for there has the intellect of woman been cherished."[8]

The Italian people immediately won her heart.

> I love much the Italians. The lower classes have the vices induced by long subjection to tyranny; but also a winning sweetness, a ready and discriminating love for the beautiful, and a delicacy in the sympathies, the absence of which always made me sick in our own country. Here, at least, one does not suffer from obtuseness or indifference. They take pleasure, too, in acts of kindness; they are bountiful.

Ever the realist, she added, "But it is useless to hope the least honor in affairs of business. I cannot persuade those who serve me, however attached, that they should not deceive me and plunder me. . . . it is absolutely necessary to be always on the watch against being cheated."[9]

She found among the Italian people an unstudied naturalness lacking in New Englanders. Her friend William Story described it with a painter's eye:

> All things are easy and careless in the out-of-doors life of the common people— all poses unsought, all groupings accidental, all actions unaffected and unconscious. One meets Nature at every turn—not braced up in prim forms, not conscious in manners, not made up into the fashionable or the proper, but impulsive, free and simple. With the whole street looking on, they are as unconscious and natural as if they were where no eye could see them.[10]

In Fuller's words, "It is to the pagans we must turn to learn the secret of a happy and virtuous life. To the Saxon, the body is a convenience, to the Italian a thing alive with beauty."[11] In Italy too she found, as Goethe had, that "the Italians have in general a deeper feeling for the high dignity of art than any other nation."[12] But it was not art in Italy that most absorbed her. "Art is dead here," she remarked. "The few sparkles that sometimes break through the embers cannot make a flame."[13]

Fuller's life in Italy from first to last was bound up with the crisis in Italian political and national life. In 1847 the political passions of nationalism and the desire for unification dominated Italy.[14] Austria controlled two of the richest states, Lombardy and Venezia. The popular liberal pope, Pius IX, ruled the Papal States, and the Bourbon king Ferdinand ruled Naples and Sicily. Revolutionary fever was rising. But though their hatred of foreign domination united the Italian patriots, they were sharply divided as to what form of government Italy should have once the despised Austrians left. There were two principal factions among the nationalists: the so-called moderates or liberals, who wanted a monarchy, constitutional or nonconstitutional, after independence; and the so-called radicals, who wanted a republic. (There was also a faction who wanted a strong Italian monarchy, and a faction in Milan who opposed national unification on the theory that autonomous local states best guaranteed individual freedom.) The liberal moderates, mostly from the landed bourgeoisie or aristocracy, feared or even hated democracy and regarded the workers and peasants with profound suspicion. This faction looked to King Charles Albert of Piedmont to lead the work of reform and perhaps to rule a united Italy.

From her earliest observations of the Italian scene, Fuller concluded that the Austrians must go. Many Americans in Italy were extremely uneasy at the prospect of revolution, but Fuller perceived its necessity:

> Her [Austria's] policy is, indeed, too thoroughly organized to change except by revolution; its scope is to serve, first, a reigning family instead of the people; second, with the people to seek a physical in preference to an intellectual good; and, third, to prefer a seeming outward peace to an inward life. This policy may change its opposition from the tyrannical to the insidious; it can know no other change.[15]

Almost immediately she cast her lot with the republicans, not the moderates, whom she loathed as much for their timidity as for their policies. "The moderate party, like all who, in a transition state, manage affairs with a constant eye to prudence, lacks dignity always in its expositions; it is disagreeable and depressing to read them."[16]

Mazzini, the charismatic leader of the republicans, embodied the national hopes. Mazzini was a visionary. He dreamed of a united republic of Italy as the spiritual center of Europe. He hoped for a magnificent new synthesis for Europe, uniting religion, political structures, and society. Churches and churchmen would give way to the religion of humanity;

despotism would dissolve into a new democratic union of nations; and the hierarchy of classes would yield to one class, The People.

Of this magnificent new world he envisioned, nationalism was the key. Mazzini had no use for the cosmopolitan, internationalist outlook of men like Goethe and Metternich. For Mazzini, people derived strength, purpose, and joy from awareness of their own nationality.[17] For him, Rome was the heart of Italy, the moral center of Europe. Twice before, he said, Rome had been the source of a great unity for the world. The Rome of the Caesars gave the world the idea of Right, of Justice. The Rome of the Popes had raised the law from earth to heaven and added Duty to Right. The third Rome, he believed, would link earth and heaven and harmonize Right and Duty. This Rome of the People, politically a centralized, independent, democratic republic, would spiritually embody a new ideal of civilization. This, then, was the shape of the future, the religion of Humanity, concentrated in Mazzini's motto *Dio e Popolo*. Because these ideals were not a matter of logic or argument but of faith, they were impervious to reason or contradictory rhetoric.[18]

But the yoke of the foreigner must first be thrown off. Only war could banish tyranny, and Mazzini conceived of revolution as a holy war of liberation motivated not by hate but by faith, by duty, even by love.[19] He preached revolution, but not primarily through armed struggle. He envisioned a fraternal union and class solidarity, all the Italian people united and rising in spontaneous and total rejection of the foreigner's rule. Mazzini had little in common with most other revolutionaries of his century. He scorned their atheism, materialism, and egotism; he rejected their advocacy of class struggle. He thought communism too destructive and materialistic. He constantly preached a higher, nobler goal, the resurrection of Italy and through Italy the resurrection of Europe. He lived entirely for that goal. His moral superiority was the source of his leadership, and he appealed to unselfish motives to get people to make sacrifices. His was a greatness of soul, a spirituality, and a generosity virtually unknown among modern political leaders.

Inevitably, he was a dangerous man to the Austrians. He had spent time in their prisons for his revolutionary activities. When Fuller met him he was living in exile in London, trailed by spies, under proscription of death if he ever returned to Italy. "By far the most beauteous person I have seen is Joseph Mazzini," she wrote home. "He is one in whom holiness has purified, but somewhat dwarfed the man."[20] Personally Mazzini possessed much dignity and sweetness. For all his mystical nationalism he was a man of reason too. His physical beauty—slender build, fine features and dark expressive eyes, high forehead, graying hair and beard—added to his charisma. He always wore black, in grief, he explained, because his country had been murdered.

Fuller always responded to masculine beauty, whether of body or soul. The combination of Mazzini's genius, his goodness, and the mystique of his imprisonment and exile attracted her. She wrote from Rome of his devotion to his country.

> The only powers he acknowledged were *God and the People*. . . . He is not an orator, but the simple conversational tone of his address is in refreshing contrast with the boyish rhetoric and academic swell common to Italian speakers in the present unfledged state. . . . The speech of Mazzini is laden with thought,—it goes straight to the mark by the shortest path, and moves without effort, from the irresistible impression of deep conviction and fidelity in the speaker. Mazzini is a man of genius, an elevated thinker; but the most powerful and first impression from his presence must always be of the religion of his soul, of his *virtue*, both in the modern and antique sense of that word.[21]

But though she admired both the man and his ideas, she never accepted them uncritically.

Fuller and Mazzini became close friends in England, and when she left with the Springs for France and Italy, they continued to correspond, although letters were difficult because of censorship and the danger surrounding Mazzini. Fuller and the Springs worked out a plot to smuggle Mazzini into Italy, first providing him with a false American passport in the name of George Moore. He was to follow them from London to Paris in disguise, and then into Italy, but the plan was never carried out.

Margaret had fallen in love with Rome, and soon she fell in love with one of Rome's sons. At Eastertime in early April 1847 she visited St. Peter's Basilica with the Springs. In the immense cathedral she became separated from her companions. A courteous, handsome young man with deep-set, melancholy eyes asked if he could be of assistance. Together Margaret and the young Roman searched chapel after chapel, but did not find the Springs. He offered to escort her to her lodgings, and soon they were frequent companions.

Marquis Giovanni Angelo Ossoli was the youngest member of an old Roman family that staunchly supported the Papacy. Two older sons were members of the Pope's palace guard. But Giovanni, alone of his family, favored the new progressive political views gaining strength all over Italy. Ossoli's mother had died when he was an infant, and though he loved and revered his aged father, he was at odds with the two older brothers who served the Pope and who would be the principal inheritors of the family patrimony. Giovanni Ossoli stood in a precarious relation to his family: the enmity of his brothers threatened his inheritance, and his politics deepened his alienation from his kin and class.[22]

Ossoli's nature was much simpler than that of the woman he loved. Kind-hearted, courageous, loyal, melancholy rather than vivacious, with an unself-conscious grace of manner and bearing, devoted to his family and his country, Ossoli made no attempt to understand or to match Margaret's intellectual and emotional complexity. He adored her, and that was enough. That is, it was enough for them: gossip has not been kind to Ossoli, and tongues were quick to wag about his ineptness and their unsuitability for each other.

"Friendship is the fruit of time, while love is the very lightning and sometimes born of the storm," said Garibaldi in his *Memoirs*.[23] Ossoli proposed marriage to Margaret, not once but several times. She persistently refused. She had long wanted a child, and love, but she had never especially wanted marriage. Indeed, she had gotten along well without it, and she knew that the disparities between herself and Ossoli made marriage unthinkable. Their background, age, education, intellect, language, and nationality were different. Neither had any money, and a Roman needed a special Papal dispensation to marry a Protestant. Ossoli's family had learned of his association with an American Protestant woman of decisively liberal views, and, predictably, they disapproved.

Their attraction and need for each other drew them together so strongly that Margaret grew alarmed. She decided to flee Rome. About this time, the Springs planned to return to America. Margaret, not yet finished with Europe, decided to stay. Alone she embarked on a rapid tour of Italy during the summer months of 1847. She may have sensed that her days as a tourist were nearly over, and she snatched one last chance to see all she could of her beloved Italy. In Milan, soon to be a center of rebellion, she met and talked with the young radicals. At Lake Como she met some aristocrats, among them Madame Constanza Arconati, who became a close friend. Because of her hectic travel pace, she fell ill from fatigue in Florence and had to be nursed back to health by the family of an American sculptor named Joseph Mozier.

Margaret Fuller's decision to accept Ossoli and his love brought her back to Rome in the autumn. She was encouraged in that decision by Adam Mickiewicz, Poland's great epic poet, whom she had met in Paris. She had described him to Emerson as "the man I had long wished to see, with the intellect and passions in due proportion for a full and healthy human being, with a soul constantly inspiring."[24] Mickiewicz, the most renowned of a group of Polish exiles in Paris, was their undisputed intellectual leader. Deeply Christian and nationalist, he preached a mystical romantic nationalism, a Polish messianism. He admired Napoleon and believed in the divine mission of great men. He believed too in the moral leadership of nations like Poland, which, transfigured by their suffering, were destined to expiate the sins of other nations and lead the world to a new, revitalized, Christian civilization. Mickiewicz's books and poems, appearing in the 1830s, had enormous influence in Europe, and he spoke so rhapsodically that he transported his listeners. Many were moved to hysteria and fainting spells.

When Fuller left Paris in early spring of 1847, she and Mickiewicz corresponded. She evidently confided to him matters she would never dream of discussing with friends like Emerson or the saintly Mazzini. The discerning Mickiewicz saw that, in spite of Margaret's independence and self-possession, she was not experienced in love, and many of her needs had not yet been fulfilled. He wrote her several letters urging her frankly to develop relationships that satisfied bodily as well as spiritual needs, to be a "liberated" woman in every sense, to think of herself as beautiful. He told her not to flee so fast from her "young Italian" and to yield to, rather than fight, her attraction to Ossoli.

It seems likely that Margaret Fuller needed the approval of a male authority figure (Emerson often had this role in intellectual and spiritual matters, Mazzini in politics) before proceeding into a relationship so fraught with danger, delight, and, as it turned out, such grave consequences. Proceed she did, and the autumn of 1847 was one of the most glorious seasons of her life. Her letters of this period reflect a tranquility and happiness seldom seen before.

Happiness, and passion at long last fulfilled, affected her writing too. Some of her best essays belong to this period. One of these, an impassioned plea to her countrymen to think of Europe's and America's failures and to be true to themselves, is as lucid and powerful a piece of patriotic writing as any produced by an American writer.[25] Fuller's acceptance of Ossoli's love intensified her love both for her native and her adopted country. She was never so truly an American patriot as when she lived in voluntary exile.

The glory of autumn gave way to the bitterness of winter, and by December Margaret knew she was pregnant. Her future now seemed out of her hands. The winter, the rain, and her gloom seemed interminable.

But the early months of 1848 brought frantic change. Insurrection exploded in France, Hungary, Bohemia, Bavaria, Vienna, Berlin, Tuscany, and Sicily. The Milanese rose up against their overlords, expelled the Austrian army from Lombardy, and set up a democratic republic. Daniele Mannin led the Venetians in ejecting the Austrians and establishing the Republic of St. Mark. Mazzini crossed the Alps and entered Italy in April. Prophetically he had predicted a general revolution in Europe as well as in Italy; now he was hailed as the leader of Italy's resurrection, and Milan received him in triumph. The Piedmont king Charles Albert, the focus of hope for the moderate reformers, led an army into a campaign against the Austrians. All Italian nationalists supported him. The call to battle went out through all the Italian states, and thousands of men hurried to join. But the Austrian military machine proved superior in numbers and strategy, and after some exhilarating initial successes, Charles Albert's army was defeated at Custoza. The Austrians reentered Milan on August 7 and began their bloody reprisals and a new reign of terror. The defeat of the acknowledged leader of the moderate liberal party meant their eclipse by the radicals, who now became the dominant force in Italian affairs.

In Rome events followed a different course. There the reign of Pius IX, begun in 1846, first appeared to be a liberal flowering. The people loved their new Pope, and he seemed sympathetic to their nationalist aspirations, their desire to rebuild society. He granted amnesty to political prisoners and the right to a people's militia, the Guarda Civica. Under his rule, plans for reform proliferated; railways, schools, workers' guilds, and scientific congresses came into being. He appointed liberal ministers, though there was no assembly or suffrage. The Romans' enthusiasm had the fervor of a religious revival.

When she first lived in Rome, Fuller saw Pius IX as a kind, loving prince, a man genuinely concerned with the welfare of his people. "He has shown undoubted wisdom, clear-sightedness, bravery, and firmness," she said in December 1847. "But it is, above all, his generous human heart that gives him his power over this people. . . . What form the issues of his life may take is yet uncertain; in my belief, they are such as he does not think of; but they cannot fail to be for good."[26] But she voiced private doubts in a letter: "From the people themselves the help must come, and not from the princes. Rome, to resume her glory, must cease to be an ecclesiastical capital."[27]

Soon she became aware of the Pope's weakness. As an outsider and a Protestant, she saw that when he was caught in the contradiction between reformer and priest, the priest would always win out. But like most Romans she continued to believe in the Pope's personal goodness, and she hoped he could lead Rome and Italy, could be "a most important agent in fashioning a new and better era for this beautiful injured land," if not by the strength of his own will and leadership, then as "the providential agent to work out aims beyond his ken. A wave has been set in motion, which cannot stop till it casts up its freight upon the shore."[28]

Early in 1848 the Pope granted a constitution, and popular hopes peaked. A new Rome seemed in the process of being born, with none of the pangs of upheaval that so often attend the birth of new societies and the death of old ones. A crisis developed for the Pope when King Charles Albert went to war with the Austrians. The Pope, who had steered a careful course between liberals and radicals, was urged by the Roman people and by his liberal ministers to join in this war of liberation against the hated foreigners. He now had to choose between the people's nationalist hopes and his position as an international Catholic ruler. He said he could not make war on a Catholic power. All over Italy the patriots felt betrayed and began to turn against their once-loved Pio Nono. His authority waned among his people. Now it became clear that, in Fuller's words, "when there was conflict between the priest and the man, he always meant to be the priest; and that he preferred the wisdom of the past to that of the future."[29]

Gradually the Pope showed himself less able to cope with popular sentiment and the radical nationalists' demands. In November 1848 the Pope's chief minister, Pellegrino Rossi (a French citizen, though Italian by birth, and despised by the Romans), was assassinated. The Pope feared for his life, and in disguise, under cover of darkness, he fled from Rome to take refuge with the monarch of Naples, the Bourbon Ferdinand (known as King Bomba after his bombardment of Messina). The Pope's abdication not only eroded most of his support among the people but left the field clear for opponents of his government. Delegations of loyal Romans went to Sicily to try to placate Pio Nono and beg him to return, but without success. Republicans filled the vacuum of leadership. In February 1849 a newly formed Assembly met and voted a Roman republic.

Margaret Fuller witnessed, narrated, and at times participated in these events, beginning with her return to Rome in the autumn of 1847. Her dispatches to the *Tribune* and her letters to friends provide one of the best existing eyewitness accounts of the crises in Rome. Her Roman essays combine an acute eye for detail, her own political and moral passion, and a sense of urgency, the drama of being in the eye of the storm. She describes Rome and Romans, leaders, processions, rituals, manifestos, and the people's hopes, all infused with her own reactions and feelings. There is a dynamic movement from specific detail to abstraction and back to detail, from the concrete to the overview, from the singular and personal to the objective and philosophic.

Her philosophic mind gave her a distaste for the sugar-coated, half-perceived half-truths by which most people lurch into the future, and she often voiced what others could not or did not. Though caught up in the Roman spring that seemed part of an Italian spring, even a European one, she wondered if it had not all happened too fast to have much substance. She wrote skeptically on April 1, 1848, "I find the news pronounced official . . . that Italy is free, independent, and one. I trust this will prove no April-foolery, no premature news; it seems too good, too speedy a realization of hope, to have come on earth."[30]

Most Americans at that time, less farsighted and toughminded than she was, could not grasp the implications of those events. A new Europe *was* in the making, and few Americans could understand that fact; few realized that they were witnessing profound social upheaval.[31] But Fuller, characteristically, did not shrink from the truth as she saw it. In New York she had realized that a new Europe was struggling to be born. In Italy she saw firsthand what had to be destroyed before the hoped-for society could come into being.

Fuller's reports on the situation in Rome contain astute political analysis. She saw, for example, that the French would not help the Roman Republic, nor could they be trusted, whereas Mazzini hoped to the last that France would prove Rome's ally. The chief villains in her accounts were the Pope's malicious advisers, his own weakness and vacillation, and the kings of Italy and Europe who lent their power and armies to defeat the Republic. History has borne out the accuracy of her analysis, made in the heat of events. Her penetrating judgments suggest her capacity for political participation on the highest levels. She knew what she was capable of doing. In another century, she said, she would ask to be made the American ambassador, "but woman's day has not come yet."[32]

Fuller's Roman essays are the culmination of an important change in her political and social outlook. She left behind a politically moderate humanitarianism for radical political convictions, a kind of socialist populism. Here the full political implications of Romanticism emerge in Fuller's thought, and all the conservative elements vanish. Many people she met and admired in Europe advocated similar leftist politics— Mazzini, for example, or George Sand, who glorified the working-class hero in her writings. But the chief catalyst in Fuller's political transformation was the conditions she observed all over Europe. The real conditions of people's lives determined her thinking more than preconceived theories. She began to assert that utter wretchedness demanded drastic social solutions, and that superficial reform was not enough. England, she wrote, needed a peaceful revolution, not to destroy, only to equalize. She began speaking of the time "when we cease to have any very poor people, and, please Heaven, also to have any very rich."

Her writings for the *Tribune* reflected her steady leftward drift. Gone now were the pleas for individual change of heart, appeals to noblesse oblige, the idea of an elite that would leaven the mass, or invocations of heavenly solutions for earthly problems. The more desperate the problems, the more she advocated a radical solution. In France she wrote:

> The fact cannot be suppressed, that the people in the provinces have suffered most terribly amid the vaunted prosperity of France. While Louis Philippe

lives, the gases, compressed by his strong grasp, may not burst up to light; but the need of some radical measures of reform is not less strongly felt in France than elsewhere, and the time will come before long when such will be imperatively demanded. The doctrines of Fourier are making considerable progress, and wherever they spread, the necessity of some practical application of the precepts of Christ, in lieu of the mummeries of a worn-out ritual, cannot fail to be felt.

Early in 1848, amid reports of insurrection, she wrote:

> The news from France, in these days, sounds ominous, though still vague. It would appear that the political is being merged in the social struggle: it is well. Whatever blood is to be shed, whatever altars cast down, those tremendous problems MUST be solved, whatever be the cost! That cost cannot fail to break many a bank, many a heart, in Europe, before the good can bud again out of a mighty corruption. To you, people of America, it may perhaps be given to look on and learn in time for a preventive wisdom. You may learn the real meaning of the words FRATERNITY, EQUALITY. You may, despite the apes of the past who strive to tutor you, learn the needs of a true democracy. You may in time learn to reverence, learn to guard, the true aristocracy of a nation, the only real nobles,—the LABORING CLASSES.

More and more she exalted the people and the new spirit at work among them, even more than she exalted leaders like Mazzini and Garibaldi who embodied the new spirit.

Unlike Mazzini, who paid little attention to the economic factors in revolution, Fuller saw that genuine social improvement for Europe would have to disturb the economic structures as well as the political. She realized that he had not fully confronted this necessity. When Mazzini returned to Italy, she wrote that during his seventeen years' exile,

> there was no hour, night or day, that the thought of Italy was banished from his heart,—no possible effort that he did not make to achieve the emancipation of his people, and with it the progress of mankind. . . . He will see his predictions accomplishing yet for a long time, for Mazzini has a mind far in advance of his times in general, and his nation in particular. . . . And yet Mazzini sees not all: he aims at political emancipation; but he sees not, perhaps would deny, the bearing of some events, which even now begin to work their way. Of this, more anon; but not to-day, nor in the small print of the Tribune. Suffice it to say, I allude to that of which the cry of Communism, the systems of Fourier, &c., are but forerunners.

As an American and an outsider, Fuller always had the alternative of remaining detached from Italy's political struggles and passions and factions, as did most of the Americans and English she knew. The Brownings, for example, who also lived and traveled in Italy during these years, kept relatively aloof. They followed the news, formed opinions, and took sides, but their personal circle consisted almost exclusively of Americans and the English. In all their years in Italy they associated with few Italians, socially and intellectually. Fuller might have done the same. Only in retrospect does it seem inevitable that she should have become so deeply involved. How much of this involvement she consciously chose and how much was inexorable personal necessity is impossible to say. Her liaison with Ossoli undoubtedly drew her more intensely into Italy's political life; but even without him, she never remained aloof and detached where great human issues were at stake. "For me, it is my nature to wish to go straight to the Creative Spirit," she once wrote to a friend. That spirit, she was convinced, dwelled in the thick of the conflict, in the uncertain, painful process of creating the future. Divinity works in the living, Goethe had said, in the becoming and changing, not in the become and fixed.

When she arrived in Italy, she sympathized with the radical party and its goals. Ossoli, by his family connections and familiarity with Roman politics, helped her to understand viewpoints other than her own and Mazzini's, and events strengthened her radical convictions. It would have been completely unlike her not to act on her convictions. She wrote to W.H. Channing on March 29:

> I have been engrossed, stunned almost, by the public events that have succeeded one another with such rapidity and grandeur. It is a time such as I always dreamed of, and for long secretly hoped to see. I rejoice to be in Europe at this time, and shall return possessed of a great history. Perhaps I shall be called upon to act. . . . A glorious flame burns higher and higher in the heart of the nations. . . . The men of straw are going down in Italy everywhere; the real men rising into power.[33]

During the spring and summer months of 1848 she became more absorbed in her private life. She was trying to cope with her pregnancy, alone except for Ossoli, penniless and homeless in a foreign land. Adam Mickiewicz, visiting Rome, told her to cheer up and not be so frightened at a natural and common condition. It was not really that simple. Fuller's natural and common condition forced her into an unnatural and uncommon dissembling, for the "fallen woman" was to the Victorians the object of a scorn unimaginable today. She had to lie to Emerson about why she could not join him and sail to America. She lied on an Italian passport about her name, age, and place of birth. She concealed her pregnancy and marriage from even her closest friends. Incognito, she left Rome first for Aquila, then Rieti, where she took lodging with a peasant family while awaiting the birth of her child. During the months of waiting she worked on her history of the Italian revolution. Letters from Ossoli, read first by censors, were her only contact with the world outside her lodgings in those tiny rural towns. Sleepless nights she spent pacing on the balcony of her room, overlooking a river. She was convinced that in giving birth she would die, and she could express her anxieties to no one but Ossoli. Though he visited Margaret as often as he could, he had duties in Rome as a captain in the Guarda Civica, the militia that Pius IX had allowed to his people during the wave of liberal reforms after his accession. Ossoli's father had died in February, and he was more than ever defenseless against his older brothers. Now truly an orphan, his poverty more certain, he and Margaret drew closer together.

In August Margaret and Ossoli had new worries. The disbanded Italian armies, after their defeat at Custoza, had drifted over to Bologna, and fighting broke out there. The Austrians attacked the city, and Pius IX was about to send Rome's Guarda Civica to defend Bologna. Margaret wisely let Ossoli decide for himself between the claims of love and war, though had he gone to Bologna to fight and perhaps die, she would have been absolutely alone.

By the end of August, the Pope decided not to send the Guarda to Bologna, and Ossoli was with Margaret in Rieti at the birth of their son on September 5. He was baptized Angelo, and the godfather by proxy was, as Margaret wished, Adam Mickiewicz. As autumn advanced, new political and economic storms brewed in Rome, setting the stage for revolt. Margaret wanted to bring the baby back to Rome with her, but Ossoli decisively rejected that plan in order to keep their secret. Though she reluctantly left Angelino, financial necessity also dictated her return to Rome: she had to be at the center of political action in order to write the *Tribune* dispatches. Thinking that the baby would be safer in Rieti, she left him in the care of the peasant family with whom she had lodged and returned with Ossoli to Rome.

The Pope fled in November 1848. On February 9, 1849, the Assembly declared the Republic of Rome. Mazzini arrived on March 5 to lead the Triumvirate, which was to govern Rome in its coming months of glory and defeat. Though he had no prior experience in practical politics, Mazzini rallied the people behind him by his enormous influence on their minds and spirits. Immediately a series of reforms ensued: church property was nationalized, clerical control of the university abolished, and the Inquisition suppressed. Censorship was ended and freedom of the press established, the death penalty was abolished, the unemployed were given work and the poor given housing, the peasants were given the church's lands. It was the only genuinely social revolution in Europe except for France's.

The Triumvirate introduced ecclesiastical reform, for example, prohibiting the practice of priests taking fees for the performance of religious duties, but Rome's was not an atheistic republic. Sporadic anticlerical violence met with disapproval, for though Mazzini had hated the church as he knew it, he declared that religious freedom meant freedom for all. That year populace and clergy celebrated Easter with as much ritual, pageantry, and devotion as ever.

Though the Republic had no police or army other than its militia, there was public order everywhere, virtually no vandalism, certainly no anarchy. All classes supported the new republican government. In England Lord Palmerston shocked the Tories by saying, "Mazzini's government of Rome was far better than any the Romans had had for centuries."[34] Like all revolutions that happen too suddenly, Rome's produced a euphoria, an exaltation at long and bitter wrongs suddenly, gloriously righted.

Fuller, between frequent visits to Rieti, sent to the *Tribune* detailed accounts of the new government. She believed that few Americans understood the life of the Italian people and said that many Americans in Italy "talk about the corrupt and degenerate state of Italy as they do about that of our slaves at home. They come ready trained to that mode of reasoning which affirms, that because men are degraded by bad institutions, they are not fit for better."[35] Now, she told her compatriots, she admired the Abolitionists, understanding that the struggle against tyranny and oppression was everywhere the same.

All lies in the future; and our best hope must be that the Power which has begun so great a work will find due means to end it, and make the year of 1850 a year of true jubilee to Italy; a year not merely of pomps and tributes, but of recognized rights and intelligent joys; a year of real peace,—peace, founded not on compromise and the lying etiquettes of diplomacy, but on truth and justice.... Hoping this era, I remain at present here. Should my hopes be dashed to the ground, it will not change my faith, but the struggle for its manifestation is to me of vital interest. My friends write to urge my return; they talk of our country as the land of the future. It is so, but that spirit which made it all it is of value in my eyes, which gave all of hope with which I can sympathize for that future, is more alive here at present than in America. My country is at present spoiled by prosperity, stupid with the lust of gain, soiled by crime in its willing perpetuation of slavery, shamed by an unjust war, noble sentiment much forgotten even by individuals, the aims of politicians selfish or petty, the literature frivolous and venal. In Europe, amid the teachings of adversity, a nobler spirit is struggling,—a spirit which cheers and animates mine. I hear earnest words of pure faith and love. I see deeds of brotherhood. This is what makes *my* America. I do not deeply distrust my country. She is not dead, but in my time she sleepeth, and the spirit of our fathers flames no more, but lies hid beneath the ashes. It will not be so long; bodies cannot live when the soul gets too overgrown with gluttony and falsehood. But it is not the making a President out of the Mexican war that would make me wish to come back. Here things are before my eyes worth recording, and, if I cannot help this work, I would gladly be its historian.[36]

Fuller did more than any other American to inform her compatriots about Rome's situation and to create sympathy in America for Rome, which gradually stood more and more alone, hated by the monarchs and reactionaries of Europe, regarded with suspicion by the moderates who distrusted the "rabble." Fuller urged her country to recognize the Republic and to send an ambassador, not some figurehead but an ambassador qualified for the work. Her efforts brought results. A consul was appointed to the Roman Republic. Unluckily, he died soon after reaching Rome, and six months passed before another consul, Lewis Cass, Jr., was sent. Cass had instructions not to recognize the Republic until he was sure it would last. Fuller blasted this diplomatic timidity and the damage it did by demoralizing the Romans. Like other nations, America was implying, "*If they can do without us,* we will help them."[37] Always faithful to her Jeffersonian convictions, Fuller asserted that the principle of self-determination was the only legitimate ground for a government's existence. Cass eventually wrote to Washington requesting that the United States grant recognition to the Roman Republic, but not until the siege had begun, and then it was too late. By the time permission arrived, Rome had fallen to the French armies.

Though preoccupied with politics and personal affairs, Fuller kept in touch with the world of art. One of her essays discusses the American artist and sculptors of Rome and their work, the reasons they came to Italy, and the excessive attention Americans were giving to Hiram Powers's statue "The Greek Slave." In the essay she refuted the common fallacy that artists could live more cheaply in Italy than in America. She attacked the philistine mentality in America and its cruelty in denying artists the economic means of subsistence, often with the sentimental idea that artists must suffer to produce art. "They [the callous American public] have read essays on the uses of adversity in developing genius, and they are not . . . afraid to administer a dose of adversity beyond what the forces of the patient can bear. Laudanum in drops is useful as a medicine, but a cupful kills downright."[38] The words seem almost written in blood, for poverty in an indifferent society had blighted her life and productivity too. A Polish countess in Rome told Fuller that she envied her, so happy, free, serene, attractive, self-possessed. Margaret wrote to a friend at home, "I do not look on myself as particularly enviable. A little money would have made me much more so; a little money would have enabled me to come here long ago, and find those that belong to me, or at least try my experiments; then my health would never have sunk, nor the best years of my life been wasted in useless friction."[39] According to Mrs. Story, she was then spending only ten or twelve cents a day for her own dinner, yet she loaned her last fifty dollars to an artist who needed it.

The life of the Roman Republic was brief, like its glory. Soon it became apparent that Europe would not let it exist. A conference of the Catholic powers of Europe—France, Austria, Spain, Naples—was held in the spring of 1849 to determine how to reestablish the Pope's rule. All but France argued for unconditional restoration of force by arms. Enough republican sentiment surfaced to cause the French to hesitate, but France kept a wary eye on the Austrian forces, lest they invade the Papal territories and upset the precarious balance of power. Louis Napoleon, who had assumed leadership of the French government the preceding December, was pressed by his Catholic ministers to intervene on behalf of the Pope's restoration, but some factions in Paris protested against crushing a sister republic. Many Romans also believed that one republic would never cooperate in overthrowing another, perhaps a measure of their political naivete. Many Catholic loyalists in Paris thought that a "fifth column" of church supporters and property owners in Rome would welcome French intervention, or even that the Roman people would welcome French troops as saving them from the worse (presumably) Austrians.

For Rome, the balance of power meant that the four Catholic governments were balanced in powerful readiness to strike. The four armies then converged on Rome, and the French general Oudinot was quickly dispatched to occupy the city "without conflict." Rome was defenseless except for her militia, the Guarda Civica. Mazzini wanted to placate the French, hoping to find in them Rome's one ally. But Fuller was never deceived by illusions that the French would help, and she explained in her dispatches why they could not be trusted.

Gradually she began to understand that the Roman Republic would not survive. In her *Tribune* columns and her personal letters, the note of bitterness, defeat, and fatalism intensifed. Still, occasionally she felt confident that if Mazzini and Rome were defeated now, what they believed in would become a reality some day. "The best fruits of the movement may not ripen for a long time."[40] Faith in the future once again assuaged the disappointments of the present.

The Roman Republic was not only threatened from without, it foundered from within on that perpetual obstacle to utopias, money. Mazzini enlisted the support of all kinds and classes of Romans. He could get people to work for and with him, but reforms took money, and Mazzini had no access to the money of the wealthy and propertied. He was no socialist, after all, and he never wanted private property to be attacked or threatened, much less confiscated. The Republic could get no credit, and despite a compulsory loan decreed from the upper classes, inflation spread.

But the most decisive factors in Rome's defeat were its isolation and

the military force of its enemies. The French armies under General Oudinot attacked on April 30. Garibaldi led a successful counterattack, but
Mazzini prevented him from driving the French into the sea, and they
soon returned to the city's outskirts. Negotiation followed. An ambassador, Ferdinand de Lesseps (of later Suez Canal fame), arrived in Rome,
but he was only a dupe of his government. Although he negotiated in
good faith, offering an armistice and protection for Rome, his mission
was a maneuver to gain time for reinforcing the French troops. Unlike
the too-trusting Mazzini, Fuller was not deceived by these pseudonego-
tiations. Oudinot attacked again on June 2, and Rome lay under siege
and bombardment for a month. A fiction spread abroad that the French
forces would "protect" Rome from other foreigners (the advancing Austrians) and "keep order" against the anarchists and the rabble. "The
world seems to go strangely wrong!," lamented Fuller to her sister.

> The bad side triumphs; the blood and tears of the generous flow in vain. I
> assist at many saddest scenes, and suffer for those whom I knew not before.
> Those whom I knew and loved—who, if they had triumphed, would have
> opened for me an easier, broader, higher-mounting road—are every day more
> and more involved in earthly ruin. Eternity is with us, but there is much
> darkness and bitterness in this portion of it. A baleful star rose on my birth,
> and its hostility, I fear, will never be disarmed while I walk below.[41]

While Ossoli fought at the walls of Rome, daily under heavy fire,
Margaret Fuller was appointed director of Fata Bene Fratelli, a hospital
for the wounded on Tiber Island. The siege prevented her from leaving
Rome to be with her baby in Rieti, and no messages could be sent out or
brought in. Cut off completely from Angelino and desperate with anxiety, Margaret also lived with the daily dread that Ossoli might be
brought in among the wounded and dying men. But she performed her
duties at the hospital efficiently and compassionately, and she remained
in frequent contact with Mazzini and Cass. It broke her heart to see
bombs fall on Rome, to see the flower of Italian youth mutilated and
dying. The last weeks of the Republic were a chronicle of heroism. The
invaders had not counted on the Romans' fierce will to resist. Fuller
knew they were dying in a hopeless contest, but no honorable terms
could be made with the enemy, so they had to fight on and not yield.

She admitted in a letter to W.H. Channing that war was too much for
her.

> You say, you are glad I have had this great opportunity for carrying out my
> principles. Would it were so! I found myself inferior in courage and fortitude
> to the occasion. I knew not how to bear the havoc and anguish incident to the
> struggle for these principles. I rejoiced that it lay not with me to cut down the
> trees, to destroy the Elysian gardens, for the defence of Rome; I do not know

that I could have done it. And the sight of these far nobler growths, the beautiful young men, mown down in their stately prime, became too much for me. I forget the great ideas, to sympathize with the poor mothers, who had nursed their precious forms, only to see them all lopped and gashed. You say, I sustained them; often have they sustained my courage.[42]

Fuller wrote her last dispatch to the *Tribune* a few days after Oudinot's forces entered the city on July 4. "In two days of French 'order,' " she wrote, "more acts of violence have been committed, than in two months under the Triumvirate."[43] The Roman Republic existed no more. Wearily she recorded its defeat.

I am sick of breathing the same air with men capable of a part so utterly cruel and false. . . . I have seen too much sorrow, and, alas! without power to aid. It makes me sick to see the palaces and streets of Rome full of these infamous foreigners, and to note the already changed aspect of her population. The men of Rome had begun, filled with new hopes, to develop unknown energy,—they walked quick, their eyes sparkled, they delighted in duty, in responsibility; in a year of such life, their effeminacy would have been vanquished. Now, dejectedly, unemployed, they lounge along the streets, feeling that all the implements of labor, all the ensigns of hope, have been snatched from them. Their hands fall slack, their eyes rove aimless, the beggars begin to swarm again, and the black ravens who delight in the night of ignorance, the slumber of sloth, as the only sureties for their rule, emerge daily more and more frequent from their hiding-place.[44]

But even in the bitterness of defeat, tasting all the cruelty of war, she was stirred by the sight of Garibaldi leading his men out of Rome, they in bright red tunics, he in a white one, their faces resolute and full of courage. Her dramatic description of the exodus captures the romance of war; of such accounts as these was Garibaldi's legend made. The dispatch ends with an eloquent plea to her own country to align itself with the progressive not the reactionary forces in the world.

The reactionaries had triumphed, at least for a time. The Assembly was dissolved; the French occupied Rome for many years, Austria occupied the other Papal States. Venice held out slightly longer than Rome, but was at last starved into submission, surrendering to the Austrians at the end of August 1849. Pius IX returned to his throne in 1850, escorted by foreign soldiers. Reaction was ruthless all over Italy. The Pope's vindictive ministers wiped out all liberal reforms; despotic rulers crammed the prisons with those who had supported rebellions and republics. In Naples 20,000 persons were in prison for political crimes. Italy would not be liberated for another twenty years.

Fuller saw Mazzini once after the French invasion, before he escaped by sea disguised as a graybearded, shuffling old steward. Her own tribulations were not yet over. The French occupied the hospitals, and their maltreatment of the wounded stunned her. Immediately after Mazzini's escape, she and Ossoli left for Rieti to reclaim their child. There they found the baby seriously ill. The peasant family, not receiving the money Margaret had regularly sent them, believed the American lady had abandoned her child. Unwilling or unable to care for him without this money, they had shamefully neglected him, barely feeding him at all. Margaret and Ossoli nursed Angelino back to health, and she resolved henceforth she would live only for her child. Because of the proscription against all who had aided the Roman Republic, the family traveled to Florence as political exiles.

Margaret Fuller Ossoli lived the last year of her life in Florence with her husband and son. Intellectually vigorous as ever, and with a heightened understanding of political struggle born in the crucible of the Roman revolution, Fuller studied socialism and corresponded with her friends about its new forms. It was a respite of serenity and happiness in a life that had known too little of either. She wrote from Florence:

> The Italian spring is as good as Paradise. Days come of glorious sunshine and gently-flowing airs, that expand the heart and uplift the whole nature. The birds are twittering their first notes of love; the ground is enamelled with anemones, cowslips, and crocuses; every old wall and ruin puts on its festoon and garland; and the heavens stoop daily nearer, till the earth is folded in an embrace of light, and her every pulse beats music.[45]

A series of beautiful and tender letters described the joy she found in her child and in Ossoli. "I feel so refreshed by [Angelino's] young life. Ossoli diffuses such a power and sweetness over every day that I cannot endure to think yet of our future. Too much have we suffered already trying to command it. . . . We have resolved to repose and enjoy being together as much as we can in this brief interval—perhaps all we shall ever know of peace."[46] She resolved never again to be separated from her husband and child.

Financial worries pressed, as always. Ossoli, now completely estranged from his family, had no hope of inheritance because of his participation in the Republic. He could not return to his home in the foreseeable future, nor was he trained for any remunerative work. Margaret borrowed money from friends and banks. Finally, believing she might earn a living for her family better in America, and hoping to find there a publisher for her history of the Italian revolution, she made plans to return.

Her letters home often reflected her weariness. Rome's defeat had been her personal defeat too. "Private hopes of mine are fallen with the hopes of Italy," she wrote to W.H. Channing. "I have played for a new stake, and lost it. Life looks too difficult."[47] Despite domestic happiness, she seemed exhausted from public struggles and private cares.

> I have been the object of great love from the noble and the humble; I have felt it toward both. Yet I am *tired out*,—tired of thinking and hoping,—tired of seeing men err and bleed. I take an interest in some plans,—Socialism for instance,—but the interest is as shallow as the plans. These are needed, are even good; but man will still blunder and weep, as he has done for so many thousand years.... I am weary, and faith soars and sings no more. Nothing good of me is left except at the bottom of the heart, a melting tenderness:— "She loves much."[48]

After the 1848 revolutions a shadow descended on the hopes of Europe. Now the shining aspirations that burned so brilliantly and sparked so many rebellions were extinguished. Politics became more cynical, power maneuvers usurped more and more of the public arena, and confidence in the ideal of freedom diminished.[49] Though some of what was fought for in the revolutions of 1848–49 became a reality later in the century, it appeared for a time that reaction and naked force used in service of tyranny were victorious. Margaret Fuller seemed crushed by the apparent triumph of all she had despised and fought against. She could not take refuge in a cynicism entirely foreign to her nature. She could not cope with total disillusionment. The defeat of Rome, together with the difficulties she faced in her own personal future, combined to overwhelm her and break her spirit at last.

If the Roman Republic had succeeded, of course, her life would have been different. She would not have fled, a penniless exile, to Florence and thence to America. Her political acumen, her friendship with Mazzini, and her writing talent would have created for her a place of honor in that republic, and Ossoli would have had his place there too as a soldier and nobleman of a distinguished family. She would have seen firsthand the development of the Roman people and the evolution of new institutions.[50] She knew all this when she wrote to W.H. Channing that her own hopes and aspirations were so closely bound up with the Republic that its failure meant for her a devastating personal failure.

But hers was not a moral failure. Perhaps in the end Europe did destroy her, and perhaps the aloof Americans, who rejected involvement in Europe's tangled and desperate affairs, were wise as well as callous and prudent. Those other American pilgrims in Italy, after all, survived more or less unscathed—the Irvings, the Emersons, the Hawthornes, the Springs, the Storys, and many others. Had Margaret Fuller likewise remained detached, as spectator and mere tourist, she would have perhaps lived longer; but she might never have really lived, as *she* defined living. In rushing toward her destruction, she found personal fulfillment

173

and the life of action, found that life was indeed sweet, as she had longed for it to be. And in the process of destruction itself she achieved her greatest heroism and compassion.

Yet the feeling persists that life dealt with her cruelly. Those who were shocked by the news of her death at sea sensed the profound injustice of that death. Many consoled themselves, like W.H. Channing, by the belief that Margaret had gone to a better world in heaven. Or, like Elizabeth Browning, they took refuge in the thought that she was better off dead: "The comfort is, that she lost little in the world—the change could not be loss to her. She had suffered, and was likely to suffer still more."[51] As if, somehow, suffering is reason enough to welcome death.

Such comments only evade the mystery and narcotize the dread impact of Margaret Fuller's death. Complacency does not penetrate the mystery. None of the known facts about her death help to reconcile us to it. Perhaps in those last hours she was reconciled. Perhaps she was not. For us the living, perhaps only one who fully understands the grandeur of her life can interpret the meaning of her death. Until then, not to evade it seems a last homage she deserves.

In the end, the pitiless sea was her grave, and that of Ossoli. Angelino's body was found washed up on the shore and was buried in a hasty grave there. The sea swallowed up the one manuscript of her best book. Of the other papers on shipboard, only her letters to Ossoli were ever found.

> Compass, quadrant and sextant contrive
> No farther tides . . . High in the azure steeps
> Monody shall not wake the mariner.
> This fabulous shadow only the sea keeps.

CHAPTER 11

The Achievement

Had Margaret Fuller lived, what might she have become? In what directions would she have grown? What further achievements would have crowned all the others? The questions are as irresistible as they are unanswerable, for the close of her life leaves us with a tragic sense of the gap between what she might have accomplished and what she did accomplish. From the start of her life to its close, she was thwarted in her aspirations and held back by limitations that would have stifled a woman of less genius, less determination, less strength of mind. Her achievements were great, but they might have been greater still.

Margaret Fuller lived a century ahead of her time, or even two centuries. She led her life and did her work entirely within the framework of man-made laws, customs, traditions, philosophy, and social structures. Elizabeth Cady Stanton once said, "Thus far women have been mere echoes of men. Our laws and constitutions, our creeds and codes, and the customs of social life are all of masculine origin. The true women is as yet a dream of the future."[1] Margaret Fuller's unshakable belief in the future consoled her for the bitter knowledge that her aspirations had not all seen fruition, that she had been held back from doing all she might have done for her country and the human race. She once wrote to Anna Barker:

> The depth of despair must be caused by the mistaken idea that this our present life is all the time allotted to man for the education of his nature for that state of consummation which is called heaven. Were it seen that this present is only one little link in the long chain of probations, were it felt that the Divine Justice is pledged to give the aspirations of the soul all the time they require for their fulfilment, were it seen that disease, old age and death are circumstances which can never touch the eternal youth of the Spirit, that, though the "plant man" grows more or less fair in hue and stature according to the soil in which it is planted, yet the principle which is the life of the plant will not be defeated but must scatter its seeds again and again till it does at last come to perfect flower, then would he who is pausing to despair realize that a new choice can *never* be too late, the false steps made in ignorance can never be counted by the All-Wise, and that, though a moment's delay against conviction is of incalculable weight, the mistakes of forty years are but as dust on the balance held by an unerring hand. Despair is for time, hope for eternity.[2]

Before her fatal voyage to¹ America, she reflected: "It seems to me that my future upon earth will soon close. . . . God will transplant the root, if he wills to rear it into fruit-bearing."³ She knew that all things lacking to the present would come about in time.

And so it seems perverse and unnecessary to dwell on what she might have been and done, when the legacy she left is so rich and so worth exploring. She thought well, loved well, and lived well, and fortunately for us, she left behind some record of these achievements. The defect of categories has worked against her, but that is not her fault; it is the fault of those who must have a proper label before they can approve. In what niche can we place her? Critic, prose poet, philosopher, feminist, essayist, social observer, reformer, revolutionary? She was all of these, yet none wholly. She eludes our categories, forcing us always to look at what she was, what she thought, what she said, and what it meant.

What of those who have declared her a failure because she was "not an artist"? Some of her friends and biographers have insisted, in rebuttal, that her life was a work of art, that her medium was not words or stones or musical tones, but her own life and spirit. There may be truth in that assertion, for to study her life and work leads to the conclusion that, if no existing definitions of the artist fit her well, then new ones must be created. Fuller used to say in her Conversations that acting in accord with the law of one's being was living poetry, "enacted poesy." The discord, the intrusions, the limitations, whatever was inferior—these were the prose of life, she said, and they were necessary. But "poesy was the natural life of the soul." When pressed for more explanation, however, she would not carry the idea further or state it too emphatically.

We would do well to be wary of the "life as art" thesis, as Fuller was wary of it. Ultimately it led to that cardinal Transcendentalist error, the denial of art as an entity. Many nineteenth-century Romantics, the Transcendentalists among them, were enamored of the "life as art" concept. The danger of the concept lies not only in its negation of art. It also leads to narcissism and the cult of personality, that is, the exaltation of personality over principle, over impersonal truth. It contains the seeds of a fatal—and lethal—egotism. Such ideas have outlived their usefulness as historical correctives. The world has suffered too much from supreme egos. It is suffering still. The "Margaret Fuller whose life was a work of art" fascinated the nineteenth century, but cannot satisfy the twentieth or twenty-first.

Four elements characterized the achievements of Margaret Fuller with remarkable consistency: her continual growth, her receptivity to experience, her affirmation of life, and her vision of unity.

When we stop judging Fuller by standards other than those she accepted for herself, we no longer see defeat or failure. By her own standards, she was triumphantly successful. "Very early I knew that the only object in life was to grow." And so she did; the metamorphosis continued to the end. Arriving at one plateau, she never long stayed, but sought further experience, further achievement. She could have remained high priestess of New England culture, successful New York critic and writer, feminist leader, or European journalist. Yet after a time she put each vocation aside and risked launching into an unknown future.

D.H. Lawrence called this the new American heroic message:

> The Open Road. The great home of the Soul is the open road. Not heaven, not paradise. Not "above". Not even "within". The soul is neither "above" nor "within". It is a wayfarer down the open road.
>
> Not by meditating. Not by fasting. Not by exploring heaven after heaven, inwardly, in the manner of the great mystics. Not by exaltation. Not by ecstasy. Not by any of these ways does the soul come into her own.
>
> Only by taking the open road. . . .
>
> Having no known direction even. Only the soul remaining true to herself in her going.[4]

Lawrence thought Whitman first broke the old "tight mental allegiance given to a morality which the passional self repudiates." It was not Whitman but Margaret Fuller who did it first.

> It is a great new doctrine. A doctrine of life. A new great morality. A morality of actual living, not of salvation. Europe has never got beyond the morality of salvation. America to this day is deathly sick with saviourism. . . .
>
> It is the American heroic message. The soul is not to pile up defences around herself. She is not to withdraw and seek her heavens inwardly, in mystical ecstasies. She is not to cry to some God beyond, for salvation. She is to go down the open road, as the road opens, into the unknown, keeping company with those whose souls draws them near to her, accomplishing nothing save the journey, and the works incident to the journey, in the long life-travel into the unknown, the soul in her subtle sympathies accomplishing herself by the way.

Margaret Fuller knew all this and lived it. This is why she is quintessentially American, as woman and writer. From Europe she wrote: "With all the abuses of America, we have one advantage which outweighs them all. Most persons reject the privilege, but it is, really, possible for one to grow."[5] It may ultimately be a privilege greater than any other.

Margaret Fuller was in the fullest sense of the word creative. For Goethe the test of creativeness, whether of act or word, lay in its continued power to operate. A quality beyond good and evil, it became manifest especially in a few very gifted persons. "Let the young poet utter what lives and is active in himself, *no matter what form it takes*," he once said.[6] In Fuller as in Goethe, we see in the growing consciousness a perpetual self-creation and re-creation, a perpetual renewal of the sources of life. John Middleton Murry said that Goethe was the first to be aware of the true human place in the realm of nature. He added, "Goethe consciously outgrew the limitations of poetry. He knew, as few of his critics have known, that poetic genius of the highest order is manifest rather in total flexibility and responsiveness of the being to the created world than in the continuous production of poetry."

I am suggesting a way to see the achievement of Margaret Fuller. She did indeed "sing the joy it is to be,—to grow," and she grew by continuously submitting to experience. Thus she saved herself from the ugly consequences of rampant egotism, because her submission required the acknowledgment of greater forces than her own intellect and will. A conscious act of subordination is involved here, or rather a series of them. It can be expressed in some formula or other: "subjective growth through objective experience," perhaps. But to formulize renders this exciting process sterile, futilely abstract, static, and utterly boring. The significance lies, not in the moral of the story, but in the story itself. It is preferable to study Fuller's experience and how she expressed it.

Such a study suggests that her greatest achievement was her apprehension of the meaning of unity. She sought, for example, to reconcile the visible and the invisible, time and the timeless, art and life. She wanted to close the gap between idea and action, between theory and practice, between thought and its incarnation. "A moment of action in one's self . . . is worth an age of apprehension through others; not that our deeds are better, but that they produce *a renewal of our being.*"[7] This Goethean motif, impatience with the life of thought and longing for the life of action, recurs consistently in her letters and journals. It was a mainspring for her life, and because of it she refused to stay imprisoned in intellectuality; she knew the futility of ideas that did not blossom into acts. Nor did she shrink from the consequences of her ideas. In the siege of Rome she saw how the "great ideas" had led to the broken, bleeding bodies carried into her hospital. But she assumed responsibility for her ideas by staying in Rome, by remaining in the midst of battle, by total commitment to the future she believed in.

We have only begun to understand the significance of Margaret Fuller's achievements. She was one of the greatest humanists of her century, one of the greatest America has ever produced. She was easily the equal of her contemporaries, Emerson and Thoreau. Unquestionably her mind was as good as either; her perception of experience was as penetrating and original as theirs; the wisdom she gained in living was as precious, her criticism of society as trenchant and far-seeing. But the conditions of her life were more difficult.

Margaret Fuller dared more and risked more than either Emerson or

Thoreau. More civilized and more fundamentally social than either man, she achieved greater balance as a thinker and human being. She was more honest than Emerson, more compassionate than Thoreau, more loving than either of them. But Fuller has been ignored, while Emerson and Thoreau have been honored and widely read. Few know her writings, while theirs are a staple of education for every American youth with any pretense to literacy. It is not a question of exalting one reputation over another; the competition for fame is not the issue here. No author's greatness is diminished because another is elevated to the galaxy. What is at stake is the opportunity to influence lives, to affect human destinies. The unknown, unread writer is denied this power to change lives, to shape minds, to destroy and create the world.

We stand on a perilous plateau in the history of civilization. The future tugs at us more and more insistently, requiring us to imagine it. Margaret Fuller heard the harmonies of a future she never lived to see. At long last, it appears that America is ready to receive her, to acknowledge her, to try to understand the truths that found expression in her magnificent life and achievement. The exile is coming home.

Notes

Principal works of Fuller cited throughout:

Memoirs of Margaret Fuller Ossoli, ed. Ralph Waldo Emerson, W.H. Channing, and James Freeman Clarke, 2 vols. (Boston, 1852). Cited as *Memoirs*.

Life Without and Life Within, ed. Arthur B. Fuller (Boston, 1860), a miscellany of essays and poems, especially two essays on Goethe and some of her *Tribune* articles.

The *New York Tribune* articles appearing between 7 December 1844 and 1 August 1846. Cited as *Tribune*.

Papers on Literature and Art, 2 parts in 1 vol. (London, 1846). Cited as *Papers on Art*.

At Home and Abroad, ed. Arthur B. Fuller, 2d ed. (Boston, 1856). This volume includes *Summer on the Lakes*, cited as *Summer*, Fuller's *Tribune* articles from Europe, a few letters, and an account of her death.

Woman in the Nineteenth Century, ed. Arthur B. Fuller (Boston, 1855). Paperbound reprint by W.W. Norton, 1971. Citations, as *Woman*, refer to the Norton reprint.

Works listed in the Bibliography are referred to in the Notes by author or brief title only.

Chapter 1

1. Welter, pp. 6–7.
2. Lerner, p. 3.
3. Douglas, p. 58.
4. *Memoirs*, 1:133.
5. Lerner, "The Lady and the Mill Girl: Changes in the Status of Women in the Age of Jackson," in Friedman and Shade, p. 83.

6. Ibid., p. 84; and Ryan, pp. 25–26.

7. Lerner, "Lady and the Mill Girl," pp. 83–84.

8. Ryan, p. 91.

9. Welter, pp. 4–5.

10. Douglas, p. 266.

11. Ibid., p. 269.

12. In the colonial era many women published newspapers, among them Elizabeth Timothy (the *South-Carolina Gazette*, 1739); Cathrine Zenger (the *New York Weekly Journal*, 1746–48); Ann Franklin (the *Newport Mercury*, 1762–63); and Clementina Rind (the *Virginia Gazette*, 1773–74). All these women were printers' widows, continuing the newspapers their husbands had begun. Frank Luther Mott, *American Journalism: A History of Newspapers in the United States Through 250 Years* (New York: Macmillan, 1947), p. 25n. A famous early woman journalist was Anne Royall, whose irascible *Paul Pry* (1831–36) was one of the earliest newspapers in the muckraking tradition. In it she interviewed such noteworthy figures as John Quincy Adams; attacked public corruption; campaigned for the dissolution of church and state; battled for sound money, liberal immigration and tariff laws, free thought, and free speech. She wrote about working women and "fallen" women and befriended them personally. *Paul Pry* had a national circulation and made its author famous, feared, and eventually convicted in court as a common scold. Royall later published *The Huntress*, altogether spending twenty-five years in journalism. Ross, pp. 27–30.

The first woman editor of an important daily paper was Cornelia Walter (the *Boston Transcript*, 1842–47), followed by Jane Grey Swisshelm, editor of the *Pittsburgh Saturday Visiter* [sic] (1848–52). Her letters from Washington to her paper and to the New York *Tribune* earned her distinction as the first woman correspondent from the capital. Lydia Maria Child, a New Englander and friend of Margaret Fuller, edited *The National Anti-Slavery Standard* in the 1840s, and Fanny Wright, with Robert Owen, co-edited the *Free Enquirer* in New York (1829–30).

Before midcentury there was no specifically female reading public for newspapers. Except for James Gordon Bennett, who in his *New York Herald* in the 1830s made a specific appeal to women readers with a weekly fashion article and descriptions of female attire in his Washington and social news, no newspaper tried to capture a female readership by appealing to its interests. Sidney Kobre, *Development of American Journalism* (Dubuque: William C. Brown, 1969), p. 236. In the 1850s, Fanny Fern and Jenny June wrote as women for women, bringing to newspapers and magazines "tears, fashions, recipes and women's problems." Ross, p. 16.

13. Van Deusen, p. 156; Hale, pp. 108, 119, 121.

14. Hale, p. 121.

15. Chevigny, pp. 382, 385, 393–95.

Chapter 2

1. Quoted in Chipperfield, p. 293.

2. *The Correspondence of Emerson and Carlyle*, p. 462, hereafter cited as *Emerson and Carlyle*.

3. James Freeman Clarke made this remark to Thomas Wentworth Higginson. It is quoted in Deiss, p. ix.

4. *The Journals of Ralph Waldo Emerson*, 11:488, hereafter cited as *Journals of Emerson*.

5. *The Letters of Ralph Waldo Emerson*, 4:254, hereafter cited as *Letters of Emerson*. One biographer of Fuller described Emerson's editing: "Emerson modified words from simple to complex, revised sentence structure from spontaneous to ponderous, ignored dates and time sequences, shifted paragraphs from one document to another, and sometimes changed names or misstated the recipients of letters." He deleted suspect material

and ripped masses of pages from her notebooks, and the effect of the *Memoirs* "was distorted, as if Emerson had used tricky mirrors." Deiss, pp. vii–ix. See also Blanchard, pp. 339–40.

6. The fullest description of this stereotype is Welter's, in Chapter 1 of *Dimity Convictions*.

7. *Emerson and Carlyle*, p. 478.

8. *Journals of Ralph Waldo Emerson, 1820–1872*, ed. Emerson and Forbes, 8:250.

9. *Dimity Convictions*, p. 145.

10. Fuller's original essay appeared in the *Tribune*, 1 February 1845. Arthur Fuller's version appeared in *Life Without and Life Within*.

11. Quoted in Miller, *The Raven and the Whale*, p. 325.

12. Gohdes, p. 208.

13. Quoted in Chipperfield, p. 20.

14. Welter argues (p. 177) that Hawthorne hoped Margaret could "dare the fates successfully," and he was disappointed when she fell. (If this is so, however, it would be more logical for Hawthorne to turn his venom on the implacable fates instead of on Margaret.) "In all his 'dark' women [like Zenobia], Hawthorne admires them for trying to be more than the general, just before he condemns them inexorably for having gone too far. . . . His 'blond' heroines, who wore the pearl of innocence rather than the carbuncle of knowledge, keep to their sphere and are rewarded by peaceful lives. Fear that to dare, to risk is the only game which makes life worth living and yet a game the prudent man is afraid to play, may have been responsible for Hawthorne's anger. His frustration was with the gods, who would treat men badly in proportion to their courage, and treat women, so much closer to the center of the divine mystery, the worst of all. . . . Hawthorne hoped she might prove the exception to the decrees of fate in a disordered world, and hated her for proving him right after all." Paula Blanchard remarks: "The 'safe' woman is pallid, pure, and a little stupid; the dark woman is dangerous because she is strong and because she represents what the author would like to suppress in himself" (p. 194).

15. The original passage appears in most editions of Hawthorne's *Italian Notebooks*, as well as in Julian Hawthorne's two-volume *Nathaniel Hawthorne and His Wife*, 1:259–62. A nephew of Margaret rebutted it; see Frederick T. Fuller, "Hawthorne and Margaret Fuller Ossoli." For the modern reassessment of the controversy, see Turner, Cargill, Randel, and Warren.

16. See Hawthorne's *American Notebooks*. Welter (p. 177) thinks too that Hawthorne's letters and diaries show that he was alternately drawn to and repelled by Margaret Fuller. The relationship between Fuller and Hawthorne is discussed in Wade, *Margaret Fuller: Whetstone of Genius*, and in Cargill.

17. Edward Wagenknecht, *Nathaniel Hawthorne: Man and Writer* (New York: Oxford University Press, 1961), p. 147.

18. Blanchard, p. 195.

19. *Journals of Emerson*, 11:503.

20. *Margaret Fuller*, p. 217.

21. Grace Greenwood (Sara Jane Clarke Lippincott), *Haps and Mishaps of a Tour in Europe* (New York, 1854), p. 49.

22. 2:433. For another example of the myth, see Charles Madison, "Margaret Fuller, Transcendental Rebel," *Antioch Review* 2 (1942): 422–38, reprinted in Madison, *Critics and Crusaders*.

23. Welter, p. 180.

24. Ellen Moers ("Madame de Staël and the Woman of Genius," *American Scholar*, Spring 1975, pp. 225–41) describes the impact Corinne had on the imaginations of nineteenth-century women writers.

25. *Memoirs*, 2:55. Perry Miller, one of Fuller's most intelligent and sympathetic modern critics, pointed out some of the parallels between the two women in the introduction to his anthology of Fuller's writings, *Margaret Fuller: American Romantic*.

26. Herold, p. 69.

Chapter 3

1. Emerson was the first to so regard her, when he wrote to Carlyle in 1846 about the arrival in Europe of one of "my luminaries." *Emerson and Carlyle*, p. 407. Others have followed Emerson's view, for example DeMille and Pritchard. In the latter's *Criticism in America*, Fuller is one of several critics discussed in a section entitled "Emerson and His Circle." A random check of standard histories of American literature and American literary criticism shows that Fuller is sometimes given a paragraph as a minor Transcendentalist and sometimes only a passing reference or two. Frequently she is omitted altogether, all of which bears out my assertion that she has been largely ignored as a literary figure.

2. *Letters of Emerson*, 2:32.

3. *Journals of Emerson*, 5:186.

4. *Letters of Emerson*, 2:398. See also his letter of 9 May 1842, 3:53.

5. Although Emerson himself acknowledged his debt to Fuller for introducing him to Goethe, the error long persisted that it was he who introduced her to Goethe. This is an example of the prevailing tendency to reduce Fuller to satellite status. See DeMille, pp. 128ff.

6. Letter of Fuller to Emerson, quoted in *Letters of Emerson*, 2:340.

7. *The Woman and the Myth*, pp. 75–80.

8. *Letters of Emerson*, 2:340.

9. *Memoirs*, 1:291.

10. *Letters of Emerson*, 2:353.

11. *Journals of Emerson*, 8:376.

12. Dall, p. 13.

13. *Letters of Emerson*, 2:352.

14. *Journals of Emerson*, 8:524.

15. *Letters of Emerson*, 2:437.

16. Ibid., 2:353.

17. Ibid., 2:324.

18. Fuller manuscripts in the collection of the Houghton Library, quoted in Warfel, pp. 576–94.

19. Ibid.

20. *Letters of Emerson*, 4:199.

21. Quoted in *Letters of Emerson*, 2:408–9.

22. *The Woman and the Myth*, p. 75. Some interesting light was shed on this triangle with the publication of one of Fuller's journals in which she details a visit to Concord. See Myerson, "Margaret Fuller's 1842 Journal."

23. There was no English translation of the *Vita Nuova* available then. Emerson began reading it in 1839 and told Fuller he thought it would not bear satisfactory translation. See Matthews. Several years later they seem to have discussed the possibility of her translating the work, but then she demurred, saying she felt it presumptuous of herself to translate Dante. Since her Italian was self-taught, she believed her education defective and her intellectual and cultural resources inadequate for such a lofty task. "When I first mentioned it to you," she wrote to Emerson, "it was only as a piece of Sunday work, which I thought of doing for you alone; and because it has never seemed to me you entered enough into the genius of the Italian to apprehend the mind, which has seemed so great to me, and a star unlike, if not higher than all the others in our sky. Else, I should have given you the original, rather than any version of mine." *Memoirs*, 1:240–41. Emerson had no such scruples about his own ability to do justice to the *Vita Nuova* and announced to Fuller in a letter in July 1843 that he had translated the work, with some help in the versification from the poet Ellery Channing, his friend and Fuller's brother-in-law. The translation was never published in Emerson's lifetime. He noted in his journal at that time, "Dante's Vita Nuova reads like the book of Genesis as if written before literature, whilst truth yet existed. A few incidents are sufficient, & are displayed with oriental amplitude & leisure. It is the Bible of Love." *Journals of Emerson*, 8:430. That same year, after one of their meetings at which Fuller gave

him some poems, he wrote: "The conversation turned upon the state & duties of Woman. As always, it was historically considered, & had a certain falseness so. For to me today, Woman is not a degraded person with duties forgotten, but a docile daughter of God with her face heavenward endeavoring to hear the divine word & to convey it to me.

Nuova Vita
Nuovissima Vita

I read again the verses of M. with the new commentary of beautiful anecdotes she had given, freshly in my mind. Of course, the poems grew golden, the twig blossomed in my hands: but a poem should not need its relation to life to explain it; it should be a new life, not still half engaged in the soil like the new created lions in Eden." *Journals of Emerson*, 8:372. Again in 1843 Emerson entered in his journal a long and impassioned eulogy of Margaret Fuller. He finds no one to compare with her except goddesses of old and concludes: "Her experience contains, I know, golden moments, which, if they could be fitly narrated, would stand equally besides any histories of magnanimity which the world contains; and whilst Dante's 'Nuova Vita' is almost unique in the literature of sentiment, I have called the imperfect record she gave me of two of her days, "Nuovissima Vita.'" *Journals of Emerson*, 8:369.

24. "Dialogue, Aglauron and Laurie," *Dial* 4, no. 4, reprinted in *Papers on Art*, Part 1, pp. 151–64.

25. Ibid., pp. 156, 155.

26. *Memoirs*, 2:68.

27. *Letters of Emerson*, 3:20.

28. *Tribune*, 30 August 1845.

29. Ibid., 1 August 1846.

30. *Letters of Emerson*, 3:401.

31. Ibid., 4:28.

32. *Memoirs*, 1:281.

33. *At Home and Abroad*, pp. 435–36.

34. Manuscript letter in the Houghton collection, quoted in Brown, p. 108.

35. *Journals of Emerson*, 11:256, 258.

36. *Emerson and Carlyle*, p. 462.

37. *Letters of Emerson*, 4:222.

38. Ibid., 4:330.

39. Letter from Fuller to Emerson, 17 November 1844, quoted in *Letters of Emerson*, 3:270.

40. *Journals of Ralph Waldo Emerson 1820–1872*, ed. Emerson and Forbes, 8:249–50.

41. *Journals of Emerson*, 11:471; *Memoirs*, 1:264, 294.

42. *Letters of Emerson*, 2:197. The other letters quoted in this paragraph are in 2:281, 378, 436, 464; and 3:62, respectively.

43. Emerson is not the only one whose recorded comments on her work are so contradictory. James Clarke praised her work lavishly in his letters to her but deprecated it in his section of the *Memoirs*. Henry James said in his biography *Hawthorne* that her work had "extreme beauty" and "real interest," but in his *William Wetmore Story and His Friends* he asserted that "her written utterance [was] naught."

44. *Letters of Emerson*, 4:230.

45. *Journals of Emerson*, 7:48.

46. Ibid., 8:381.

47. Ibid., 8:149–50.

48. Ibid., 9:148.

49. Ibid., 9:108.

50. "Woman," *Miscellanies*, pp. 339, 340, 348. The following two quotations are from pp. 343–44.

51. *Memoirs*, 1:321–22.

52. For example, *Journals of Emerson*, 9:107, 115, 164; and 8:391.

53. *Journals of Emerson*, 7:400.

54. *On Literature,* in *Madame de Staël,* trans. and ed. Morroe Berger, p. 219.
55. *Letters of Emerson,* 3:442–43.
56. Quoted in Rusk, p. 343.
57. *Letters of Emerson,* 3:54.
58. *Memoirs,* 1:236.
59. Ibid., 1:234.
60. *Letters of Emerson,* 2:336.
61. *Memoirs,* 2:67.
62. *Journals of Emerson,* 8:238.
63. Manuscript journal, quoted in Warfel, p. 593.
64. *Memoirs,* 1:237.
65. Ibid., 2:68.
66. Quoted in Chipperfield, p. 217.
67. *Memoirs,* 1:195 and 2:69.
68. Ibid., 2:67.

Chapter 4

1. Goethe, "Ein Wort für Junge Dichter," quoted in Murry, p. 250.
2. The connections between the Transcendentalists and Germany have been thoroughly explored in such studies as Pochmann's, Vogel's, and Miller, *The Transcendentalists, An Anthology.*
3. Pochmann's study is the most thorough and the best existing study so far of Fuller's connections with German writers. Braun, *Margaret Fuller and Goethe,* is good but needs updating.
4. The quotations in this paragraph are from *Memoirs,* 1:119, 117.
5. 11 October 1828, in *Conversations of Goethe with Eckermann,* hereafter cited as *Eckermann.* The Oxenford translation, which became the standard English-language version of this classic, was based on Fuller's translation, which appeared in 1839. Both Oxenford's and Fuller's translations are long out of print.
6. Quoted in Murry, pp. 245–46. Madame de Staël noted this response too: "L'admiration pour Goethe est une espèce de confrérie dont let mots de ralliement servent à faire connoitre les adeptes les uns aux autres. Quand les étrangers veulent aussi l'admirer, ils sont rejetés avec dedain. . . . Un homme ne peut exciter un tel fanatisme sans avoir de grandes facultés pour le bien et pour le mal; car il n'y a que la puissance, dans quelque genre que ce soit, que les hommes craignent assez pour l'aimer de cette manière." *De L'Allemagne,* part 2, chapter 7.
7. Vogel, p. 90. The phrase appears in a letter from Emerson to Carlyle in 1834.
8. *Memoirs,* 1:242.
9. *Complete Works of Ralph Waldo Emerson,* Centenary edition, (Boston: Houghton Mifflin, 1904), vol. 12, *Natural History of Intellect,* pp. 331, 326.
10. Ibid., pp. 331–32.
11. Ibid., p. 332.
12. *Representative Men,* p. 261.
13. Ibid., p. 266.
14. This comparative evaluation was made by Vogel, pp. 100–101.
15. For example, William Ellery Channing, Andrews Norton, James Marsh, Samson Reed, George Ripley, Emerson, Orestes Brownson, F.H. Hedge, Theodore Parker, James Freeman Clarke, John Sullivan Dwight. Poet Christopher Cranch was once a divinity school student too, but eventually he went to Italy and became a hedonist.
16. For a discussion of women and religion in nineteenth-century America, see Douglas and Welter.
17. "New Year's Day," *Tribune,* 1 January 1845.
18. James, *Literary Reviews and Essays,* p. 271.

19. *De L'Allemagne*, part 2, chapter 13.
20. *Eckermann*, 31 January 1827.
21. *Woman*, p. 129.
22. Ibid., p. 128.
23. Ibid., p. 130.
24. *Memoirs*, 1:133–34. One modern scholar of Transcendentalism states that though the literary source of "self-culture" was Goethe, the ideal was also a legacy of Unitarianism, as interpreted by Dr. Channing, who thought that self-cultivation was "the quintessence of the Unitarian principle that religion consists chiefly in the improvement of the character." Buell, p. 90. If this is so, then the rejection of the ideal by Clarke, himself a Unitarian minister, is all the more difficult to understand.
25. *Memoirs*, 1:133–34.
26. Ibid., 1:222.
27. *Truth and Fiction Relating to My Life*, 2:423.
28. *Eckermann*, 2 March 1831.
29. "Goethe," *Life Without and Life Within*, p. 32; *Journals of Emerson*, 11:477.
30. *Memoirs*, 1:225–26.
31. "Clairvoyance: Seeress of Prevorst," *Tribune*, 23 July 1845. See also "The New Science, or the Philosophy of Mesmerism or Animal Magnetism," *Life Without and Life Within*, pp. 169–73.
32. *Eckermann*, 13 February 1829.
33. Hochfield, p. xvii.
34. *Eckermann*, 17 February 1831.
35. Ibid., 6 March 1831.
36. "Goethe," *Life Without and Life Within*, p. 35.
37. Rose, p. 170.
38. The second part of Wilhelm's story, the *Wanderjahre*, has structural problems for the reader. Goethe wrote a first version of the *Wanderjahre*, calling it Part One on publication in 1821, but he did not finish it until the last years of his life. The *Wanderjahre* was a pastiche when it finally appeared in this second version in 1829: on the thread of Wilhelm's travels were hung a series of episodes, tales, and aphorisms. Friedenthal, p. 357. The English-speaking world knew the story of Wilhelm chiefly through Carlyle's translation, and he translated only the first, earlier version of the *Wanderjahre*, not the second. Neither the first nor the second version is now in print in English translation. Fuller had read the longer version of the *Wanderjahre*, especially admiring the character of Macaria, and she insisted that the meaning of Wilhelm Meister's education and development was incomplete if taken from the *Lehrjahre* alone without reference to the *Wanderjahre*.
39. Viëtor, *Goethe the Poet*.
40. For this illuminating comparison I am indebted to Karl Viëtor's discussion, *Goethe the Poet*, pp. 118–19.
41. *Journals of Emerson*, 5:407.
42. See the extensive definition of humanism in Chapter 1 of Paul Fussell, *The Rhetorical World of Augustan Humanism* (London: Oxford University Press, 1965).
43. *Summer*, p. 101.
44. Quoted in Braun, *Margaret Fuller and Goethe*, pp. 80–81.
45. Quoted in Viëtor, *Goethe the Poet*, p. 73.
46. *Memoirs*, 1:287.
47. Viëtor, *Goethe the Poet*, p. 76.
48. Quoted in Viëtor, *Goethe the Poet*, p. 76.

Chapter 5

1. *Hawthorne*, p. 62.
2. *Letters*, 1:445.
3. Ibid., 2:59. See also 1:459–60.

4. *William Wetmore Story and His Friends*, 1:127–28.

5. Frothingham, p. 300.

6. *Memoirs*, 1:294.

7. Ibid., 1:263–64. Though Emerson's judgments of Fuller today seem insufferably condescending and superficial, they continue to dominate the thinking of most contemporary scholars and critics. See, for example, Buell, pp. 145–46.

8. *Memoirs*, 1:78.

9. Ibid., 1:94.

10. *Hawthorne*, p. 62.

11. Ibid.

12. Quoted in Pritchard, p. 68.

13. *Memoirs*, 1:107.

14. Ibid., 1:295–96.

15. Ibid., 1:296.

16. "The Literati of New York City," pp. 81–82. The following two quotations in this paragraph are on pp. 82 and 79, respectively.

17. *Memoirs*, 1:128.

18. Ibid., 1:295.

19. Ibid., 1:125.

20. Ibid., 1:189.

21. Ibid., 1:297.

22. Ibid., 2:36–37.

23. Ibid., 1:295.

24. Ibid., 1:73.

25. Ibid., 2:138.

26. Larousse, quoted in *French Symbolist Poetry*, trans. C.F. MacIntyre (Berkeley and Los Angeles: University of California Press, 1964), p. vi.

27. *Memoirs*, 2:138.

28. Letter to Paul Demeny, in *Rimbaud: Complete Works, Selected Letters*, trans. Wallace Fowlie (Chicago: University of Chicago Press, 1966), p. 309.

29. *A Room of One's Own*, p. 80.

30. *Memoirs*, 2:138.

31. Ibid., 1:295.

32. *Letters of Emerson*, 2:202.

33. "Swedenborg and His Disciples," *Tribune*, 7 July 1845.

34. *Memoirs*, 1:296.

35. Ibid., 2:164.

36. Ibid., 2:8.

37. "First of January, 1846," *Tribune*, 1 January 1846.

38. Review of Raumer's *America and the American People*, *Tribune*, 4 December 1845.

39. Review of Mrs. Sigourney's *Scenes in My Native Land*, *Tribune*, 28 January 1845.

40. *At Home and Abroad*, p. 207.

41. *Margaret Fuller*, pp. 84, 42.

42. See, for only a few examples, Letter 5 of the series she sent to the *Tribune* from Europe; Chapter 1 of *Summer; Memoirs*, 1:198, 2:97, and 2:333. She once told Emerson that in the woods she did not think, but that she "finds herself expressed." Quoted in Hawthorne, *The American Notebooks* (Columbus: Ohio State University Press, 1972), pp. 605–6.

43. *At Home and Abroad*, p. 183.

44. "The Literati of New York City," p. 79. See also Poe, "About Critics and Criticism," p. 195.

Chapter 6

1. "A Short Essay on Critics," *Papers on Art*, part 1. p. 4.

2. "Lowell's 'Conversations on Some of the Old Poets,'" *Tribune*, 21 January 1845.

3. Among them Goddard, 1:343; Barbour, p. 618. There are several good studies of Fuller's criticism, for example, Durning, *Margaret Fuller, Citizen of the World;* Ebbitt; and McMaster. The most extensive so far is Golemba's "The Balanced View in Margaret Fuller's Literary Criticism."

4. "A Record of Impressions Produced by the Exhibition of Mr. Allston's Pictures," *Papers on Art*, part 2, pp. 110–11. These remarks anticipate similar ones later by Hawthorne in *The Marble Faun* and Henry James in his biography of Hawthorne.

5. "Canova," *Dial*, 3:454.

6. "Entertainments of the Past Winter," *Dial*, 3:48–50.

7. "Lowell's 'Conversations,' " *Tribune*, 21 January 1845.

8. "Ole Bull," *Tribune*, 20 December 1844. Fuller sometimes sounded like a schoolmistress talking to mischievous children: "The frequent rudeness of talking during the finest [musical] performance, has shown that no small part of the audience were regardless of the divine expressions of thought they thus insulted, no less than of the feelings of those who might have enjoyed them, but for the neighborhood of these intruders. It ought to be understood that half a dollar buys a seat, and the privilege of hearing, but not that of making the same useless to all around. Strange, strange, that it should be necessary to say such things! Das versteht sich: that is understood of itself, say the Germans." *Dial*, 3:533.

9. "Entertainments of the Past Winter," *Dial*, 3:60.

10. Ibid., p. 46. The following quotation is on the same page.

11. "Gesta Romanorum," *Tribune*, 31 May 1845.

12. "On Didactic Poetry," *Goethe's Literary Essays*, p. 130.

13. Smith, pp. 37–38.

14. "Impressions of Allston's Pictures," *Papers on Art*, part 2, p. 110. See also "A Dialogue: Poet, Critic," *Papers on Art*, part 1.

15. "A Dialogue: Poet, Critic," *Papers on Art*, part 1, p. 13.

16. *Memoirs*, 1:113.

17. "Poets of the People," *Papers on Art*, part 2, p. 2.

18. "English Writers Little Known Here," *Tribune*, 4 March 1845.

19. "The Balanced View."

20. "American Literature," *Papers on Art*, part 2, pp. 132, 128.

21. *French Poets and Novelists*, p. 114.

22. "Goethe," *Life Without and Life Within*, p. 48. The two following quotations are on pp. 50–51.

23. Ebbitt also takes these works as a focal point for a discussion of Fuller's moralistic critical standards and concludes that the fusion of the esthetic and the spiritual in Fuller's criticism is never quite accomplished.

24. "Supplement to Aristotle's Poetics," *Goethe's Literary Essays*, p. 107.

25. "The Magnolia of Lake Ponchartrain," *Life Without and Life Within*, p. 330.

26. *Papers on Art*, part 2, p. 2.

27. "American Literature," *Papers on Art*, part 2, pp. 150–51.

28. "Headlong Hall," *Tribune*, 12 May 1845.

29. "Francisco de Noronha," *Tribune*, 9 May 1846.

30. "Life of Beethoven," *Tribune*, 7 February 1845.

31. "Modern Drama," *Papers on Art*, part 1, p. 104.

32. "The Two Herberts," *Papers on Art*, part 1, p. 33.

33. "Lives of the Great Composers," *Papers on Art*, part 2, p. 88.

34. "Goethe," *Life Without and Life Within*, p. 46.

35. For an extensive account of Fuller's role as author-editor, see Cooke.

36. *Memoirs*, 2:7.

37. "Entertainments of the Past Winter," *Dial*, 3:48. See also "Modern Drama," *Papers on Art*, part 1.

38. "American Literature," *Papers on Art*, part 2, p. 124. The following quotation is from the same source, same page. See also "Italy," *Tribune*, 13 November 1845.

39. "Italy," *Tribune*, 13 November 1845. The quotation in the following paragraph is from the same source.

40. "Mr. Hosmer's Poems," *Tribune*, 11 December 1844.
41. "American Literature, *Papers on Art*, part 2, p. 129.
42. "Emerson's Essays," *Tribune*, 7 November 1844.
43. "Poets of the People," *Papers on Art*, part 2, p. 4.
44. "American Literature," *Papers on Art*, part 2, p. 126.
45. Ibid., p. 140.
46. *Eckermann*, 4 January 1827.
47. "American Literature," *Papers on Art*, part 2, p. 142.

Chapter 7

1. Quoted in Ruland, p. 212.
2. *Papers on Art*, part 2, pp. 2–4, my italics in the last paragraph.
3. It appears in *Wilhelm Meisters Lehrjahre*, book 5, chapter 4, in a discussion of dramatic art: "The artist was required to present his guests with silver apples in platters of silver," and again in *Eckermann*, 22 October 1828, in this interesting variation: "Women are silver dishes into which we put golden apples."
4. "A Short Essay on Critics," *Papers on Art*, part 1, p. 7.
5. Lawrence in *Studies in Classic American Literature* (1923), Williams in *In the American Grain* (1933), and Rourke in *The Roots of American Culture* (1942).
6. Golemba's "The Balanced View" contains a more detailed discussion of Fuller's concept of a golden age.
7. "Poets of the People," *Papers on Art*, part 2, p. 4.
8. Preface to *Philosophical Miscellanies*, quoted in Ruland, p. 275.
9. *Papers on Art*, part 2, p. 10. The following quotation is on p. 17.
10. "Modern Drama," *Papers on Art*, part 1, pp. 103–4.
11. "American Literature," *Papers on Art*, part 2, pp. 151–52.
12. This was observed by Stuart Sherman: see Foerster, *Toward Standards*, p. 87. V.L. Parrington is another example of the running-river school of critics.
13. "American Literature," *Papers on Art*, part 2, p. 151; "A Short Essay on Critics," *Papers on Art*, part 1, p. 3.
14. *Papers on Art*, part 2, p. 47. The following quoted passages are on pp. 48, 106–7, 70–71, and 46, respectively.
15. *Memoirs*, 2:58.
16. For example, by McMaster; Miller, *Margaret Fuller: American Romantic;* and Parrington, 2:426–34.
17. Smith, pp. 31–32, 66.
18. Pritchard, pp. 63–64, has noted the fusion of romantic theory with classical principles in Fuller's criticism, but he has not explored their implications.
19. "Philip van Artevelde," *Life Without and Life Within*, pp. 127–40.
20. "Charles Anton's 'A System of Latin Versification,' " *Tribune*, 12 May 1845.
21. "Lanman's 'Letters from a Landscape Painter,' " *Tribune*, 18 January 1845.
22. "Browning's Poems," *Papers on Art*, part 2, p. 31.
23. "Modern Drama," *Papers on Art*, part 1, p. 101.
24. "Lowell's 'Conversations,' " *Tribune*, 21 January 1845.
25. "Charles Anton's 'A System,' " *Tribune*, 12 May 1845, my italics in the last sentence.
26. "Miss Barrett's Poems," *Papers on Art*, part 2, p. 29.
27. "Noted on Dilettantism," *Goethe's Literary Essays*, p. 76, and *De La Littérature*, part 1, chapter 12.
28. Glicksberg, p. 57.
29. Golemba, "The Balanced View."
30. "Prose Works of Milton," *Papers on Art*, part 1, p. 38.

Chapter 8

1. *Memoirs*, 1:149.
2. Ibid., 2:58.
3. For these paragraphs on nineteenth-century America, I have used standard historical studies, such as Furnas, Handlin, Morison, and others.
4. The Fuller manuscripts in the Houghton Library contain copious notes about Jefferson recorded in her journals. See also *Memoirs*, 1:124, 149.
5. From the Fuller manuscripts, volume 2, by permission of the Harvard College Library.
6. *Memoirs*, 2:29.
7. Golemba, *George Ripley*, p. 69. Golemba's account of Brook Farm in chapters 3 and 4 gives a good overview of this enterprise.
8. *Memoirs*, 2:73. The two following quotations appear on pp. 28 and 58–59.
9. "Books of Travel," *Tribune*, 18 December 1845.
10. *Hawthorne*, p. 66.
11. Golemba, *George Ripley*, pp. 81–82.
12. *Harriet Martineau's Autobiography*, 1:381.
13. *The Woman and the Myth*, p. 213. See also Higginson, p. 129.
14. "Farewell," *Life Without and Life Within*, p. 355.
15. The most notable of these are: Review of the *Life of Frederick Douglass*, 10 June 1845; "Cassius M. Clay," 14 January 1845; "First of August [1845]"; and the ironic fable about racism in America, "What Fits a Man to Be a Voter?" 31 March 1846, all reprinted in *Life Without and Life Within*. For a lengthier discussion of Fuller and the Abolition movement, see Kearns.
16. Quoted in *Letters of Emerson*, 2:280.
17. At least one scholar of Transcendentalism thought Thoreau's *A Week* received its impetus from Fuller's *Summer* (Miller, *Margaret Fuller, American Romantic*, p. 116). A more recent study of literary Transcendentalism dismissed *Summer* as "a concoction of gossip, preachment, platonic dialogue, and Indian lore." Buell, p. 204. Elsewhere in his study (pp. 189 ff.) Buell outlined the reasons for the popularity of travel writing in nineteenth-century America, which helps to explain why books like Fuller's and Thoreau's were well received.
18. *Summer*, p. 101. The five following quotations are on pp. 62, 61, 65, 99, and 96.
19. "Thomas L. McKenney's *Memoirs*," *Tribune*, 8 July 1846.
20. "United States Exploring Expedition," *Life Without and Life Within*, p. 142.
21. "McKenney's *Memoirs*," *Tribune*, 8 July 1846.
22. "Frederick Douglass," *Life Without and Life Within*, p. 123.
23. "Schoolcraft's *Oneota, or Red Races of America*," *Tribune*, 12 February 1845.
24. "McKenney's *Memoirs*," *Tribune*, 8 July 1846.
25. *Summer*, p. 49. The following quotations are on pp. 62, 100, 99, 112, 35, 10, 14, 34–35, 21, 5, 21, and 30, respectively.
26. "Mrs. Sigourney's *Scenes in My Native Land*," *Tribune*, 28 January 1845. The following two quotations are from the same source.
27. *Summer*, p. 7. The following two quotations are on p. 62.
28. Van Deusen, p. 149.
29. "Christian Dancing, Hunting, Angling," *Tribune*, 16 May 1846.
30. *Summer*, p. 45. The following quotation is on p. 14.
31. "Fourth of July," *Tribune*, 4 July 1845.
32. "The Rich Man," *Life Without and Life Within*, p. 287.
33. "The Poor Man," *Life Without and Life Within*, pp. 301–2.
34. "St. Valentine's Day—Bloomingdale Asylum for Insane," *Tribune*, 22 February 1845.
35. "The Irish Character," *Tribune*, 24 July 1845.
36. "Farewell to New York City," *Tribune*, 1 August 1846.
37. In *Life Without and Life Within*, p. 212. The following quotation is on p. 213.
38. "The Celestial Empire," *Life Without and Life Within*, p. 307.

39. "New Year's Day," *Tribune*, 1 January 1845.
40. "American Facts," *Tribune*, 19 May 1845.
41. "First of January 1846," *Tribune*, 1 January 1846.
42. "Victory—On Schiller's Ode to Joy," *Tribune*, 21 May 1846.
43. "Lives of the Great Composers," *Papers on Art*, part 2, p. 99.
44. "Headley's *Napoleon and His Marshals*," *Tribune*, 1 May 1846. The following quotation is from the same source.
45. "First of January 1846," *Tribune*, 1 January 1846.
46. "New Year's Day," *Tribune*, 1 January 1845.
47. "J.A. King's *Twenty-Four Years in Argentine*," *Tribune*, 5 June 1846.

Chapter 9

1. *Memoirs*, 1:229.
2. "Medical Miscellany," *The Boston Medical and Surgical Journal* (15 December 1841): 311; reprinted in *Victorian Poetry* 11 (Summer 1973): 172.
3. *Memoirs*, 1:135.
4. Crow, p. 149.
5. P. 37.
6. Flexner, pp. 23, 30.
7. *Society in America*, 2, part 3, p. 229.
8. *Memoirs*, 1:95.
9. Ibid., 2:21.
10. *Letters from New York* (1843), quoted in Parker, p. 91.
11. *Society in America*, 2, part 3, p. 227.
12. *Memoirs*, 1:98. The two following quotations are on pp. 98–99.
13. *Woman*, p. 41.
14. *Memoirs*, 1:195.
15. Ibid., 1:235.
16. *Society in America*, 2, part 3, p. 228.
17. Ibid., p. 259.
18. Welter, p. 146.
19. Flexner, p. 68.
20. Ibid., p. 82.
21. *Woman*, p. 172. The following five quotations are on pp. 43, 40, 116, 117, and 37.
22. "Mrs. Jameson's *Memoirs*," *Tribune*, 24 July 1846.
23. *Woman*, p. 172.
24. *Memoirs*, 2:138.
25. *Woman*, p. 174.
26. Quoted in Higginson, p. 112.
27. *Woman*, p. 177.
28. Ibid., p. 121.
29. Crow, p. 41.
30. *Woman*, p. 150.
31. Welter, p. 184.
32. *Woman*, p. 77.
33. *Journals of Emerson*, 8:95.
34. Welter, p. 146.
35. *Woman*, p. 109. The following four quotations are on pp. 19, 118, 173, and 174.
36. Quoted in the New York *Tribune*, 12 February 1845.
37. Quoted in Hope Stoddard, p. 188.
38. Ibid., p. 187.
39. p. 537.
40. Parrington, 2:427.

41. "The Literati of New York City," pp. 74–75.
42. Barbour, pp. 623–25.
43. Ibid., p. 623.
44. Quoted in Julian Hawthorne, 1:257.
45. Ibid., 1:258.
46. *Memoirs*, 2:135.
47. For an extensive examination of women authors in nineteenth-century America, see Douglas.
48. Showalter, p. 332.
49. Ibid., p. 330.
50. Pritchard, p. 103.
51. Ibid., p. 104.
52. Showalter, p. 333.
53. Barbour, p. 623.
54. *Harriet Martineau's Autobiography*, 1:518.
55. Ibid., 1:382–83.
56. H.L. Stoddard, p. 98.
57. Wade, *Margaret Fuller: Whetstone of Genius*, pp. 91, 93.
58. *The Writings of Margaret Fuller*, ed. Mason Wade, p. 587.
59. *Life Without and Life Within*, p. 349.
60. *Woman*, p. 63.
61. *Memoirs*, 2:136.

Chapter 10

1. *Memoirs*, 2:184.
2. *At Home and Abroad*, p. 193.
3. Ibid., p. 171.
4. Ibid., p. 170.
5. *Memoirs*, 2:205.
6. Ibid., 2:220.
7. Priscilla Robertson, pp. 312–13.
8. *Memoirs*, 2:211.
9. *At Home and Abroad*, pp. 425–26.
10. *Roba di Roma*, quoted in Deiss, p. 48.
11. Harvard manuscript, quoted in Deiss, p. 5.
12. *Wilhelm Meister*, book 8, chapter 7.
13. *At Home and Abroad*, p. 426.
14. For the accounts in this chapter of Italian political life, I have drawn on these sources: Barr, Deiss, Griffith, Hall and Davis, Hibbert, Langer, Priscilla Robertson, Thomson, Janet P. Trevelyan, and Fuller's *Tribune* dispatches and letters from Europe.
15. *At Home and Abroad*, p. 240.
16. Ibid., p. 243.
17. Priscilla Robertson, p. 366.
18. Griffith, pp. 64–70.
19. Ibid., pp. 67–68, 79.
20. *Memoirs*, 2:173.
21. *At Home and Abroad*, pp. 365, 367.
22. See Deiss's biography for an extensive account of Ossoli and his family.
23. P. 88.
24. *Memoirs*, 2:207. For details of the Fuller-Mickiewicz friendship, see Wellisz.
25. Letter 18, *At Home and Abroad*, pp. 250–56.
26. *At Home and Abroad*, p. 264.
27. *Memoirs*, 2:226.

28. *At Home and Abroad*, p. 284.
29. Ibid., p. 321.
30. Ibid., p. 309.
31. Most Americans in Italy in the mid-nineteenth century "found themselves recoiling before a new Europe in the making below its restoration structure, and they were affected by profound shock and surprise when the revolutionary Europe of 1848–1849 burst in their faces. . . . The American intelligence and conscience of the Emersonian era found themselves pursuing the myths and ghosts of the European past and the fictions and masks of the European present. . . . that response had ensued from the subtle cultural dialectic that during the nineteenth century had strangely tended to pit a fixed American consciousness of Italy against a series of moving, changing realities in contemporary American, European, and Italian history. . . . All of the outstanding and active leaders of the Italian national revolution—Gioberti no less than Mazzini, Carlo Cattaneo no less than Cavour—were in fundamental agreement that the *Risorgimento* had to destroy a great part of the foundations and structure of the classic order of things in Italy. Even those among the early and later 'passionate pilgrims' to Italy, like Cooper, Washington Irving, Ticknor, Hawthorne, and [Charles Eliot] Norton himself before 1860, who enjoyed the company and confidences of either the conservative or the liberal ruling classes or both, of either the moderate-radical or the revolutionary Italian elites, only vaguely and sentimentally or momentarily and reluctantly attempted to comprehend this. Fuller had been the shining exception: her friendship with Mazzini had not remained a mere emotional experience; rather, it had become an intellectual bridge leading from 'talk to life,' from contemplation to commitment, from sentimental experience to sustained action." Salomone, pp. 1373, 1364, 1378.
32. *At Home and Abroad*, p. 344. The following five quotations are on pp. 187, 205, 305–6, 320, and 425.
33. *Memoirs*, 2:235, 238.
34. Quoted in Griffith, p. 220.
35. *Memoirs*, 2:227.
36. *At Home and Abroad*, pp. 326–27.
37. Ibid., p. 389.
38. Ibid., p. 375.
39. *Memoirs*, 2:223.
40. *At Home and Abroad*, p. 343.
41. Ibid., p. 437.
42. *Memoirs*, 2:269–70.
43. *At Home and Abroad*, p. 415.
44. Ibid., p. 418.
45. *Memoirs*, 2:333.
46. Letter to Caroline Sturgis Tappan, quoted in Deiss, p. 297.
47. *Memoirs*, 2:267.
48. Ibid., 2:302.
49. Priscilla Robertson, p. 419.
50. Chevigny, p. 390.
51. Quoted in James, *William Wetmore Story*, 1:130.

Chapter 11

1. Address to the International Council of Women, 1888, quoted in Schneir, p. v.
2. Undated manuscript letter, quoted in Durning, *Margaret Fuller*, p. 138.
3. *Memoirs*, 2:337. The following quotations are in 1:341, 1:342, and 1:133.
4. *Studies in Classic American Literature*, p. 172. The following two quotations are on pp. 171 and 172–73.
5. Manuscript notebook, quoted in Higginson, p. 224.
6. Quoted in Murry, p. 250, my italics. The following quotation is on pp. 257–58.
7. *Memoirs*, 1:31, my italics.

Bibliography

Alcott, A.B. *The Journals of Bronson Alcott.* Edited by Odell Shepard. 2 vols. Boston: Little, Brown, 1938.
Anthony, Katherine. *Margaret Fuller: A Psychological Biography.* New York: Harcourt, Brace and Howe, 1920.
Barbour, Frances M. "Margaret Fuller and the British Reviewers." *New England Quarterly* 9 (1936): 618–25.
Barr, Eileen S. "Margaret Fuller D'Ossoli." *Western Humanities Review* 6 (1951–52): 37–52.
Barr, Stringfellow. *Mazzini: Portrait of an Exile.* New York: Henry Holt, 1935.
Bell, Margaret. *Margaret Fuller.* New York: C. Boni, 1930.
Berger, Morroe, ed. *Madame de Staël.* New York: Doubleday, 1965.
Berkeley, George Fitz-Hardinge. *Italy in the Making: June 1846 to 1 January 1848.* 2 vols. Cambridge, England: University Press, 1932, 1936.
Berry, Edward G. "Margaret Fuller Ossoli, 1810–1850." *Dalhousie Review* 30 (1951): 369–76.
Blanchard, Paula. *Margaret Fuller.* New York: Delacorte/Seymour Lawrence, 1978.
Blankenship, Russell. *American Literature as an Expression of the National Mind.* New York: Henry Holt, 1949.
Bradford, Gamaliel. "Margaret Fuller Ossoli." In *Portraits of American Women.* Boston: Houghton Mifflin, 1919, pp. 133–63.
Braun, Frederick A. *Margaret Fuller and Goethe.* New York: Henry Holt, 1910.
———. "Margaret Fuller's Translation and Criticism of Goethe's *Tasso.*" *Journal of English and Germanic Philology* 13 (1914): 210–13.
Brooks, Van Wyck. *The Dream of Arcadia.* New York: Dutton, 1958.
———. *The Flowering of New England.* New York: Dutton, 1936.
Brown, Arthur W. *Margaret Fuller.* New York: Twayne, 1964.
Browning, Elizabeth Barrett *Letters.* Edited by F.G. Kenyon. 2 vols. New York: Macmillan, 1897.
Buell, Lawrence. *Literary Transcendentalism.* Ithaca: Cornell University Press, 1973.
Cargill, Oscar. "Nemesis and Nathaniel Hawthorne." *Publications of the Modern Language Association* 52 (1937): 848–62.
Carlyle, Thomas. "Goethe" and "Goethe's Works." In *Critical and Miscellaneous Essays.* Philadelphia: A. Hart, 1853, pp. 79–94 and 345–65.
———. *Letters of Thomas Carlyle.* Edited by Alexander Carlyle. New York: F.A. Stokes, 1923.
Carpenter, Richard V. "Margaret Fuller in Northern Illinois." *Journal of the Illinois State Historical Society* 2 (1910): 7–22.

Bibliography

Cassirer, Ernst. *The Myth of the State.* New Haven: Yale University Press, 1946.

Chevigny, Bell Gale. *The Woman and the Myth: Margaret Fuller's Life and Writings.* Old Westbury, N.Y.: Feminist Press, 1976.

Chipperfield, Faith. *In Quest of Love.* New York: Coward-McCann, 1957.

Clarke, James Freeman. *Autobiography.* Boston: Houghton Mifflin, 1892.

———. *The Letters of James Freeman Clarke to Margaret Fuller.* Hamburg: Cram, de Gruyter and Co., 1957.

Clough, Shepard B. and Salvatore Saladino. *A History of Modern Italy.* New York: Columbia University Press, 1968.

Colville, Derek. "The Transcendental Friends: Clarke and Margaret Fuller." *New England Quarterly* 30 (September 1957): 378–82.

Conrad, Susan Phinney. *Perish the Thought: Intellectual Women in Romantic America, 1830–1860.* New York: Oxford University Press, 1976.

Cooke, George Willis. *A Historical and Biographical Introduction to the Dial.* Cleveland: The Rowfant Club, 1902.

Crow, Duncan. *The Victorian Woman.* New York: Stein and Day, 1972.

Dall, Caroline Healey. *Margaret and Her Friends.* Boston: Roberts Bros., 1895.

Deirdre, Kathleen. "Margaret Fuller d'Ossoli: Modern American Humanist." Ph.D. Dissertation, University of Minnesota, 1975.

Deiss, Joseph Jay. *The Roman Years of Margaret Fuller.* New York: Crowell, 1969.

DeMille, George E. *Literary Criticism in America.* New York: Dial Press, 1931.

Douglas, Ann. *The Feminization of American Culture.* New York: Knopf, 1977.

Durning, Russell E. *Margaret Fuller: Citizen of the World.* Heidelberg: Carl Winter, Universitätsverlag, 1969.

———. "Margaret Fuller's Translation of Goethe's 'Prometheus.'" *Jahrbuch für Amerikastudien* 12 (1967): 240–45.

Ebbitt, Wilma R. "Margaret Fuller's Ideas on Criticism." *Boston Public Library Quarterly* 3 (July 1951): 171–87.

Eliot, George. Review of Fuller's *Memoirs.* In *Westminster Review* 57 (1852): 665–66.

———. *The George Eliot Letters.* Edited by Gordon S. Haight. 7 vols. New Haven: Yale University Press, 1954–55.

Emerson, Ralph Waldo. *The Journals of Ralph Waldo Emerson.* Edited by William H. Gilman, Alfred R. Ferguson, et al. 14 vols. Cambridge: Harvard University Press, 1960–1978.

———. *Journals of Ralph Waldo Emerson, 1820–1872.* Edited by Edward Waldo Emerson and Waldo Emerson Forbes. 10 vols. Boston: Houghton Mifflin, 1910–14.

———. *The Letters of Ralph Waldo Emerson.* Edited by Ralph L. Rusk. 6 vols. New York: Columbia University Press, 1939.

———. *Miscellanies.* Boston: Houghton Mifflin, 1884.

———. *Representative Men.* Philadelphia, 1906.

——— and Thomas Carlyle. *The Correspondence of Emerson and Carlyle.* Edited by Joseph Slater. New York: Columbia University Press, 1964.

Fehrenbacher, Don. *The Era of Expansion: 1800–1848.* New York: John Wiley, 1969.

Flexner, Eleanor. *A Century of Struggle.* Cambridge, Mass.: Belknap Press, 1959.

Foerster, Norman. *American Criticism.* Boston: Houghton Mifflin, 1928.

———. *Toward Standards.* New York: Farrar and Rinehart, 1930.

Friedenthal, Richard. *Goethe: His Life and Times*. Cleveland: World Publishing Company, 1963.

Friedman, Jean E., and William G. Shade. *Our American Sisters: Women in American Life and Thought*. Boston: Allyn and Bacon, 1973.

Frothingham, O.B. *Transcendentalism in New England*. New York: Putnam, 1876.

Fuller, Frederick T. "Hawthorne and Margaret Fuller Ossoli," *Literary World* 16 (10 January 1885).

Fuller, Margaret. *Love Letters of Margaret Fuller*. New York: D. Appleton, 1903.

Furnas, Joseph C. *The Americans: A Social History of the United States, 1587–1914*. New York: Putnam, 1969.

Fussell, Edwin S. *Frontier: American Literature and the American West*. Princeton, N.J.: Princeton University Press, 1965.

Garibaldi, Giuseppe. *Autobiography*. 3 vols. London, 1889.

———. *Memoirs*, trans. R.S. Garnett. New York: Appleton-Century, 1931.

George, Sharon Kaye. "Margaret Fuller: American Literary and Social Critic." Ph.D dissertation, University of Texas at Austin, 1975.

Gerlach, Walter. "Goethe as a Scientist." *Times* [London] *Literary Supplement*, 3 August 1973, pp. 907–8.

Glicksberg, Charles I., ed. *American Literary Criticism 1900–1950*. New York: Hendricks House, 1952.

Goddard, H.C., "Transcendentalism," in *Cambridge History of American Literature*, vol. 1. New York: Putnam, 1917, pp. 326–48.

Goethe, Johann Wolfgang von. *Conversations of Goethe with Eckermann*. Translated by John Oxenford. London: J.M. Dent, 1930.

———. *Goethe's Literary Essays*. Edited by J.E. Spingarn. New York: Ungar, 1921, 1964.

———. *Italian Journey, 1786–1788*. Translated by W.H. Auden and Elizabeth Mayer. New York: Schocken Books, 1968.

———. *Torquato Tasso*. Translated by Charles E. Passage. New York: Ungar, 1966.

———. *Truth and Fiction Relating to My Life*. Translated by John Oxenford. 2 vols. in one. Boston: Wyman-Fogg, 1902.

———. *Wilhelm Meister's Apprenticeship*. Translated by Thomas Carlyle. New York: Crowell-Collier, 1962.

———. *Wilhelm Meister's Apprenticeship and Travels*. Translated by Thomas Carlyle. 2 vols. Boston: S.E. Cassino, 1882.

Gohdes, Clarence. *The Periodicals of American Transcendentalism*. Durham, N.C.: Duke University Press, 1931.

Golemba, Henry L. "The Balanced View in Margaret Fuller's Literary Criticism." Ph.D. dissertation, University of Washington, 1971.

———. *George Ripley*. New York: Twayne, 1977.

Gornick, Vivian, and Barbara K. Moran, eds. *Woman in Sexist Society*. New York: Basic Books, 1971.

Greeley, Horace. *Recollections of a Busy Life*. New York: J.B. Ford, 1868.

Griffith, Gwilym O. *Mazzini: Prophet of Modern Europe*. New York: Howard Fertig, 1970.

Griswold, Rufus. *The Female Poets of America*. 1848, rev. 1874.

———. *The Prose Writers of America*. Philadelphia: Porter and Coates, 1870.

Hale, William Harlan. *Horace Greeley, Voice of the People*. New York: Harper, 1950.

Hall, Walter Phelps, and William Stearns Davis. *The Course of Europe Since Waterloo.* New York: Appleton-Century-Crofts, 1957.

Handlin, Oscar. *The Americans.* Boston: Little, Brown, 1963.

Hart, John S. *The Female Prose Writers of America.* Philadelphia, 1852, rev. 1855.

Hawthorne, Julian. *Nathaniel Hawthorne and His Wife.* 2 vols. Cambridge, Mass.: University Press, 1884.

Hawthorne, Nathaniel. *American Notebooks.* Centenary Edition, vol. 8. Columbus: Ohio State University Press, 1972.

———. *Italian Notebooks.* Riverside Edition, vol. 10. Boston: Houghton Mifflin, 1883.

———. *The Blithedale Romance.* Centenary Edition, vol. 3. Columbus: Ohio State University Press, 1964.

Hennessy, Helen. "The *Dial:* Its Poetry and Poetic Criticism." *New England Quarterly* 31 (March 1958): 66–87.

Herold, J. Christopher. *Mistress to an Age: A Life of Madame de Staël.* Indianapolis: Bobbs-Merrill, 1958.

Hibbert, Christopher. *Garibaldi and His Enemies.* Boston: Little, Brown, 1966.

Hicks, Granville. "Margaret Fuller to Sarah Helen Whitman: An Unpublished Letter." *American Literature* 1 (1930): 419–21.

Higginson, Thomas Wentworth. *Margaret Fuller Ossoli.* Boston: Houghton Mifflin, 1884.

Hochfield, George. "Introduction." *Selected Writings of the American Transcendentalists.* New York: New American Library, 1966.

Hopkins, Vivian. "The Influence of Goethe in Emerson's Aesthetic Theory." *Philological Quarterly* 27 (1948): 325–44.

———. "Margaret Fuller: American Nationalist Critic." *Emerson Society Quarterly* 55 (1969): 24–41.

Houghton, Walter E. *The Victorian Frame of Mind, 1830–1870.* New Haven: Yale University Press, 1957.

Howe, Julia Ward. *Margaret Fuller.* Boston: Roberts Bros., 1888.

———. *Reminiscences, 1819–1899.* Boston: Houghton Mifflin, 1900.

Hoyt, Edward A., and Loriman S. Brigham. "Glimpses of Margaret Fuller: The Green Street School and Florence." *New England Quarterly* 29 (March 1956): 87–98.

James, Henry. *The Art of the Novel.* New York: Scribner's, 1962.

———. *French Poets and Novelists.* London: Macmillan, 1893.

———. *Hawthorne.* 1879. Reprint: Ithaca: Cornell University Press, 1967.

———. *Literary Reviews and Essays.* Edited by Albert Mordell. New York: Twayne, 1957.

———. *William Wetmore Story and His Friends.* 2 vols. Boston: Houghton Mifflin, 1903.

Jones, A.E. "Margaret Fuller's Attempt to Write Fiction." *Boston Public Library Quarterly* 6 (April 1954): 67–73.

Kearns, Francis E. "Margaret Fuller and the Abolition Movement." *Journal of the History of Ideas* 25 (January–March 1964): 120–27.

Lange, Victor, ed. *Goethe: A Collection of Critical Essays.* Englewood Cliffs, N.J.: Prentice-Hall, 1968.

Langer, William L. *Political and Social Upheaval, 1832–1852.* New York: Harper and Row, 1969.

Lawrence, D.H. *Studies in Classic American Literature.* New York: Viking Press, 1964.

Lerner, Gerda. *The Female Experience: An American Documentary.* Indianapolis: Bobbs-Merrill, 1977.

Loewenberg, Bert James, and Ruth Bogin. *Black Women in Nineteenth-Century American Life.* University Park and London: The Pennsylvania State University Press, 1976.

Lowell, James Russell. *A Fable for Critics.* New York: Putnam, 1848.

———. *New Letters of James Russell Lowell.* Edited by M.A. DeWolfe Howe. New York: Harper, 1932.

Lukács, Georg. "Wilhelm Meisters Lehrjahre." In *Goethe: A Collection of Critical Essays.* Edited by Victor Lange. Englewood Cliffs, N.J.: Prentice-Hall, 1968, pp. 86–98.

McMaster, Helen. "Margaret Fuller as a Literary Critic." *University of Buffalo Studies* 7, no. 3 (1928).

McNeal, Thomas H. "Poe's Zenobia: An Early Satire on Margaret Fuller." *Modern Language Quarterly* 11 (1950): 205–16.

Mack Smith, Denis. *Garibaldi.* London: Hutchinson, 1957.

———. *The Making of Italy 1796–1870.* New York: Harper and Row, 1968.

MacPhail, Andrew. *Essays in Puritanism.* Boston: Houghton Mifflin, 1905.

Madison, Charles A. *Critics and Crusaders.* New York: Henry Holt, 1947.

Markley, O.W. "The New Image of Man." *New York Times,* 16 December 1974, p. 33.

Marraro, Howard. *American Opinion on the Unification of Italy, 1846–1861.* New York: Columbia University Press, 1932.

Martin, Willard E., Jr. "A Last Letter of Margaret Fuller Ossoli," *American Literature* 5 (1933): 66–69.

Martineau, Harriet. *Harriet Martineau's Autobiography.* Edited by Maria Weston Chapman. 2 vols. Boston: J.R. Osgood, 1879.

———. *Society in America.* 2 vols. New York and London: Saunders and Otley, 1837.

Matthews, J. Chesley. "Emerson's Translation of Dante's *Vita Nuova.*" *Harvard Library Bulletin* 11 (1957): 208–44 and 346–62.

Mazzini, Giuseppe. *Life and Writings.* 6 vols. London, 1890–91.

Mill, John Stuart. *The Subjection of Women.* London: Oxford University Press, 1966.

Miller, Perry. "I Find No Intellect Comparable to My Own." *American Heritage* 8 (February 1957): 22–25 and 96–99.

———. Introduction, *Margaret Fuller: American Romantic.* Ithaca: Cornell University Press, 1963.

———. *The Raven and the Whale: The War of Words and Wits in the Era of Poe and Melville.* New York: Harcourt, Brace and World, 1956.

———. *The Transcendentalists: An Anthology.* Cambridge, Mass.: Harvard University Press, 1950.

Morgan, Robin, ed. *Sisterhood Is Powerful.* New York: Random House, 1970.

Morison, Samuel Eliot. *The Oxford History of the American People.* New York: Oxford University Press, 1965.

Munsterberg, Margaret. "Margaret Fuller Centenary." *Boston Public Library Quarterly* 2 (1950): 245–68.

Murry, John Middleton. "Goethe." In *Selected Criticism 1916–1957.* London: Oxford University Press, 1960, pp. 245–65.

Myerson, Joel. *Margaret Fuller: An Annotated Secondary Bibliography.* New York: Burt Franklin, 1977.

———. "Margaret Fuller's 1842 Journal: At Concord with the Emersons." *Harvard Library Bulletin* 21 (July 1973): 320–40.

Orr, Evelyn W. "Two Margaret Fuller Manuscripts." *New England Quarterly* 11 (1938): 794–802.

Parker, Gail. *The Oven Birds: American Women on Womanhood 1820–1920.* New York: Doubleday, 1972.

Parrington, V.L. *Main Currents in American Thought.* 3 vols. in one. New York: Harcourt, Brace, 1948.

Peacock, Ronald. "Goethe's Version of Poetic Drama." In *Goethe: A Collection of Critical Essays.* Edited by Victor Lange. Englewood Cliffs, N.J.: Prentice-Hall, 1968, pp. 33–49.

Perloff, Marjorie. "Yeats and Goethe." *Comparative Literature* 23 (1971): 125–40.

Pochmann, Henry A. *German Culture in America 1600–1900.* Madison: University of Wisconsin Press, 1957.

Poe, Edgar Allan. "About Critics and Criticism." In *The Complete Works of Edgar Allan Poe.* Edited by J.A. Harrison. 17 vols. New York: Crowell, 1902. Vol. 13.

———. "The Literati of New York City." In *The Complete Works of Edgar Allan Poe.* Edited by J.A. Harrison. 17 vols. New York: Crowell, 1902. Vol. 13.

Pritchard, John Paul. *Criticism in America.* Norman: University of Oklahoma Press, 1956.

Randel, William P. "Hawthorne, Channing and Margaret Fuller." *American Literature* 10 (1939): 472–76.

Robertson, J.G. *A History of German Literature.* Edinburgh and London: Blackwood, 1966.

Robertson, Priscilla. *Revolutions of 1848: A Social History.* Princeton, N.J.: Princeton University Press, 1952.

Rose, Ernst. *A History of German Literature.* New York: New York University Press, 1960.

Ross, Ishbel. *Ladies of the Press.* New York: Harper, 1936.

Rossi, Alice S., ed. *The Feminist Papers.* New York: Columbia University Press, 1973.

Rossi, Joseph. *The Image of America in Mazzini's Writings.* Madison: University of Wisconsin Press, 1954.

Rostenberg, Leona. "Margaret Fuller and Elizabeth Barrett Browning." *American Notes and Queries* 2 (February 1943): 163–65.

———. "Margaret Fuller's Roman Diary." *Journal of Modern History* 12 (1940): 209–20.

———. "Mazzini to Margaret Fuller, 1847–1849." *American Historical Review* 47 (1941): 73–80.

Rourke, Constance. *The Roots of American Culture.* New York: Harcourt, Brace, 1942.

Ruland, Richard. *The Rediscovery of American Literature.* Cambridge: Harvard University Press, 1967.

Rusk, Ralph L. *The Life of Ralph Waldo Emerson.* New York: Scribner's, 1949.

Ryan, Mary P. *Womanhood in America: From Colonial Times to the Present.* New York: New Viewpoints, 1975.

Salomone, A. William. "The Nineteenth-Century Discovery of Italy: An Essay in American Cultural History." *American Historical Review* 73 (1963): 1359–91.

Salvemini, Gaetano. *Mazzini*. Stanford, Calif.: Stanford University Press, 1957.

Schneir, Miriam, ed. *Feminism: The Essential Historical Writings*. New York: Vintage Books, 1972.

Sforza, Carlo. *Contemporary Italy: Its Intellectual and Moral Origins*. New York: Dutton, 1944.

Showalter, Elaine, "Women Writers and the Double Standard." In *Woman in Sexist Society*. Edited by Vivian Gornick and Barbara K. Moran. New York: Basic Books, 1971, pp. 323–43.

Slochower, Harry. "Margaret Fuller and Goethe." *Germanic Review* 7 (1932): 130–44.

Smith, Bernard. *Forces in American Criticism*. New York: Harcourt, Brace, 1939.

Spencer, Benjamin T. *The Quest for Nationality*. Syracuse: Syracuse University Press, 1957.

De Staël, Madame Germaine. *Corinne, or, Italy*. New York: Derby and Jackson, 1859.

———. *Madame de Staël*. Edited by Morroe Berger. New York: Doubleday, 1965.

———. *Oeuvres Complètes de Madame La Baronne de Staël*. Paris: Treuttel and Würtz, 1820–21.

Stern, Madeleine B. *The Life of Margaret Fuller*. New York: Dutton, 1942.

———. "Margaret Fuller and *The Dial*." *South Atlantic Quarterly* 40 (1941): 11–21.

———. "Margaret Fuller's Schooldays in Cambridge." *New England Quarterly* 13 (1940): 207–22.

Stoddard, H.L. *Horace Greeley*. New York: Putnam, 1946.

Stoddard, Hope. *Famous American Women*. New York: Crowell, 1970.

Story, William Wetmore. *Roba di Roma*. London, 1876.

Stovall, Floyd, ed. *The Development of American Literary Criticism*. Chapel Hill: University of North Carolina Press, 1955.

Strauch, Carl F. "Hatred's Swift Repulsions: Emerson, Margaret Fuller and Others." *Studies in Romanticism* 7 (Winter 1968): 65–103.

Swift, Lindsay. *Brook Farm*. New York: Macmillan, 1900.

Thomas, J. Wesley. "A Hitherto Unpublished Poem by Margaret Fuller." *American Literature* 15 (1944): 411–15.

———. "James Freeman Clarke, Margaret Fuller, and Emma Keats, Some Previously Unpublished Manuscripts." *Filson Club Historical Quarterly* 28 (1954): 21–27.

———. "New Light on Margaret Fuller's Projected 'Life of Goethe.' " *Germanic Review* 24 (1949): 216–23.

Thomson, David. *Europe Since Napoleon*. New York: Knopf, 1957.

Trevelyan, George M. *Garibaldi's Defence of the Roman Republic, 1848–9*. London: Longmans, Green, 1919.

Trevelyan, Janet P. *A Short History of the Italian People*. London: Allen and Unwin, 1956.

Turner, Arlin. "Autobiographical Elements in Hawthorne's *The Blithedale Romance*." *University of Texas Studies in English*, no. 15 (1935): 39–62.

Van Deusen, Glyndon G. *Horace Greeley, Nineteenth-Century Crusader*. Philadelphia: University of Pennsylvania Press, 1953.

Viëtor, Karl. *Goethe the Poet*. Cambridge: Harvard University Press, 1949.

———. *Goethe the Thinker*. Cambridge: Harvard University Press, 1950.

Violette, Augusta Genevieve. *Economic Feminism in American Literature Prior to 1848.* University of Maine Studies. Second Series, no. 2. Orono, Me.: University Press, 1925.

Vogel, Stanley M. *German Literary Influences on the American Transcendentalists.* New Haven: Yale University Press, 1955.

Wade, Mason. *Margaret Fuller: Whetstone of Genius.* New York: Viking Press, 1940.

———, ed. *The Writings of Margaret Fuller.* New York: Viking Press, 1941.

Warfel, Harry R. "Margaret Fuller and Ralph Waldo Emerson." *Publications of the Modern Language Association* 50 (1935): 576–84.

Warren, Austin. "Hawthorne, Margaret Fuller, and 'Nemesis.' " *Publications of the Modern Language Association* 54 (1939): 615–18.

Wellek, Rene. *A History of Modern Criticism.* 4 vols. New Haven: Yale University Press, 1955–65.

———. "The Minor Transcendentalists and German Philosophy." *New England Quarterly* 15 (1942): 652–80.

Wellisz, Leopold. *The Friendship of Margaret Fuller D'Ossoli and Adam Mickiewicz.* New York: Polish Book Importing Co., 1947.

Welter, Barbara. *Dimity Convictions: The American Woman in the Nineteenth Century.* Athens: Ohio University Press, 1976.

Whyte, A.J. *The Evolution of Modern Italy.* New York: Norton, 1959.

Wilkinson, Elizabeth M. "Goethe's Conception of Form." In *Goethe: A Collection of Critical Essays.* Edited by Victor Lange. Englewood Cliffs, N.J.: Prentice-Hall, 1968, pp. 110–31.

Willis, Frederick L.H., ed. *Alcott Memoirs.* Boston: Badger, 1915.

Wilson, Edmund. *The Shock of Recognition.* New York: Doubleday, 1943.

Woolf, Virginia. *A Room of One's Own.* New York: Harcourt, Brace, 1929.

Zabriskie, Francis Nicoll. *Horace Greeley.* New York, 1890.

Index

Index

Buell, Lawrence, 190
Bull, Ole, 82, 188
Bumpo, Natty, 64
Burke, Edmund, 61
Burns, Robert, 35
Byron, Lord (George Gordon), 12, 71, 124, 153

Calvinism, 49. *See also* Puritanism
Cambridge (Mass.), 3–4, 7
Cambridgeport (Mass.), 1
Canton (Mass.), 2
Capitalism, 127
Capital punishment, 126
"The Captured Wild Horse," 71
Carlyle, Jane, 10, 153
Carlyle, Thomas, 40, 103, 126, 141; as friend of Emerson, 14–15, 33, 42, 47, 183, 185; German literature and, 45–47; Goethe and, 48–49, 186; MF and, 10, 15–16, 21, 76, 103, 141, 153
Cass, Lewis, Jr., 34, 168, 170
Catholicism, family of Ossoli and, 11, 158; Irish, 113; religion of, 80; rulers of Europe and, 11, 162, 169. *See also* Pius IX (pope)
Cattaneo, Carlo, 193
Cavour, Camillo Benso di, 193
Celibacy, 143–44
Censorship, 158, 165–66. *See also* Writers, censorship and *A Century of Struggle* (Flexner), 133
Cervantes, Miguel de, 90
Channing, Ellery, 28, 88, 183
Channing, William Ellery, 87, 185, 186
Channing, William Henry, 8, 92, 115, 165, 170, 172–74; MF's *Memoirs* and, 14–16, 33, 70, 74, 135
Charles Albert (king of Piedmont), 156, 160–61
Cherokee Indians, 120
Chevigny, Bell Gale, 28, 31, 116
Child, Lydia Maria Francis, 135, 139, 146, 181
Children, 30, 38, 41, 79, 139, 154; literature and, 84; mentally retarded, 131, 154
China, 128
Chopin, Frederic, 10, 153
Christ. *See* Jesus Christ
Christianity, 15, 17–18, 53–54, 56, 135, 147; American life and, 48–49, 145; humanism and, 59; Indians and, 118–20; Mickiewicz and, 159–60
Church. *See* Catholicism; Christianity; Clergy and clericalism; Religion
Civilization, 59, 62, 105, 117, 139, 157,

179. *See also* Nature, civilization and, in *Summer*
Civil War, 9, 75
Clarke, James Freeman, 8, 18, 26, 69, 86, 149, 185, 186; Goethe and, 14, 47–48, 54; MF's *Memoirs* and, 14–16, 54, 67, 85, 133, 184
Clark, Lewis Gaylord, 146
Classicism, in America, 104–5; German, 46, 59; in Goethe, 46, 60, 63; in MF's thought, 51, 61, 97–98, 104–6, 126, 145
Classics, Greek and Latin, 2–3, 5, 53, 105, 139. *See also* Greece
Clergy and clericalism, 89; in Europe, 114, 156; in New England, 50, 74; slavery and, 120; in Rome, 166–67
Coleridge, Samuel Taylor, 31, 65, 78
Cologne (Germany), 107
Colonial era. *See* United States, colonial; Women, colonial
Comedy, 90
Communism, 128, 157, 164
Community, 60, 145, 151. *See also* Brook Farm; Utopian communities
Como, Lake, 159
Comprehensive critics, 85–86
Concord (Mass.), 18, 25, 29–30, 32–33, 183
Conservatism, 61–62, 148, 163
Conversation, of MF, 6, 15, 19, 23, 31, 35, 67–68, 77
Conversations, Boston, 8, 19, 62, 116, 137–39, 146, 176
Convicts, 126, 131
Cooper, Anna Julia, 138
Cooper, James Fenimore, 94, 117, 193
Copyright laws, 77, 80
Corinna (Greek poet), 35
Corinne (De Staël character), 22–23, 29, 155
Correspondances, 71
The Correspondence of Fraülein Gunderode and Bettina von Arnim, 8
Cosmopolitanism, of Goethe, 52, 157; of MF, 13, 52, 94, 97, 128, 145
Coverdale, Miles (Hawthorne character), 19–20
Cranch, Christopher, 185
Crane, Major Peter, 2
Crawford, Thomas, 80
"Criticism in England" (Eliot), 78
Criticism. *See* Art criticism, of MF; Literary criticism, theory and practice of; Literary criticism, of MF
Cromwell, Oliver, 129
"Cult of true womanhood," 6, 15–16, 20

Index

Index

Faust (Goethe), 47, 58
Faust (Goethe character), 58, 60–61, 87, 105
Federalist party, 3
Felix (Goethe character), 60
Feminism, of MF, 16, 18–19, 39, 92, 132–51, 176–77
Feminist movement, nineteenth-century, 18, 36–38, 113, 132, 139–41, 144, 146, 148–49. See also Women
Ferdinand (king of Naples), 156, 162
Fern, Fanny, 181
Ferrara, 63–65
Festus (Bailey), 87
Fichte, Johann Gottlieb, 46
Fire Island (N.Y.), 12–13, 33
"First of January 1846," 128
Flanders, 153
Flaubert, Gustave, 134
Fleurs du Mal (Baudelaire), 102
Flexner, Eleanor, 133
Florence (Italy), 12, 66, 159, 172–73
Foerster, Norman, 61
Form. See Literary criticism, of MF, form and meter in
Fourier, Charles, and Fourierism, 13, 40, 164
France, 88, 163, 169; invasion of Rome, 11, 168–72; law in, 132; MF in, 153–54; Napoleonic, 23, 132; social conditions in, 152–54, 160, 163–64; writers and intellectuals of, 17, 32, 71
Franklin, Ann, 181
Freudianism, 110
Friends and friendship, 3, 6–8, 14–17, 21–22, 27–29, 46, 64, 67, 137, 176
Frontier. See Western frontier
"The Frontiers of Criticism" (Eliot), 79–80
Fuller, Arthur (brother), 2, 17–18, 148, 182
Fuller, Ellen (sister), 2, 10, 33, 134, 170
Fuller, Eugene (brother), 2
Fuller, Lloyd (brother), 2
Fuller, Margaret Crane (mother), 1–3
Fuller, Richard (brother), 2, 17–18, 34
Fuller, Timothy (father), 1–4, 6, 21, 23, 112, 114
Fuller, William Henry (brother), 2
The Future of America (Wells), 110

Garden metaphor, in MF's criticism, 97–99, 101–2
Garibaldi, Giuseppe, 159, 164, 170–71
Garrison, William Lloyd, 117
Genesis, Book of, 102, 183
German literature, 23, 45–46, 62, 92–93.

See also Romanticism, German; and names of specific authors
Germany, 45, 122, 153, 155, 185
Gioberti, Vincenzo, 193
Glasgow (Scotland), 154
Goethe, Johann Wolfgang von, 45–65, 70, 83, 91–92, 99, 104, 109, 153, 177–78, 186; art and, 62–65, 84–86, 88–89, 92, 94–95, 107–9, 177–78, 186; concept of growth in, 57–58; cosmopolitanism of, 52, 157; dämonisch and, 54–56, 62; humanism of, 52, 58–63, 89; ideal of self-development of, 53–54, 115, 186; Italy and, 155; as liberator, 45, 52–53, 65; MF's defense of, 13, 51, 88–89; MF's writings on, 35, 47, 50, 53, 55, 63–64, 69, 72, 88–89, 185; popularity of, 47–48; sayings of, 1, 14, 47, 81, 84, 89, 95, 165, 177; women and, 52–53. See also Emerson and Goethe; names of specific works
Goethe, Ottilia, 153
Golden age, 99, 102, 145
Golemba, Henry L., 86, 189
Gothic cathedrals, 107
Great Lakes, 8, 117
"The Great Lawsuit," 8, 10
Greece, 53, 58–59, 139, 145, 155; mythology of, 8, 116
"The Greek Slave" (Powers), 83, 168
Greeley, Horace, 9–10, 13, 39, 67, 125, 150; as MF's employer, 9, 17, 31, 72–73; MF's Memoirs and, 14–15, 17
Greeley, Mary, 9, 125
Greene Street School, 7
Greenough, Horatio, 80
Greenwood, Francis P., 149
Grimké, Sarah, 144
Grimké sisters, 139
Griselda (myth), 38
Griswold, Rufus, 78, 147
Groton (Mass.), 2, 4, 26
Guarda Civica (Rome), 11, 161, 166, 169
Guercino (Giovanni Francesco Barbieri), 27
Guiccioli, Countess, 153

Hamlet, 59
Harbinger, 45
Harring, Harro, 76–77
Harvard University, 2, 4, 9, 134
"The Haunted Palace" (Poe), 109
Hawthorne (James), 184, 188
Hawthorne, Julian, 18
Hawthorne, Nathaniel, 18–21, 83, 94, 102, 116, 144, 173, 182, 188, 193
Hawthorne, Sophia Peabody, 20, 147–48

206

Index

Index

210